1

HARBOURING SECRETS

THE SUITCASE WASHED UP ON THE NORTH SHORE IN THE EARLY hours of Saturday morning, 17 November 1923. The tidal waters of Port Jackson pushed it onto the small and gentle curve of Athol Beach, Mosman, only a short distance across the harbour from Sydney's busy metropolis. Greasy and stained from the seawater, the beaten-up case seemed out of place against the neatly clipped backdrop of Ashton Park.

At around 9.45 a.m., a large Sunday school group from the north-west suburb of Gladesville began arriving at Athol. Some of the children scattered across the beach, while others began playing in the bushland and gardens.

William Lodder, a young schoolboy from Drummoyne, was playing near the water when he spied the silhouette of an upright suitcase at the other end of the beach. The boy was drawn to it. Guided by the age-old childhood rule of finders keepers, he claimed the prize. He unfastened the clips on the case and swung its lid open. The odd dank smell intrigued him more.

Inside the case, an object shaped like a pork loin was wrapped in a towel and secured with a piece of string. Although seaweed and sand had been tossed about within the case, the parcel remained secure, chocked by a block of wood.

William lifted the parcel out of the case for closer inspection, holding it up by the piece of string. Pulled taut by the wet weight of the parcel, the string promptly snapped and the parcel dropped onto the sand. The thud made William feel more uneasy, and he later described to police an 'unsettling smell'. He poked at the parcel with his toe. It felt strangely soft. His courage crumbled. Something seemed wrong.

Reluctant to touch the parcel again and too timid to look at it more closely, William raced up the beach. He urged a group of boys to follow him, hoping he could lead a party back for a more forensic examination of the fascinating and mysterious object. But the boys ignored William's boasting and dismissed the object as swimming trunks wrapped in a towel. He quickly forgot about it.

About an hour later, Eunice Clare, a twelve-year-old school-girl also attending the church picnic, made her way down the beach flanked by a small posse of friends. Eunice was less hesitant than William: on sight of the parcel, she walked directly to it and commenced a systematic examination. She

THE SUITCASE BABY

TANYA BRETHERTON

hachette
AUSTRALIA

Published in Australia and New Zealand in 2018
by Hachette Australia
(an imprint of Hachette Australia Pty Limited)
Level 17, 207 Kent Street, Sydney NSW 2000
www.hachette.com.au

10 9 8 7 6 5 4 3 2 1

National Library of Australia
Cataloguing-in-Publication data

Bretherton, Tanya, author.
The suitcase baby/Tanya Bretherton.

978 0 7336 3922 7

Boyd, Sarah.
Olliver, Jean.
Infanticide – New South Wales – Sydney.
Infants – Crimes against – New South Wales – Sydney.
Newborn infants – Death.
Sydney (NSW) – History.

Cover design by Christabella Designs
Cover photographs courtesy of NSW Police and Forensic Photography Archive, Sydney Living Museums
(Sarah Boyd 617 LB; Jean Olliver 616 LB)
Typeset in 12/18.6 pt Sabon LT Pro by Bookhouse, Sydney
Printed and bound in Australia by McPherson's Printing Group

The paper this book is printed on is certified against the
Forest Stewardship Council® Standards. McPherson's Printing
Group holds FSC® chain of custody certification SA-COC-005379.
FSC® promotes environmentally responsible, socially beneficial
and economically viable management of the world's forests.

CONTENTS

picked it up thinking it was 'what appeared to be costumes rolled in a towel'. The parcel had now been exposed to the air for some time and the dank smell had dispersed a little. Eunice knelt on the soft sand. She began to unwrap the towelling, hoping some treasure might be inside – perhaps a forgotten piece of jewellery stashed carefully by a wealthy Mosman lady during a beach swim or, even better, money. Within moments Eunice stumbled back in fright as a baby's head flopped loose from the wrappings.

Eunice was swift in sounding the alarm. Followed by her band of young cronies, she ran up the beach until they located the nearest adult – a man working near the wharf.

Athol Beach was only a short distance away from Mosman Police Station on Bradleys Head Road, so it did not take long for local police to arrive. At around 12.30 p.m., William O'Reilly, sergeant of the Mosman unit, walked the length of the beach starting at the wharf end. He easily found the suitcase, still resting near the high-water mark with a parcel alongside it; a baby's head was clearly visible at one end. The string remained tightly wrapped around the towel coiled over the torso and legs of the child's body. The scene was jarring. The child was clearly dead, but not repugnant: the small face was cherubic and uninjured. The child had been carefully swaddled, as if put to sleep, and then gently set afloat. The sight before Sergeant O'Reilly seemed somehow sacred: a baby Moses consigned to the Nile with only a basket of reeds for protection.

The police typed up statements of the children's observations at the scene. At the bottom of these pages, small handwritten signatures reflect the two very different personalities of the young beachcombers whose discovery would launch the highest-profile child murder case in Sydney's history.

Eunice's signature, 'E. C. Clare', is indistinguishable from that of a well-educated adult of the time. Her cursive is perfectly formed and justified neatly to the right of the page. Each initial is expertly spaced with a full stop. In her sworn statement, Eunice is careful to note the presence of other possible witnesses and calmly explains her inability to recall more detail: 'I picked up the parcel and saw a child's head in it. When I saw that I put the parcel down again. A lot of other children were there and saw what I saw ... I did not notice whether the towel was wet or dry as I was upset at finding the baby.'

In contrast to Eunice's clinical notes, William Lodder's statement reveals the true horror of what had occurred on Athol Beach: a young child had discovered the dead body of an even younger child. Despite him being almost exactly the same age as Eunice, the immaturity and innocence of William Lodder's words is undeniable. His signature provides a clear reminder of how traumatic this discovery must have been for all of the Sunday school group. 'W Lodder' is written erratically, inconsistently. The oversized loops skip down the page in an impulsive way, much like William on his fateful skip down the beach.

That morning, Sergeant O'Reilly had handled the suitcase baby gently, reacting with a protective instinct that he couldn't explain. He placed the child's body back in the suitcase and proceeded directly to Mosman Wharf to catch a ferry to the city morgue. Like an ancient ferryman carrying a soul to the underworld, O'Reilly solemnly crossed the harbour. A police sergeant carrying a well-beaten port in his hand as if on holiday, but in full uniform, must have been a curious sight for his fellow travellers. He disembarked at Circular Quay and walked the short distance to the city morgue, located right near the water's edge on George Street, where the metropolis of Sydney empties into the harbour.

Sergeant O'Reilly and Charles Broomfield, keeper of the morgue, began preparations for the formal medical examination. Both men were highly experienced and not likely to be shaken by the grim undertaking before them. O'Reilly was an officer of long standing, having risen to a senior supervisory position on the North Shore. Charles Broomfield was a second-generation morgue keeper, closely apprenticed by his father, with over twenty years' experience in the job.

O'Reilly placed the child's body face up on the examination table. He freed the legs and lower body from the towel. It was a baby girl. Her size indicated that she could be newborn. Both men suspected her body had spent a good deal of time floating in the harbour, given the quantity of seaweed and sand inside the case. It had definitely emerged from the water and had not been abandoned by someone trudging along the beach.

This fact added another level of strangeness to the discovery. Sydney Harbour beaches are rough, hazardous, and known for their aggressive and destructive rips that typically smash anything washed ashore. And the harbour is deep, capable of safely accommodating large-scale steamships and cargo vessels with the biggest hulls ever created. Should a parcel successfully sink, it is unlikely to surface again. The harbour does not usually surrender its captives so easily. To this day, its floor is a junkyard of wrecked vessels, motor vehicle bodies, and industrial debris from two hundred years of European settlement.

Yet the harbour had somehow been kind to this child's body, and the mysterious suitcase raft had proved to be a more-than-adequate vessel. The body's exposure to the sea had also afforded it a level of preservation and protection from the insect infestations commonly found in bodies left exposed on land, especially in the warmer months of a Sydney spring. There was no evidence of adipocere: the crumbly white particles, known as grave wax, that form through saponific-ation – the same process used to make soap – when a body is stored in moisture-rich environments that lack oxygen. Against all odds, the unusual coffin had drifted atop the water and safely landed on a stretch of sand less than 100 metres long, located on one of the least hazardous beaches in all of Sydney Harbour.

Given their combined amount of experience, Broomfield and O'Reilly would have most likely conjectured back and forth about the child's age. However, before the autopsy took place and medical expertise was brought to bear on the matter, it would have been difficult to estimate the bracket of hours, days, weeks or months.

It was Broomfield's job, grim and methodical task that it was, to enter the baby's particulars in the heavy-bound and oversized tome known officially as the morgue book. His formal entries resemble a macabre parody of a cherished mothercraft tradition of growth milestones in a family keepsake album. The morgue keeper, not the baby's mother, recorded the weight, height and key measurements.

The body was 21.5 inches (over 54 centimetres) long, using the perinatal convention of measuring from the top of the head to the heel. Her weight was recorded to be a healthy and 'well nourished' 7 pounds 2 ounces (3.2 kilograms).

In addition to those of the body, details of all other items – including the condition of the suitcase and noteworthy observations of its characteristics and contents – were carefully recorded. In the presence of Broomfield, who also acted as a witness, O'Reilly examined everything again, more closely. He now had time to be more attentive, sheltered from the hot mid-November Sydney sun by the cool, contemplative stone environment.

While it would be the medical practitioner's job to perform an internal examination of the body and thereby officially determine the cause of death, it was obvious to both officers that they were looking upon the result of something wicked and violent. A string was tied tightly around the body's neck, the string still attached, a length of it dangling slack and twisted. The tip of a pretty and delicate piece of mauve stitching protruded from the mouth. Both officers recognised the design as one common to the decorative border of a woman's handkerchief.

The body was dressed in basic and commonplace items of baby apparel for the late nineteenth century and early twentieth century. A napkin. A garment known as a baby binder or corset, made of flannel, which wrapped around the torso and remained laced in the front. It was a slightly old-fashioned item as binders were not used by all mothers at the time, but investigators did not see the item as particularly significant. A loose flannel undershirt hung over the corset.

A small number of items remained in the suitcase. A block of wood. An empty gin bottle. Part of a cigarette packet. There was also a photograph – an eerie echo of the scene on the morgue slab: the baby girl lay alone, with no carer in sight, as if sleeping.

At 2.15 p.m. that day, the medical practitioner, Stratford Sheldon, commenced the autopsy. Sheldon was the closest thing that Sydney had to medical royalty. He came from a dynasty of doctors. His father, William Sheldon, was a popular North Sydney doctor. Both Stratford and his brother had become doctors with thriving independent practices in the city centre and in the burgeoning suburb of Granville in the west.

Sheldon was one of the best in his field, and his set of specialisations was directly relevant to the examination of a suitcase baby. He had a rare knowledge of deaths in

Sydney Harbour and experience in undertaking post-mortems of watery deaths. In 1921 he had conducted the autopsy of Isabel Lippe, a Victorian woman involved in a complex and high-profile case. Lippe's body had been found at the bottom of The Gap, a cliff edge on South Head with a reputation for both fatal accidents and suicide jumps from its 21-metre drop into the Tasman Sea.

Everyone in law enforcement wanted Lippe's death to be ruled as murder. She had been pursued and deceived by a well-known con man, Charles MacAlister, and the police wanted a reason to arrest him. But Sheldon held firm in the face of immense pressure. After a long and complex inquest, he argued that by analysing multiple sources of evidence – the number and placement of broken bones, estimated time in the water and position of the body on impact – only one scientific conclusion was possible. Suicide. His post-mortem report ruined the case that police had been building against MacAlister. Sheldon's opinion was respected but he wasn't always liked by Sydney's metropolitan police.

Sheldon looked first at the suitcase baby's clothing, seeing that it comprised only the most basic of necessities. The empty gin bottle found inside the suitcase also suggested to Sheldon that indigence had played some role in the death. Gin was popular with the inner-city underclass because it was cheap. Its easy availability meant that gin had become a home remedy for common ailments from cradle to grave. The elderly used it to treat arthritis, while mothers used it as a sedative and tonic for restless and colicky babies.

As a legally qualified medical practitioner engaged to under-take work for the morgue, Sheldon was under instruction to determine the cause of death, and this meant performing an internal examination. Though the making of social commen-taries did not fall within Sheldon's immediate brief, he knew, before he even started his examination, that he was looking at the body of a child born into poverty. In his daily comings and goings as a city doctor, Sheldon would rarely if ever have encountered a baby so common, but in the morgue there was no social hierarchy. In this cold and damp place, the lowest and the highest of society assembled to participate in the ritual of the post-mortem. The perverse logic of the social welfare system in 1923 meant that while the suitcase baby had most likely not received any professional medical care in life, her body was being subjected to the best post-mortem that money could buy.

Sheldon estimated the baby to have been between three and four weeks old. On the umbilicus there remained a small amount of 'dry epithelial string'. This meant the umbilical cord stump had healed, but only recently, because new tissue was visible.

Sheldon repositioned the baby's body on the slab, elevating the torso to ensure the chest and abdomen could be sliced open cleanly and the ribs sawn through neatly. An internal examination found all of the organs to be healthy. The heart showed no signs of a common and potentially serious vulner-ability such as a hole. The foramen ovale, a hole between the two halves of the heart which remains open before birth, had closed, as it should, shortly after birth. Sheldon was looking down on the body of what had been, at one time at least, a perfectly healthy baby.

While the general condition of the body indicated that the baby had been fed and cared for, the stomach was empty at the time of death. The baby had been dead when the suitcase was put in Port Jackson as there was no evidence of water in the lungs – a hallmark of drowning.

Using a magnifying glass and drawing the lamp as close to the body as possible, Sheldon leaned in to examine the lungs. In his final sworn statement, lodged with the Central Criminal Court, he said that he had found unequivocal evidence of death due to suffocation. Petechial haemorrhages were dappled on the tissue of the lungs; these red marks appear when blood leaks from ruptured vessels. Sheldon was methodical, noting the significance of this observation by drawing on other contextual evidence. As petechial haemorrhages can also occur as a result of cardiac arrest, Sheldon examined the heart closely to see if it exhibited signs of rupturing. It was unspotted and perfectly formed. Sheldon's conclusion: death had occurred as a result of strangulation, with the airways purposefully obstructed by some external source.

The string was still tied so tightly around the neck that it told a story of the force and determination in the perpetrator's mind. A white muslin handkerchief, decorated with the mauve stitching, was stuffed deeply into the mouth. It was as if the baby was frozen in time, trapped in a silent theatre of her last struggles for breath.

Sheldon's summary of the post-mortem evidence concluded: 'Either the string around the neck or the handkerchief in its mouth would have been sufficient to cause death.' The murderer had not hesitated and had fully committed to the undertaking. There was no doubt the suitcase baby had suffered a horrible death. Not only had her body been discovered twice, but in a manner of speaking she had also died twice.

2

CORNERING A SUSPECT

THE MATTER WAS TRANSFERRED FROM THE SMALL POLICE station in Mosman to a larger and better-resourced unit: No. 2 Head Station, Regent Street, Central Sydney. Sergeant Ernest Green, Sergeant Don Alchin and Constable Wright Sherringham assumed responsibility for investigation of the criminal case.

Each officer faced a professional challenge. Police force operations in New South Wales were governed by a 'deploy first, ask questions later' approach to rostering. Police historians note that it was not until the 1960s in New South Wales that more specialised areas of police work formally emerged as part of operations; as a result, leaders and managers often found it difficult to accumulate detailed knowledge in one area of law enforcement. In the 1920s, officers could literally be assigned to any criminal investigation, whether it matched their skill set or not.

Sergeant Green, the chief investigator on the case, offered special insights as a local. He was more street smart than book smart. Born and bred in Sydney, he knew the social and economic peculiarities of the city and its residents. Green had worked the constabulary beat of the inner-city streets and back lanes, and he understood what kind of seedy crime could happen there. He also knew infanticide cases were widely regarded in the force to be career poison because they were nearly impossible to solve. Many hundreds of unsolved case files for dead babies were attached to No. 2 Head Station already. He was not eager to be involved in yet another dead-end case.

Sergeant Alchin and Constable Sherringham were country boys recruited from rural towns over 300 kilometres out of Sydney.

Alchin was from Young in the south-west – a burgeoning flour and timber mill town surrounded by farming and grazing plains. He was mid-career, and represented an emerging breed of more specialised and expert officers. He was part of the NSW police elite hand-picked for a secondment scheme designed to deepen the level of deductive reasoning throughout the Australian force. By swapping roles with a counterpart in another state, each senior officer honed his investigative skills in a new setting. Only a few months before the discovery of the suitcase baby, Alchin led a high-profile investigation in Western Australia that had received national media coverage. A man (Don Pizzatti), camped in the bush to cut timber sleepers, was found dead with bullet wounds to the head. It had been a tricky case. Pizzatti had been reported missing by his fellow cutters, but given the dense forest, it had taken days to find him. A fellow sleeper cutter, a seventeen-year-old boy called Thomas Brookes, had been found with Pizzatti's eleven pounds in savings. Initially, at least, it seemed a straightforward robbery and murder case. Thanks to careful and somewhat compassionate investigation by Alchin, the complexities of the case came to light. Brookes had been shooting roos. The death had been an accident. Brookes had stolen Pizzatti's money after the accident. Brookes was also intellectually disabled. It was information critical to the deliberations in court. Brookes was found guilty of manslaughter and not murder. He would serve a few years in prison for robbery and for careless operation of his rifle, but was found not guilty of murder.

Alchin was as experienced as any officer on the NSW force at that time, but he was a poor fit for infanticide, a niche area of criminology. Alchin's specialty was money-related crime and, much like Sergeant Green, he had a sense of foreboding about the case. He understood crime as a craft and an enterprise. *Why* the crime had occurred was less relevant to Alchin's usual investigations, as the primary motive was always financial gain; it was *how* the crime had been committed that was important. Alchin was an expert in understanding the criminal mind, but his criminals were cunning, not complex. He knew how to capture petty pickpockets, to uncover fraud and graft, and to find bank robbers and safe crackers. Alchin knew the technical proficiencies needed to forge notes and mould pennies into florins. He had captured every kind of robber from street-corner swindlers through to large-scale fraudsters. In the previous year alone, he had developed water-tight cases against fencers of stolen watches in George Street, and decoded a major investment fraud in which a local Sydney charlatan duped one investor out of a staggering £125 000 in a primitive version of a Ponzi scheme.

As an experienced officer, Alchin knew what an infanticide case meant. In rare circumstances where a perpetrator was identified and located, it was almost always a woman – and he did not like locking up women. In his mind, women were generally victims not perpetrators.

In Sydney, Alchin had recently led an investigation into what journalists at the time ridiculed as 'the doings' of a philanderer. In reality, the crime was a sophisticated dallier-turned-crook scam. One persuasive fraudster had single-handedly swindled wealthy young women out of their fortunes by convincing them to sign over significant estates of property and family heirlooms well before the intended marriage had occurred. Alchin did something highly unconventional for a police officer – he brought together the two very different female victims of the same crime. He tracked down the abandoned wife of the romancing rapscallion and encouraged her to meet with her husband's wealthy mistress. He then drove the heiress to the wife of the crook so she would witness the financial impact of the man's desertion on not just his wife but also his brood of children. The experience so touched the heiress that she offered monetary assistance to the family of the very rogue who had swindled her.

Alchin had a reputation for being sharp-witted if unorthodox. He also had a reputation for his social conscience. The problem of destitution in the inner city, particularly among returned soldiers, had become increasingly visible in 1923. Five years since the war had ended, it was not unusual to see homeless veterans wandering the streets still in the civilian clothes they had been issued with on demobilisation. Alchin led an unusual and somewhat unsavoury recycling initiative to clothe the destitute by stripping suits from unclaimed cadavers at the Coroner's Court and handing them out to ex-diggers.

Constable Wright Sherringham was, like Alchin, a determined and committed police officer. But in many ways he was Alchin's polar opposite. Alchin was experienced. Sherringham was a novice. Alchin was a practical man and not afraid to bump shoulders with the masses. Sherringham was an unapologetic snob.

Sherringham had moved to Sydney from a tiny town in the central west of New South Wales, even smaller than Alchin's home town of Young. Cumnock was dominated by pastoral families and was an archetype of early European agricultural settlement, having been built on the holy farming trinity of sheep, cattle and grain production. For an ambitious young police officer, however, it offered little opportunity. The

Sherringhams were well known in the area as aspirational pastoralists who had made a shrewd acquisition of land. Wright Sherringham was well bred and had married into an equally influential family in the district. He also shared his father's aspirational tendencies but he set his sights on law enforcement, not farming. While nearby Bathurst had a regional gaol and grand courthouse, offering opportunity for a young officer to cut his teeth in a criminal justice career, the constable had his sights set even higher.

In the suitcase baby investigation, the challenges to be faced by these three officers would not come from within the police force alone. The macabre use of a suitcase as a coffin was splashed as a sensational headline across all of the major newspapers and had been picked up by regionals as far west as the *Kalgoorlie Miner* and as far south as the Launceston *Examiner*. Journalists and their editors immediately recognised the potential for the story and began milking it. Rather than release one article encompassing all known details of the case, editors employed a tactic to stimulate appetite for the story and help build public hysteria. In modern-day news circles, this tactic is sometimes referred to as 'salami-ing' – one story, cut into thin slices, is slowly released over successive days, creating the impression that discoveries are being made by police on a daily basis and encouraging readers to keep buying the paper.

By the end of a fortnight of reporting, journalists had developed their own jargon for the event. The tomb of the small corpse was no longer a 'suit-case': it was imprinted on the minds of the public as a 'baby-case'.

While journalists found the suitcase fascinating, Alchin, Green and Sherringham took a different view. Despite their varying skill sets and backgrounds, they agreed wholeheartedly on one thing – the suitcase would not be much use to the investigation. It was a modest, mass-produced, off-the-shelf port, identical to hundreds sold from the many department stores in all major Australian cities. The owner of the case had chosen not to add detailing to the exterior in the form of embossed initials or a personalised monogram – a fashion among both tourists and immigrant travellers at the time.

The investigators turned their attention to the other items. An empty gin bottle – no markings. An empty cigarette packet – a generic brand that could have been bought from anywhere. Sherringham, the least experienced officer present, asked his two seniors if this suggested a male perpetrator. Alchin, a thoughtful profiler of the criminal mind, said it was too early in the investigation to jump to that kind of conclusion. Green shook his head. This was a baby, and that almost always meant a mother, he said. The other officers had to agree. The string tied around the baby's throat was an ordinary kitchen item – exactly the kind used by a housewife to tie a rolled pork loin.

The clothes were store-bought and not personalised in any way. Hand-stitched needlework, a popular pastime of many mothers and grandmothers, did not adorn the clothing. The same could be said of the towelling in which the body had been wrapped. It was a Turkish towel of woven cotton with a fringe at each end. There was nothing in these items that might offer some clue to the identity of the baby or the family to whom she belonged.

All evidence of the baby's existence appeared to have been surrendered to the water. The inclusion of the single photograph suggested that no personal keepsake was wanted. The perpetrator had not just sought the death of the baby; they wanted to forget she had ever existed.

By the end of Tuesday, two business days into the investigation, the officers had begun assembling a likely location for the crime. The location of the suitcase near the harbour would have usually presented the police with a deluge of challenges. Port Jackson is about 55 square kilometres, and many tributaries feed into it, including the Parramatta and Lane Cove rivers. The suitcase could have been discreetly dropped into the harbour by anyone from any embankment or bridge near the shoreline, anywhere within the greater Sydney region. The Parramatta is the largest of the rivers culminating in a tidal estuary that feeds directly into Port Jackson. The suitcase baby could have commuted a long distance, swept by an energetic tidal movement to arrive at her resting place.

But the presence of the wood block undermined the idea that the murder might have occurred outside of the city. The block offered police the broad design of the crime, and suggested a story of desperation and deceit as well.

Sydney had relied primarily on wood pavers for road construction since the 1880s, and these blocks were indistinguishable from one another. Many of the city's older roads were now rotting at the edges. Crumbled chunks of wood were in abundance and loose on the hems of the streets. The roads were also in a state of continual repair, with piles of fresh pavers stacked on street corners in preparation for resurfacing. But while the pavers were virtually everywhere in the city, they were not everywhere in Sydney – by 1923 they were confined to the metropolis. The paver therefore positioned the perpetrator with an efficiency akin to the tracking of a mobile phone by its proximity to tower signals. In the hours leading up to the disposal of the body, the perpetrator had in all likelihood been in the city and thrown the suitcase into an inner-city harbour.

The paver suggested desperation, as it had surely been grabbed opportunistically. The investigators suspected that the perpetrator had chocked it into the suitcase with the expectation that the mass would help to weigh the item down and ensure its sea burial. Ironically, the perpetrator had unwittingly made the vessel seaworthy by increasing its buoyancy. They had shown determination but had certainly not been artful in covering their tracks.

The most important piece of evidence would turn out to be no bigger than a fingernail.

The handkerchief that had been violently crammed into the mouth and upper throat of the victim was laid flat on the table of an interview room at No. 2 Head Station. It particularly intrigued Green, Alchin and Sherringham because of all the items it was the most personal and offered the most direct link to the murderer. In stark contrast to the wicked and violent crime, the item was pretty and delicate. Small mauve flowers dotted the corner, and even the coronial doctor had used a somewhat poetic description in his post-mortem report: 'A decorative and delicate heliotrope border.' It suggested something romantic or whimsical about the object and, by association, the perpetrator.

Sergeant Alchin noted how the pattern reminded him of a handkerchief owned by his wife, which she had purchased in the city centre. This observation initially stumped the investigators. The item was unremarkable, with little to distinguish it from the thousands of mass-produced embroidered handkerchiefs on the market.

It was the rookie, Constable Sherringham, eager to make an impression on his senior officers, who stepped forward to turn the handkerchief over. On one corner, visible only from the underside where knotted threads were present, '2/14' had been written in tiny and almost invisible print where the fabric had been carefully hemmed in. The officers recognised what the lettering meant: a commercial laundry code. At some point in time, and perhaps not recently, the handkerchief had been professionally laundered.

The laundry code system was used to track individual orders, and represented an industry-wide practice common to commercial laundries across Britain, the United States and Australia. Each business assigned a unique identification number to each customer, which they used every time they booked in a cleaning order. These mark codes were a core part of business practice, allowing laundries to create economies of scale by washing large volumes of clothing based on the specifications of the items. Linens, cottons and woollens each required different levels of heat, and different quantities and chemical compositions of soap. By sorting orders into lots, then sorting them back into individual customer orders, laundries significantly reduced the cost per item. The mark codes were indelible and designed to sustain multiple wash processes so they could not easily be dissolved by the harsh commercial soaps and solvents used for stain removal.

The mark on the handkerchief suggested the possibility of solving what was widely identified across the police force to be an unsolvable crime. If the code could be deciphered, the perpetrator had effectively signed their name and address on the body of the unknown baby, indelibly, in laundry code ink.

But the investigators still had a problem – where and how to start looking for the laundry. During the 1920s in Sydney, cleaning services represented one of the strongest areas of small business and cottage industry growth. They were easy and low-cost to run, and required little more than access to piped water and adequate floor space. They were also in high demand, with residential households, commercial businesses (particularly catering and hospitality operators), itinerant workers and travellers all using commercial operators to launder their clothing and household linens. This demand had created huge growth in the sector, and businesses had mushroomed across the city to launder its unwashed and washed masses alike.

Investigating the origin of the laundry mark could involve interviews with hundreds of operators, requiring them to explain their bookkeeping and customer account records. While No. 2 Station was better staffed than most other police units in the state, it was still far from well resourced. Its officers' capacity to undertake a time-intensive criminal investigation was limited, and with vice saturating the streets of the inner city, Surry Hills and Haymarket, the murder of an unknown and unwanted newborn represented the very lowest of police priorities.

To come up with a list of the most likely laundries, Green and Alchin narrowed the geographical parameters of the crime as much as possible. They already knew that the road paver suggested that the suspect had been in the city centre while disposing of the evidence. The suitcase seemed relatively new and had most likely been sold by a large department store; Anthony Hordern & Sons was the biggest in Sydney, with expansive retail frontage on the corner of George, Pitt and Goulburn streets at the southern end of the city centre.

With the examination of the evidence completed, the suitcase and the baby parted company forever. The suitcase and its contents were treated with great care. Each was carefully photographed. The practice of police photography at the time was artful, with meticulous attention paid to capturing the elements of dark and light in each item. Tagged and catalogued, the evidence was preserved in the catacombs of police storage.

While the authorities took great care in handling the evidence, no memorial nor respect was afforded to the baby, who was scheduled for disposal in an unmarked mass grave designated for paupers.

3

WALKOVER

As the senior investigator, Sergeant Green set the pace. He determined the direction of the legwork for the case. It would be outward-moving, starting in the city centre – terrain that was well known to him – and roaming as far as resources would permit.

Delegating the menial task of laundry doorknocking, Green sent Constable Sherringham out on foot to a local destination: one of the largest commercial laundries in the city and surrounding area, the Model Laundry Company. Sherringham took a fifteen-minute walk from No. 2 Station on Regent Street to the nearest laundry-receiving depot in Goulburn Street, Haymarket.

Violet Finney, wife of the laundry proprietor and manager of the receiving depot, oversaw customer accounts across the entire business and had a comprehensive ledger on hand. After a short interview Sherringham held the name and a street address of a 'Mrs Gore', with laundry customer number 2/14, firmly in his hand.

If Sherringham had not been fully cognisant of the clock ticking in the investigation as he'd walked into the laundry, he was certainly aware of time pressure as he left. On the surface, it appeared to be a walkover for the police – both metaphorically and literally. The murder weapon could be directly linked not only to a name but also to an address, and this had been handed to the officer at the very first interview. The distance between the laundry and the street address now represented a door-to-door stroll.

But there remained a challenge. The street address wasn't residential but was for the Square and Compass Hotel on George Street, in an area known for its turnover of transient workers in temporary accommodation. Sherringham was now in pursuit of a suspect who might not be a permanent resident of Sydney. Had the suspect already fled? If the suspect was still at the hotel, could they be alerted by associates and dart out before he had a chance to interview anyone?

This would also be an unsavoury task for Sherringham. Although the hotel was used by produce purveyors who had travelled from around the state to trade at Haymarket, it was also known as a place where people liked to cut loose. It didn't have the reputation of hotels located in the more dangerous Surry Hills, but gambling was common, and therefore the hotel was frequented by opportunistic thieves. Many police reports of excessive drinking and drunken brawls had been filed in the past year. The Square and Compass was precisely the kind of establishment of which the constable's family, who perceived themselves as the landed gentry, would not have approved. It was therefore the kind of establishment of which Sherringham himself did not approve.

At that moment, the constable stood less than five minutes' walk from the laundry depot and less than five minutes' walk to the hotel. Sherringham was sorely tempted to go directly to the hotel, but he also feared that Green would be unimpressed by his failure to follow protocol. He was required to check in with a senior officer prior to attending. He hurried back to the station and reported to Green.

At around 5 p.m. that day, Thursday 22 November, Sherringham and Green, now both dressed in plain clothes, arrived at the Square and Compass. The proprietor pointed out a broad-shouldered man standing in the bar downstairs as Mr George Gore.

Sherringham and Green introduced themselves to Gore, and began asking questions. Gore asked them to follow him to the first floor of the hotel, where the accommodation was located. He approached a bedroom door close to the stairwell and knocked while calling out, 'Can we come in, Jean?'

A woman's voice answered, 'No.'

Gore began to push the door open, cautiously, announcing loudly, 'We are coming in. We are here, Jean.'

A woman stood next to the bed, her head down. As soon as the officers caught sight of her, they recognised her type.

The thin frame, dark lipstick, well-cut dress and fashionable shoes – this was a woman who dressed to attract the attention of men. From head to toe, the girl was a flapper, albeit a bit of an ageing one.

Sherringham and Green looked at each other but before either could say anything – and indeed before they had even properly entered the room – the woman spoke rapid fire. 'I know I have been accused of killing my baby but I never had one.'

Sherringham was floored, and although it was customary for the supervising officer to take the lead in interviews, his surprise at Jean's utterance was so great that he spoke first. 'That is a most remarkable statement for you to make seeing that you don't know us and we have not spoken to you. Can you say what made you say it?'

The woman kept her head down and did not answer.

Sherringham, on the front foot again, repeated what he had said. 'That is a most remarkable statement to make. Can you say what made you say it?'

The woman would not look up. She was staring at the floor.

'We want to know what you know about a dead baby found at Athol on Saturday 17 November last.'

To this, the woman responded in a way that to the officers seemed a childlike attempt at subterfuge: defiant, but simple and unsophisticated.

'I know nothing about it. I never had a child and a doctor can prove that.'

'You take the name of Mrs Gore, don't you?' asked Sherringham.

'Yes.'

'And what is your first name?'

'Jean.'

'You took some laundry to 35 Goulburn Street to be laundered on 5 October last.' Sherringham cleverly framed the words as a statement rather than a question. He wanted to communicate to Jean that the police already knew what had occurred – all they needed now was for her to confirm it all.

'Yes.'

'Among that clothing were a number of ladies' handker-chiefs.'

'Yes.'

'Have you any of them now?'

'Yes.'

Sherringham's confidence shocked Green, but it seemed to be working – the woman seemed compliant. Her head was still down. But Green also knew from experience what inner-city criminals could be like. They were fast and sharp. He kept a close eye on George Gore.

Jean walked to a large wardrobe in the corner and pulled a pile of handkerchiefs from a drawer inside.

Outwardly, Sherringham and Green remained composed; however, they quietly made eye contact, sharing the acknowl-edgement that they had achieved a huge breakthrough.

Sherringham continued to take the lead. He pointed out the laundry mark on the corner of every handkerchief, each with a heliotrope border identical to the one that they had at the police station.

'The handkerchief that was found in the mouth of the dead baby bears a similar laundry mark to these handkerchiefs. Can you account for that?'

Jean held her breath for a moment. Then she answered, 'No.' She followed with a response that was more considered. 'I have a friend with a baby and I gave her some handkerchiefs but I knows she did not kill her baby. She gave it to a woman to look after.'

'What is the name of your friend? Where can she be seen?'

'I can't tell you that.'

'Why?'

'Because if she killed her baby I would be the last in the world to give her away.'

Sherringham's tone lowered to reinforce the gravity of the situation that Jean was now in. 'This is a very serious matter and that is a most peculiar attitude to take up.'

Green and Sherringham insisted that Jean and George Gore accompany them to the station. The suspects were taken to an interview room and seated before a table. Sherringham picked up the line of questioning and brandished the physical evidence to heighten the suspects' fear. He produced two photographs of the handkerchief. One clearly showed the laundry mark; the other showed the whole handkerchief laid flat, its heliotrope border almost squarely framing the image. He showed both photographs to Jean and Gore, laying them on the table in front of Jean. Her head remained down, but she cast her eyes up long enough for a glance.

'That is a photo of a handkerchief found in the mouth of the dead baby at Athol,' Sherringham told her. 'Would you say it was a photo of one of your handkerchiefs?'

'Yes, that is my laundry mark all right.'

'Can you tell us what you have done with that handkerchief?'

'Yes, I gave it to my friend that has a baby.'

'Can you tell us her name and where she can be seen?'

The to-and-fro of the interview continued for some time. Green noticed the way that the woman responded to Sherringham. He was young, handsome. She seemed to be leaning forward more closely than was needed, every time that he spoke. She also seemed keen to keep the conversation going. But while she was responding to the questions, she was far from being cooperative. She refused to offer up any information about the friend she had implicated. She kept denying personal involvement in any baby murder. Green wanted a result. He took an unconventional approach. He went out of the room, leaving Jean and Gore alone with the constable. If Sherringham could get her to talk, it was very likely she would do so if the conversation seemed more private.

Slowly, Jean began to reveal details. To the questions relating to whom the baby might belong, where in the country they might now be, and when she had last heard from them, Jean now offered up a series of answers:

'Cissie.'

'A place beyond Gosford.'

'I do not know who she has gone to there.'

Jean also stated that she had received a letter that very morning from Cissie, but had ripped it up because 'it had nothing in it'.

To Sherringham's surprise, George Gore started to do the job for him. Gore spoke tersely to Jean. More tersely than the constable had expected.

'It is no use saying that, Jean. Why don't you tell the man the truth?'

Jean, in response, said, 'I am sure Cissie never murdered her baby. She would never do anything like that.'

'That is all the more reason you should tell them where she is. Why don't you tell them?'

'I cannot do that,' said Jean.

Gore then became angry. He seemed more concerned with saving his own hide than his wife's. He clearly did not want to be implicated any further. 'I think I can tell you where she lives.' He wrote an address on a blank piece of paper lying on the table in front of him.

Sherringham nodded approvingly and thanked him.

Jean followed suit and began behaving much more cooperatively. She now seemed very concerned that Sherringham would perceive her husband as the cooperative one and define her as uncooperative. 'I will tell you where she can be seen. But I do not want her to get into trouble. I am sure she did not kill her baby. She gave it to a woman to look after. Her name is Cissie Boyd and she takes the name of Mrs Jackson. She is living with a man named Shorrock on an orchard in Kulnura, out from Wyong.'

4

GONE TO GROUND

Sergeant Green commended Constable Sherringham on his efficiency. In less than a day, Sherringham had progressed the case significantly. In the context of an abandoned baby investigation, his achievement was remarkable indeed.

Green, Alchin and Sherringham met in the evening of Thursday, 22 November to discuss the new information. Green said he believed that Jean was being evasive. He suggested that the name she'd offered was a red herring, and perhaps she had more to do with the baby's murder than she was willing to admit. Though Alchin had not interviewed Jean, he listened carefully to the assessments of his fellow officers and agreed that her behaviour seemed guarded. He argued that it was not for the reason Green suggested. 'George is not Jean's husband, there's just no way. I can guarantee she is married and the husband is off living somewhere else,' he said with great confidence.

Around 9 p.m., Green sent the constable home for the night. For Green and Alchin, the workday was far from over. They travelled about two hours north on a train from Sydney's Central Station to Wyong, a tiny town wedged between small crop-farming communities to the south and west, and the South Pacific Ocean to the east. They arrived just after midnight, walked a short distance to collect a car at the local police station, and set out on the 35-kilometre road trip to the small inland settlement of Kulnura and the farm owned by Shorrock.

The trip from the coast to Kulnura was difficult enough during the day, but close to impossible at night. This was not the outback, nor a country road bordered by sheep pastures, terrain with which Alchin felt well acquainted. Even to those unfamiliar with it, the outback offers the advantage of an open and visible horizon, but what lay before the two men was bush track, and barely so. It was relentlessly rough and rocky, and in some places hardly wide enough to accommodate the car. Overhanging branches scratched and clawed at the car as it wound along the curling road, vibrating and moving sideward as gravel rolled beneath its wheels. Through their boots, the officers felt the constant and loud rhythmic beat of the stones that showered the belly of the car. The officers pitched left to right and jostled hard against the seat as the car dropped into and groaned out of the many unseen potholes.

At least the clear sky that evening was fortuitous for the men. The near-to-full moon cast its glow across the face of Mangrove Mountain. By 1923, the inner-city streets of Sydney had the brilliancy of electric lighting and the certainty of purified gas lamps when electricity failed. The officers were grateful for the moonbeams in such a remote place as this.

At many points Alchin slowed the car to a crawl, giving the officers time to study the shadows and depth of the forest through the window. They comforted themselves with discussion about the good fortune of the weather. It was dry and had been one of the driest months that year. If it had rained that day, and rained enough, the road would have been impassable.

The communities along their route were small. The farmhouses were highly dispersed and not visible to each other by line of sight. For someone determined not to be found, the area represented the perfect place to burrow and quietly hide.

Seclusion and solitude were precisely what many residents of Kulnura sought. Since the end of the war, many new inhabitants of the area were returned soldiers making use of land settlement grants. It was believed the act of farming – the peace and tranquillity of a rural setting, the natural rhythms of cultivation and the prospect of a stable income stream – were restorative to men suffering the traumatic effects of war. From the reconnaissance that the officers had undertaken before setting out, the farmer they sought was one of those returned servicemen. Shorrock had enlisted in the Australian Imperial Force in March 1917 at Mosman. He was single.

His nearest relative was a married sister who also lived in the Kulnura region.

A preliminary background search for the woman known as Cissie Boyd or Cissie Jackson (the other name provided by Jean) hadn't yielded anything. They knew nothing whatsoever about their prime suspect.

When Alchin and Green pulled up outside Shorrock's property at 2 a.m., no lights were visible inside the house. Green knocked heavily on the door. After some time, the house showed quiet signs of life. The officers could hear footsteps shuffling across a wooden floor, then the fumbling of someone in search of a source of light.

A gentleman opened the door holding a small hurricane lamp. When he lifted it so that he might see the faces of his mysterious visitors more clearly, he inadvertently cast more light on himself. He was an older man, his light brown hair peppered with grey. This fitted the description of his service records, which indicated that he was in his late forties.

Alchin spoke first. 'We are detectives from Sydney.'

The man's face tensed in alarm.

'Are you Joseph Shorrock?' Green asked.

'Yes,' he replied, with some hesitation. It was clear that this man had absolutely no idea why the police might be at his door in the middle of the night.

'Is there anyone else in your house at this time?'

To the surprise of the officers, a dark figure appeared behind Shorrock and became slowly illuminated by the glow of the lamp.

'Yes,' replied Shorrock. 'I have a friend who works on my property living here.' He motioned to the figure beside him. 'This is Mr Pepper.' Shorrock held his breath before he added, 'And I have a Mrs Jackson staying with me. A guest who has travelled from Scotland.' He spoke with a soft tone, and his voice had the lilting, song-like rhythm distinctive to the far north of England.

'Sir, we will need to speak to Mrs Jackson. We need to come inside now,' said Green firmly.

At this, Shorrock stepped back, swung open the door and invited the detectives inside. As he hurried to light more lamps, he called out, 'Mrs Jackson, are you awake? There is someone here to speak to you.'

Shorrock led Alchin and Green to a bedroom a little further down the corridor. He knocked politely, but there was no answer. He felt the presence of the sergeants behind him. He nudged the door open slowly, with the policemen closely flanking him.

Green set eyes on the woman first, through the crack in the opening door. She was towards the corner of the room attempting to hide, though not very convincingly, behind a closet door. She was dressed in men's pyjamas. She looked tiny and sickly.

The officers asked only enough of the woman to establish that she had some involvement in the case. They wanted to take her back to Sydney to be interviewed formally at No. 2 Station in a controlled environment.

'What is your name?' Alchin asked.

'Jackson,' she answered. She looked vulnerable, scared.

Alchin pressed on, but a little more reluctantly. 'A week ago you had a baby girl with you in Sydney. What did you do with it?'

She was cornered, in a small room, the dim lamplight no doubt amplifying her fear as the looming figures of the three men cast slender and exaggerated shadows up the wall and ceiling of the small bedroom. They blocked her only exit. There was simply no way out.

'I want to tell the truth,' she said.

She then hung her head and did not speak again for what felt to the officers like a long time.

'I want to tell the truth,' she repeated.

'And you should tell the truth,' urged Alchin.

The officers and Shorrock waited again, while Albert Pepper listened from the corridor.

'I strangled it,' she said matter-of-factly.

Alchin felt his stomach start to turn. 'How did you do that?' he asked.

'I put a handkerchief in its mouth and I shoved it tightly.'

To the surprise of all the men present, she continued without prompting.

'And I tied its ankles together with another piece of string but by that time it was dead.'

The floodgates had been opened.

'I then rolled it in a towel and put it in a grip [suitcase] and my friend Jean and I got a tram to Circular Quay and Jean picked up a wood block there and I put it in the grip.

We got on a boat to North Sydney but it was too light, and I was not game to throw the hamper over going across. We were on the front of the boat. We remained on the boat. When coming back we were at the back of the boat and it was dark and I dropped the suitcase into the harbour.'

Shorrock stared away. Lowering the lamp he still held in his hand, he could not look her in the face.

'You had better dress,' said Green. 'We need you to come to Sydney with us.'

As Green opened the car door to assist the woman they knew as Mrs Jackson into the back seat, Shorrock and Pepper watched on. In the moonlight, Alchin, an expert in reading deception in the faces of criminals, stood close enough to the men to observe their genuine shock. He spoke to them quietly, 'You will both need to be interviewed shortly, but for now, Mrs Jackson will need to be returned to the police station without delay.'

Eager to return with their key suspect to Sydney, Alchin quickly gathered more thorough contact details and inform-ation regarding the movements of the men. As he stepped towards the car, Shorrock called out, 'But, Sergeant, what is to be done with the boy?'

'Pardon me, Mr Shorrock, I'm not sure I understand your meaning?' replied Alchin.

'The little boy. Mrs Jackson's boy – James. He is asleep in the back room of the house as well. He's only three.'

•

Alchin drove. Green sat in the back with Mrs Jackson. About thirty minutes passed before any of them spoke and, to the surprise of the police, it was Jackson who spoke first. Alchin listened intently from the driver's seat.

'What will you do with me for this?' she asked.

Green answered bluntly, without emotion. 'This is a very serious matter and you will have to be charged with murder.'

Alchin backtracked around the base of Mangrove Mountain, following the winding road in the moonlight away from the humidity and heavy scent of the forest and towards the fresher air of the sea. Unlike Green, Alchin had trouble retaining his composure. His criminals were men of corruption and graft – those who denied, connived and deceived to the bitter end of a prosecution. The tiny, unassuming woman riding quietly in the back of the police car sat at odds with everything he knew to be criminal. And the ease with which she admitted to such debased capabilities chilled him to the bone.

5

ABLACH

Ablach *[Scottish origin, noun]*
1 *Mangled carcass. Body not necessarily dead but maimed or reduced to a pitiable condition.*
2 *Since late 19th century used in Scotland to refer to an insignificant person.*
3 *Can be used playfully to describe a child.*

Merriam-Webster Dictionary

OF MURDER IT IS SAID THAT ONLY TWO PEOPLE EVER KNOW the truth of what occurs – the killer and the killed. Of course, the suitcase baby cannot be counted as one of these two: she had no awareness of what occurred beyond physical pain.

But the maxim of murder as a macabre bond between two people still applies here. Only two people knew the truth of the suitcase baby murder. And those two were sitting in police custody at Darlinghurst Gaol as dawn broke on Friday, 23 November 1923.

The police knew that the statements of the two women now held in custody would be the most important pieces of evidence collected during the course of the investigation. Ultimately, the conviction of one or both women would be determined by the choices the police made in the next twenty-four hours, and they had been made acutely aware of this through messages trickling down from the most senior levels of the force.

The suitcase baby murder was the highest-profile case that metropolitan police in Sydney had faced that year. It had been a leading national news story in every local rag, broadsheet and tabloid for six straight days. It had also become an important case politically, hence the pressure from above. Securing a conviction was now essential for the police force.

The suitcase baby murder was also important politically for the police in the inner city. The turn of the century had seen the economic decline of the inner-city fringe in Sydney. As the middle class had migrated to detached and therefore larger and cleaner accommodation offered by large-scale suburban development, the central business district had become encircled by poverty. While hundreds of working-class people earnestly made a living and raised families in these areas, destitution and crime were part of the fabric of day-to-day life in Woolloomooloo, Surry Hills, Haymarket, Redfern, Newtown, Camperdown, Glebe, Darlinghurst and

Paddington. The illegal drug and alcohol trade was growing, along with the amount of prostitution.

In the 1920s, newspaper reports of police activities presented a curious blend of official business and celebrity gossip. What police did was of great interest to the community. Journalists were eager to deliver up stories on which senior police sergeant had been seen in a certain country town, or who was attending a funeral, who'd got married, or who was going on holiday. Maintaining public confidence in the police force was vital, and convictions on high-profile cases were required for two main reasons.

First, the NSW police force had an image problem, and big moves were required to restore the confidence of the public in law enforcement. A historian at Deakin University, Richard Evans, describes in detail how corruption in the police force grew throughout the 1920s in Sydney. Police officers were increasingly working undercover, pretending to be criminals with a view to infiltrating and ultimately cracking the growing problem of vice rackets. The problem was that some officers had taken their acting roles a little too seriously and decided to pocket bribes while turning a blind eye to drug trafficking, illegal bookmaking and the sly grog trade. In some parts of Sydney, the police were perceived to be no better than the criminals.

Second, the force needed to demonstrate its value as a locally grown and trained organisation, otherwise it was at risk of being displaced by imperial imports. At several points over the previous two years, the NSW police commissioner had been put under strong political pressure to absorb excess staff from the imperial forces – in particular, those in Ireland.

In 1920, Ireland had implemented a unique security policy in an attempt to deal with increasingly violent religious unrest. The Irish police had undertaken a massive recruitment drive in order to increase the number of officers on the ground in communities. An auxiliary force had been built with a view to supporting the local police. Unfortunately, many of the men had received very little training and were either incompetent or engaging in criminal behaviour and 'eye for an eye' violence with local protestors. From 1920 to 1922, the reserve forces, colloquially known as the 'Black and Tans' for their distinctively coloured uniforms, were found to be responsible for trashing and ransacking towns, and besieging the town of Tralee. They were believed to be responsible for the abduction and murder of high-profile Catholic priests as payback for attacks on and murders of Black and Tans.

Throughout 1922, commissioners of police Australia wide had been under great political pressure to assist in retraining and relocating the now overstaffed Irish police force. NSW Commissioner James Mitchell had pushed back hard, but good press that praised the integrity and competence of the locally grown force remained a top priority. The superintendent had communicated the meaning of this to the local area command: confidence in the force would translate directly into a better working life for all officers – more funding, better recruits, better resources, and more public respect for men working the beat. Mitchell wanted the suitcase baby murder solved quickly and was closely monitoring the efforts of local area command. He insisted on daily briefings on progress.

At around two that morning, the officers had apprehended a woman who called herself Mrs Jackson. Six hours later, the woman had abandoned her pseudonym and admitted to her real name – Sarah Boyd.

When Constable Sherringham arrived at work around the time of this admission, Sergeants Alchin and Green were still at the station after more than twenty-four hours on duty. The sergeants were exhausted. Alchin, in particular, was rattled by the loathsome act of infanticide, and the cold and logical description of this undertaking offered by the woman who freely confessed to it. Alchin and his wife, both staunch Catholics, had prayed for children throughout their married life but after many years of failure had resigned themselves to childlessness. As a man who had struggled with the under-standing that his God was denying him a son or daughter, Alchin was deeply troubled by such a gross tragedy as an unwanted child. The baby had not mattered to her mother – and now, from the position of an objective investigator, Alchin knew that the testimonies of the two suspects mattered much more to the securing of a conviction than even the discovery of the body. The child, it seemed, mattered to absolutely no one.

Both sergeants were in an interview room taking a formal statement from Sarah. Present also was Constable Wallace, one of the junior officers conscripted to undertake transcription, retrieve items of evidence and see to any other administrative tasks required for the case that morning.

Sherringham knocked on the interview-room door. Green quietly and respectfully exited the room, conscious of not disturbing the momentum of Alchin's interview with the suspect.

Green was impressed with Sherringham's abilities for interrogation. The constable was young and inexperienced to be sure, but he was also clever and seemed to intuitively know how to respond to the tactics of evasion, concealment and half-truths commonly used by suspects. Green assigned to him the collection of one of the most vital pieces of evidence associated with the case. The woman who now admitted her real name to be Jean Olliver would outline her level of involvement in the murder to Constable Sherringham.

While the interview process was important to both mapping the full arc of the crime and eliciting admissions from individuals regarding their involvement, the official statements of Sarah and Jean provided something further. They revealed a complex relationship between the two women – more complex than the police had first imagined.

Sarah made her formal statement first. She gave the appearance of one who had surrendered entirely to the process.

Alchin asked if she wished to make a statement. 'I want to tell the truth,' was her reply.

The statement was short, confirming all the major elements of the case that the police had pieced together. The baby had died because Sarah had strangled it, she said. Her statement was consistent with Stratford Sheldon's assessment.

'I wrapped the child in a towel, and placed it in a travel case,' said Sarah.

According to Sarah, Jean had scooped a block of wood off the roadside near Circular Quay and placed it in the suitcase in the belief that it would weigh down the package. She had accompanied Sarah to the water. They had ridden the North Shore ferry and dropped the suitcase overboard.

The officers read the statement back to Sarah. 'That is true,' she replied, and signed it.

Alchin behaved professionally throughout, but he appeared to struggle with the question of 'why' more than the other officers involved. At one point, he posed the question to Sarah in a direct, almost pleading way. 'Why did you do it?' he asked.

The answer offered him no sense of peace, as Sarah spoke again of cold practicalities. Alchin interpreted this as her having no moral reckoning of the crime. 'I did not get any word from its father,' said Sarah. 'I have written him a couple of letters and he has not replied.'

Alchin made detailed notes while the events of the previous night were still clear in his mind. He also made the appropriate copies of the statement and debriefed with Green. However, when Alchin left the station that morning, this signalled his official exit from the investigation. He wanted no further involvement and requested that the superintendent assign him elsewhere. The Crown's case would move forward to the Supreme Court without Alchin giving direct evidence and without his appearance at the trial. He requested leave and left Sydney on 'holiday' about ten days later.

Jean made her formal statement with Sherringham in attendance.

The baby had died because Sarah had killed it, claimed Jean. She had left Sarah alone for only ten minutes, some time after 6 p.m. on Thursday, 15 November. When she returned, the baby was dead, the string wrapped around its throat, a handkerchief in its mouth. 'Its face was black,' she added.

Jean tried to persuade Sarah to give herself up to the police, but when Sarah pleaded that she could not, Jean's only thought was to protect her.

Sarah asked Jean to pick up the road paver as they alighted the tram at Circular Quay. Sarah placed the block in the suitcase.

Jean accompanied Sarah on the ferry across the harbour. She saw Sarah throw the case overboard.

Jean's testimony also helped to sketch out the events after the suitcase was thrown into the harbour. It was Jean who insisted that Sarah could not go back to her accommodation at the Brighton Residential Boarding House that night. It was Jean who insisted that Sarah stay with her at the Square and Compass. Jean was concerned for Sarah's safety, she said. She was scared about what Sarah might do. 'It was like she had gone mad,' said Jean.

Sherringham read the statement back to Jean. 'That is true,' she replied, and signed it.

Green and Sherringham then pooled their efforts and confronted the two women together. This was most likely done with the expectation that anything the women had concealed up to this point would be exposed, and that openly discussing their confessions would expose any betrayal between them and sever their friendship. This would make it easier for the police to construct their case. They wanted the alliance between the women broken.

Green addressed them both. He stood looking down on them, after seating them face to face at the interview table, intensifying the pressure on them.

'Each of you women has made a statement in reference to the killing of the baby found at Athol Gardens,' said Green. 'I want you to listen attentively to them. Proceed reading, Sherringham.'

The women listened and then reacted in a way that the police had not expected.

Jean didn't seem concerned that Sarah had identified her as the one largely responsible for hiding the crime. It was Jean's idea to weight the suitcase; it was Jean who had steadied Sarah's hand and supported her in throwing the case over-board. Jean agreed this was true.

Yet, Jean objected firmly to one part of Sarah's testimony. Sarah claimed that she had returned to her own room at Brighton Residential, and this wasn't true, according to Jean. She interrupted Sherringham as he read the statement back. 'No, Cissie! You did not go back there, you stayed with me that night!'

'Oh yes, so I did,' said Sarah matter-of-factly.

Sherringham continued. Jean disputed another part of Sarah's statement, but this time she waited until he had finished reading before she spoke up, directly to Sarah. 'I was not in the room, Cissie, when you killed the baby.'

'Oh yes you were, Jean,' Sarah replied.

To this, Jean did not respond.

During the course of the entire investigation, the coronial inquest and ultimately the trial, these few words would be the only crossed ones recorded to pass between the women.

6

PLOTTING A BOYD CURVE

A LIST OF FACTS CAN BE GATHERED ABOUT THE SOCIOECONOMIC backdrop of Sarah's early life. Can plotting a course back to the place and time coordinates of Sarah's birth and upbringing, and even further back through her family history, provide a grand theory to explain the suffocation of her baby?

When dissected into a set of statistics, the Boyds read like a grim profile of poverty typical of nineteenth-century Scottish industrial towns. They were situated in the largest sector of employment, in one of the most important industries for Scotland at the time: factory workers in the textile mill town of Paisley, Renfrewshire, 20 kilometres west of Glasgow. The local county statistical profile of the era is characterised by high fertility and high infant mortality, low average annual income and low life expectancy. Communities were worked to death. A range of chronic health problems such as respiratory diseases, fostered by poor working and living conditions, contributed to an average life expectancy that did not exceed forty.

For each statistical observation made about Sarah's early life, a poignant image is evoked. Father's country of birth: Ireland. Occupation: chemical combiner. A bearded man in a woollen work suit with buttoned-down pockets. Mother's country of birth: Scotland. A mother in a bell-shaped skirt and puffed sleeves, a silhouette of corseted moral restraint. Religion: Presbyterian, Free Church of Scotland. Their lives captioned by the text: typical textile mill family, Paisley, Victorian era. Household size: eight.

In 1895, a sixth child is recorded. Child born: alive. Sex: female. Christian name: Sarah.

From the moment that Sarah's father and mother were married and commenced their life together, they were not focused on achieving prosperity but rather on maintaining survival. This required a capacity to read and anticipate the shifting fortunes of Ireland and Scotland to find work and sustain their growing family.

Born in Larne in 1855, on the east coast of Northern Ireland, William Boyd was cradled by the social and economic angst left in the wake of the worst famine in Irish history. It affected him so deeply that once he made his escape, he never returned to his homeland.

Between 1845 and 1849, an airborne pathogen caused the widespread failure of potato crops and reduced thriving plants to decayed waste in the fields. The potato represented the foundation of the working peasant diet: eaten as a staple, drunk as the heady liquor poteen, and baked into their daily bread. Those living on the brink of survival at the best of times – rural, impoverished and with dependants – were the hardest hit, and the Boyds were no exception.

While this was not Ireland's only potato famine, more than any other it left a scar on the Irish psyche. More than a million people died from starvation, disease or both, and the number of citizens who emigrated as a result of the famine is conservatively estimated to be at least double this number. In the short term, famine poses a threat to the life and livelihood of families; in the long term, it destroys the labour markets and economies that support them. In Ireland, the majority of those taking flight from the crisis were able-bodied workers, the raw machinery that the country would need to rebuild. This only further accelerated the collapse of the national economy. Early twentieth–century analyses of the event describe mass migration from Ireland as one of the most significant economic and social movements in history.

The famine shaped the fortunes and affected the resilience of the Boyd family. Larne was hit hard. Historian Dr Frank Costello, an expert on the Great Famine, describes Larne's experience of it as 'harrowing'. In modern parlance, William Boyd was a survivor of childhood trauma on a national scale. According to Robert Dodgshon, an emeritus professor at the University of Aberystwyth, the context of subsistence crises faced by many small rural towns across Ireland, Scotland and the North of England in this period meant that small and vulnerable families had to develop astute coping strategies in order to survive. William Boyd was one of these astute survivors.

Larne offered him grim prospects indeed. East of the town, the scene is gothic and dramatic, with low-lying grey beach covered in shards of stone that blend into a flat charcoal sea. The seabed is peat and mud, gravel and stones. In the mid-1800s, Larne would have felt especially vulnerable to the vagaries of the raw coast on which it rested, with etern-ally rough swells buffeting the town's edge. At night, winds howled, shutters banged and terraces groaned under the force of the wind blowing in from the Irish Sea.

Facing west, the view that young William gazed upon was worse. Thanks largely to the famine, the spectre of a notorious workhouse loomed over the town. Built in the early 1840s, the workhouse comprised five acres of hospital (labelled at the time as an 'infirmary for idiots') and emergency accommo-dation for the destitute (or 'inmate wards'). In one of the only evaluations of its kind, a report on workhouse conditions was particularly damning of Larne in particular. Though the local government's inspector of workhouses, Colonel Spaight, conducted his assessment many decades later (in 1892), he identified Larne as a woeful under-provider of welfare, even among Irish workhouses, which had a particularly dismal reputation for cramped conditions, rancid meat and putrid pit latrines. In an official national inquiry on welfare, Spaight pinpointed Larne's workhouse as particularly unsavoury, with many 'sanitary defects' and described the 'cells for idiots' as 'wretchedly cold'. Outbreaks of typhus had been documented as one of the most common causes of death. Larne had earned its reputation as a provider of 'poor' relief for the poor.

Locals, and indeed residents of the entire county of Antrim, felt the after-shocks of the famine for years. The deeply held aversion to the workhouse remained long after the famine was officially declared to be over. While no official records remain to verify this, it is highly likely that William's parents, along with the vast majority of impoverished families in the area, had sought food from or had been sheltered by the workhouse during the darkest days of the famine. While this had no doubt saved their lives by sparing them from starvation, association with the 'poorhouse' was experienced as a profound loss of dignity. The ticket of admission to the workhouse was more akin to a travel visa to an offshore island of shame and exile. Entering the workhouse required paperwork, approvals and an interview, and it required a person to leave their community entirely behind and enter another, while agreeing to abide by the laws that governed life inside its walls. Workhouses were more than welfare institutions as they typically functioned as self-contained economies that traded with the local town and had their own workforces, services and products. Inmates were required to wear uniforms and were not permitted to wear civilian clothes.

The Larne workhouse was originally designed to house four hundred, but was known to often accommodate many beyond this. While those who sought refuge would have entered because they had absolutely nowhere else to turn, in many cases the stigma of staying at the workhouse ensured that they remained that way – it was similar to serving time in prison, and not diluted by the fact that your neighbours and members of your parish had lived there as well.

Rather than waning, by 1870 the disgrace of receiving poor relief from the workhouse intensified in Larne. For post-famine generationers like William, historians suggest that fear of the workhouse was even greater than for their parents. The dark mythology of the workhouse had firmly entered the public consciousness. Steven King, Professor of Economic and Social History at the University of Leicester, and Emeritus Professor of Health History at Glasgow Caledonian University John Stewart argue that there formed 'an association in the public mind between workhouses and famine deaths' and this 'intensified public aversion to the institution'. As William neared his fifteenth birthday, and the worst impacts of the famine were lifting from Larne, it faced a blight of its own – a growing reputation as a rough and beggarly workhouse town. For women who spent time in the workhouse, 'immoral character' was assumed. Men who were eventually released from the workhouse were seen as drunk, defective or disinclined to honest work. Larne's reputation and legacy were at odds with a young man who self-identified as smart and industrious.

William had to set his sights not on better work opportunities but on any work opportunities. He swept into Scotland with a flood of economic refugees. Shortly after, Glasgow was struck with an epidemic of typhus and one of the worst outbreaks of rheumatic fever the city had ever known. In the minds of locals, the Irish were to blame. A racial epithet was born. Glaswegians nicknamed typhus, and the influx of migrants, the 'Irish fever'.

Jane Marshall, Sarah's mother, was a Glasgow local, and like William had faced significant social and economic insecurity in childhood. Her father was unskilled and took work wherever he could. He worked for a short period as a city street lamplighter. While the shifts were from dusk till dawn, it was easy work compared to the very poorly paid and inconsistent general labouring that he usually managed to secure.

In early childhood, Jane almost died from rheumatic fever. She contracted a streptococcus throat infection that became systemic and, unlike many children in her neighbourhood, she was lucky enough to survive. But it left her with a weak constitution – involving symptoms such as heart palpitations, fainting spells and shortness of breath – for the remainder of her life.

Though it can't be known how the two young lovers met, Jane was clearly swept off her feet by William. Whether weakened at the knees by a rheumatic spell or by affection for the newly arrived immigrant with the playful northern Irish accent, Jane's heart was fluttering and she easily swooned.

With a shared history of socioeconomic fragility, William and Jane quickly took two important steps to increase the opportunities available to them. First, they accessed the only institutional provision for security afforded to them by welfare law and capable of providing a safety net in the event of sickness, infirmity, care of dependants, and old age – they got married. Second, William encouraged Jane to do something that he had already done: leave her family and homeland.

Before the marital bed was cold, William and Jane migrated to the north-eastern coast of the United States in search of better opportunities. And they were not lonely on the boat. Like the Great Famine, the Irish economic collapse of the 1870s also drove record numbers of families from home soil to the shores of the United States, Canada, England and Australia.

Over the next twelve to eighteen months, the events that unfolded back in Britain must have made William feel vindicated. In 1879, signs emerged that the dark pathogenic cloud of fungal spores had returned to the potato fields of Ireland. Conditions in England and Wales were little better, with heavy and unrelenting rains causing widespread destruction of crops and livestock. Cattle and sheep were suffering and sodden, the flesh literally rotting off their backs while they stood in the flooded fields. Even thirty years later, turn-of-the-century historian and agricultural expert W. R. Curtler continued to describe 1879 as 'the black year of agriculture'. As Jane adjusted to not only motherhood but also life in a new nation, and William worked on the factory floor of a large textile producer, widespread failure of potato crops occurred in western Ireland. While it was not in his home county of Larne, the news must have stirred William on some level. He had successfully outrun the return of blight to his homeland.

While living in the United States, the Boyds had two – and what would be their only – sons: William Junior (named after his father and paternal grandfather) and John (named after Jane's father). Along with many Irish immigrants, William ensured the family took up residence in and around Boston, not far from the port in which they had disembarked.

For unskilled immigrants, the opportunities for entry-level manufacturing work seemed boundless. The area was one of the fastest-growing local economies in the Americas, with textile and footwear production shaping the fortunes of many arrivals from Ireland. Prior to the 1880s, despite New England representing only 8 per cent of the US population, the region employed 20 per cent of the country's manufacturing sector.

By 1880, however, economic conditions in New England began to change. Growth slowed, with 'the erosion of the region's industrial leadership especially pronounced in textiles, and boots and shoes – the industries largely responsible for New England's early industrialisation'. William, figuratively reading the writing on the factory wall, packed up his family and left.

Rather than return to Ireland, where economic conditions continued to look bleak, William followed the thread of cotton spooling out from the United States to where he believed opportunities still existed: West Scotland. Their first three daughters were born in 1884, 1886 and 1888. And all the while, the family town-hopped as they sought textile work opportunities. It was not that William had any particular interest in textiles, but economic circumstances and the availability of jobs had made him a man of cloth. The eldest girls, Janet and Margaret, were born in Lanarkshire, while the third girl, Agnes, was born in Irvine, North Ayrshire, about 70 kilometres away.

Modern understandings of the quality of working life during early industrialisation are woven tightly with Dickensian impressions of Victorian London: poor living conditions; terrible treatment of the powerless by the powerful; and the blood, sweat and tears of those who hauled the back-breaking weight of the Industrial Revolution forward. In Scotland, modes of production were cut from the same cloth. Male labour, particularly of those perceived to be strong, was absorbed by the Scottish coal industry. Women and children were generally preferred by the cotton and jute mills – the operation of spinning and weaving machinery was hard work but little of it involved heavy lifting.

Business owners designed the mills to maximise production, and the Boyds lived in mill towns. Square footage of floor space was carefully measured so production lines could be compacted as tightly as possible. The machines needed to run continuously, facilitated by attentive workers. The access lanes between the lines were so narrow that only small-framed workers could move between, under and around the rotating, sliding and rolling mechanical arms. While machinery was now used to spin and weave, fingers were still required to load, guide, brush, oil, snag, twist and fix to ensure production was not halted. Strong backs were needed to shift cotton bales on arrival and to load bolts of cloth for departure.

In the production of textiles, women and children were considered more important than men, but not important enough to be paid comparable wages.

The Boyds managed remarkably well. Despite the financial demands of feeding a large family, Jane and William did it alone and without the children having to work in the mills from a very young age. Child labour was not only common but also a necessary part of the labour process, with minors required to crawl beneath or climb atop machinery in order to clear lint that might cause a jam. While laws were in place that limited the ways in which child labour was used by textile factories in the late 1800s, there was a general acceptance among both families and employers that working children were good for both the factory and household bottom lines.

There is much evidence that these laws were in many cases ineffective. The *Ten Hours Act 1847* legislated that shifts be no longer than ten hours, placed limits on start and finish times (no work before 6 a.m. or after 6 p.m.), and defined the length of working days on Saturday. However, with few inspectors to patrol the thousands of large-scale factories across Britain, business owners could easily ignore the law. The *Factory and Workshops Act 1878* – the year that William Junior was born – sought to limit the exploitation of women and children in textile mills. However, it still allowed children ten and over to be employed on shifts comparable to those undertaken by adults.

William and Jane worked hard to keep their family together, and they succeeded in insulating their children from some of the horrors of industrial life in a textile town. William worked shifts of up to fifteen hours. Jane, with a brood of children to keep in line and a home to look after, worked shifts of twenty-four. But they were resolute. They had seen what factory work had done to the moral fabric of families in the many towns in which they had lived. The Boyds, not the factory, would raise their children.

As the turn of the century approached, William and Jane must have felt some satisfaction. Their laneway housing had a reputation for being dirty, blackened by the smoke that spiralled around the homes as they burned fires continually to remain warm. But for William and Jane, hope rose too. They had kept moving for years, while William had chased and caught slightly better work each time. They continued to be impoverished, but they had achieved a measure of economic and familial stability, albeit on the cusp of calamity, by avoiding vagrancy through migrancy. Each of their children had received a substantive education, not just a few classes here or there squeezed around factory shifts. And the Boyds had managed to remain together, unlike many families of the era who effectively signed away their parental rights when their children joined the factory apprentice system.

William and Jane had achieved the baseline aspiration of any parent: they had given their children better opportunities and prospects than the world had offered them.

Now in their forties, the couple witnessed their older children entering employment and contributing to the household budget. The family appeared to be achieving more stability as the elder siblings established themselves in steady employment. The second eldest, John, followed his father into chemical work in carpet production, receiving a wage better than his father's and comparable to the higher incomes in England. Janet, Margaret and Agnes attended school full time, well into their teenage years and beyond the legal requirement of the *Education (Scotland) Act 1872* that made schooling compulsory only until age thirteen.

In 1895, seventeen years after having her first child, Jane named her sixth child Sarah, after her own mother. Like Agnes, Sarah was born in Irvine. Very soon after, however, the family was again on the move. This time the destination was the town of Paisley, about 30 kilometres north and closer to Glasgow. William had developed a skill set around the dyeing and bleaching of cloth and had again secured factory work, but now in the more specialised alchemy of mixing chemicals that softened fabric and also made it more receptive to dye.

Though the Boyds were strong, and seemed held together fast like the bolts of cloth they worked to produce, it was not to last. Even the strongest of cloths can be ripped, torn in half, with one sudden movement. For the Boyds, it happened soon after Sarah's birth.

Jane was at home when she began to feel chest pains and suffered what appeared to be a fainting spell. At first, the family was not too concerned, as Jane had suffered rheumatic weakness and shortness of breath most of her life. However on this occasion the pains did not go away. Jane collapsed and did not regain consciousness. At autopsy, she was determined to have had mitral stenosis – permanent damage to her heart sustained as a result of her childhood rheumatic fever. It was 1896 and Jane was forty-two.

With the loss of Jane, the climate and culture of the family changed. The household environment in which Sarah was raised was vastly different from the one that had been experienced by her older siblings. While William had worked long hours, Jane's skills and capacities as a mother had ensured that the family could always remain ready, poised for change. Despite her reputation as a 'sickly rheumatic', Jane's strength and adaptability had held the large family together. It was she who had managed and coordinated their relocations to follow William as he'd sought work. And she had done so for almost two decades, while either being pregnant or recovering from childbirth, and while nursing a chronic respiratory and heart condition.

The Boyd family had always chosen an existence that both physically and metaphorically rested between two working-class survival strategies: being nested or nomadic. Whether it was because Jane was gone or because William himself was getting older, the family's longstanding survival strategy was over. They did not leave Paisley again. They moved once more, many years later, just around the corner to Clarence Street.

As a young child in Paisley, Sarah lived in a low row of housing on Canal Street, populated by workers who represented a cross-section of textile, cloth, thread and yarn jobs – both factory and some smaller cottage-based enter-prises. They made shirts, mops and shoes. They loomed and weaved. Others tailored, or they worked in draperies. And the rest prepared the paperwork that kept the monolithic mill enterprise running.

One side of the street was resolutely nomadic: a boarding house, populated by men who were tramping to survive. Census and district court sessional records contain many accounts of workers who tramped. More commonly men, they drifted from place to place to pick up labouring work in factories or on farms, staying in boarding houses. While they gave the appearance of being single men, in many cases they had dependants living where work was not available. Peter Drylie, a miner who lived in Paisley and had tramped for years, eventually just never went home. His wife and children were 50 kilometres away to the south, in Muirkirk, now alone and destitute. Because local parishes assumed responsibility for the management of welfare and charity to families, the Muirkirk church reported the matter to the authorities. In the year after Sarah was born, Drylie was captured by the Paisley police, charged and sent to gaol for desertion.

On the other side of Canal Street, neighbours to the Boyds – the Cowdens – were the archetype of a nested working-class family at the time. They had raised their entire family in that house. John Cowden, now well into his seventies, had begun work as a weaver when he was a newly married man. For more than fifty years, he had woven his way along the same winding path to the factory, which was walking distance from home. And as each of the children grew, they followed in his footsteps along the very same path, to the very same factory, to do the very same job.

Sarah was a stranger within her own family, her life different in almost every respect from those of her siblings. Her brothers were more than a decade older than her. Her sisters had been born closely together, with two years between each of them. Although Agnes was only three years older than Sarah she still aligned more closely with Janet and Margaret. Sarah was the only member of her family who shared no memories whatsoever of their mother.

And it wasn't just age that separated Sarah from her siblings. The older Boyds had seen beyond Paisley, and her father and brothers had seen the world. Sarah knew only a few miles in the radius of streets encircling Paisley Abbey at the centre of town.

Sarah's neighbourhood became known for instability and sudden tragedy. Suicide rates increased. In the first year of her life, a neighbour retired in a manner that was becoming increasingly common. A sixty-year-old local labourer – who had given his whole life to the mill – hanged himself, at home, using a length of twine he had taken from work. Before Sarah's fourth birthday, another neighbour shot his wife and himself, both unsuccessfully. In what could be described as a symbolic and ugly act of rage towards the longstanding respiratory illness from which his wife suffered, he aimed at her lung with a revolver and fired. She fell hard to the floor and, assuming her dead, he put the gun in his own mouth and pulled the trigger. He and his wife, after significant time in the infirmary, both survived. But the bullet had lodged in his cheek and could not be removed.

Within a short period, Paisley gained a reputation for being not just a dirty place but a dangerous one as well. In 1897, crime rates increased significantly. Violent attacks and theft were on the rise, and the police were required to break up a growing number of brawls between drunks in the open street. The number of people apprehended for criminal activity increased by almost 20 per cent in one year alone. Paisley now had a dissociative sense of identity; its once pitiful but pious working class began to be regarded as reprobates. As Sarah reached puberty, Paisley's local culture was one conflicted, filled with tension and at odds with itself – disorderly and drunk, but devout as well.

By sixteen she had left formal schooling and taken up work at the factory, in the heddle room. She was younger than her sisters had been when first entering the labour market. The work would have made the world seem even smaller to her, requiring a focus on fine details. It would also have been exacting, tiring and numbingly tedious. Each day would have been filled with repetitive hours of monitoring thousands of tiny heddles, watching the eye in the centre of each heddle, trying to seek order in the confusion of moving parts and dangling threads. Sarah's life was hemmed in, bordered by choices that were not her own, shaped by the decisions of the seven people who had come before her.

Her weekly wage was pitiful – less than half of the income that the cottage-industry women hand weavers of Paisley had earned a hundred years before. Though there were signs the market for Paisley-made goods and textiles remained strong, and jobs were still available, the pressure to produce at a lower cost became intense as cheaper wages and more efficient production in Lancashire squeezed Scottish producers. The expectations on Sarah as a worker would have been more intense than those that had been placed on her sisters. She would have worked longer hours for less pay.

The social environment of Paisley continued to fracture as Sarah entered late adolescence. It remained a church town, with a strong reputation for branches of puritanical Presbyterianism, and it had long represented the stereotype of a Victorian industrialised mill town – overcrowded and polluted, albeit on a smaller scale than Glasgow. By the turn of the century, Paisley had begun to change for the worse. There were signs that its industrial power was weakening. The first generation of factory workers who had fuelled Paisley's rise were now aged and suffering lifelong health problems as a result of their jobs. Younger workers, with less stable work to occupy them, were starting to carouse, steal and fight. Sarah's Paisley was far more dangerous than the one her brothers and sisters had come of age in. She also faced limited prospects for marrying up in a town with a reputation for being grimy.

Renfrewshire had long maintained a reputation for being more genteel and cleaner than the coal-mining districts of

Scotland, because locals could make the unusual claim that the sheep in their fields had not turned black. But by the start of World War I, this reputation had changed. In the first-ever health census of its kind, Paisley was identified as one of the sickest towns in Scotland, with the women of Paisley the sickest of all.

Brown lung disease had been documented as a side effect of exposure to dust and fibre fragments that accumulated in the upper respiratory tracts of workers in fabric, yarn and thread manufacturing. Known colloquially as 'Monday fever' because workers typically felt better on weekends when away from the debris and dust, by the 1870s it had been medically defined and acknowledged as the condition known as 'byssinosis'. It is a painful condition, described as a crushing weight on the chest and the sensation of being strangled. But if nineteenth-century mill workers wanted to be paid, they worked through it. They were also likely to experience bronchial diseases, skin irritations and diseases, and 'influenza-like' symptoms.

•

During the years of World War I and its aftermath, Sarah became lost to both her family and to anyone trying to sharpen their focus on her using a historical lens. Sarah's young adulthood is dark, peppered with difficult decisions that would ultimately lead to her awaiting trial in a lonely Darlinghurst Gaol cell. A viable document trail that might shed light on the years immediately preceding her emigration from Scotland is missing.

The closer we get to Sarah, the more difficult she becomes to understand. Even with careful and compassionate examination of her relationships and everyday life, it's still hard to envision how she came to be a woman capable of strangling her own child.

However, when she is compared to her contemporaries, the picture slowly comes into focus. The further away we get from Sarah as an individual, the easier she is to see.

In the summer of 1920, two Scottish women called Sarah, unknown to each other and unrelated, faced an identical quandary. Both were young, both lived in the same region of Scotland (one in Paisley and one in Glasgow), both fell pregnant out of wedlock and both were named Sarah Boyd. Both were also prepared to go to extreme lengths in order to shield themselves and their families from the shame and stigma of illegitimate children.

Glasgow Sarah tried to conceal her pregnancy until the day of the baby's birth. Sometime after her father left for work, she was alone at home. After going into labour and successfully delivering a healthy newborn girl on her own, Glasgow Sarah acted quickly. She placed the baby under blankets and suffocated her. But she did not dispose of the baby immediately. She slept one night with the corpse concealed in her bedding. The next morning, after her father left for work, she again had the house to herself. She stuffed the body behind woodwork beneath the sink.

The crime was only discovered through the testimony of neighbours who reported to police that they had suspected she might be pregnant and then suddenly observed that she was not. When police arrived a few days later to question her, Glasgow Sarah's first response was denial. Within a few short minutes, however, she was peeling back the board beneath the sink. 'I did not know what to do with it,' she said. 'I had made no provision for it.'

Glasgow Sarah was found guilty of murder and received a prison sentence of twelve months. When asked why she had done it, she placed one person at the centre of her motive, and it was not the father of the child. Her only option, she had believed, was to make the child completely disappear because 'of the shame it would bring on her and her father'.

In July 1920, Paisley Sarah, daughter of William and Jane, was also pregnant with an illegitimate child and still living at home with her family. She, too, elected to make her pregnancy disappear, but she used an entirely different method.

She had successfully used the dropped-waist, billowing and oversized fashions of 1920 to conceal the pregnancy. As the birth neared, she knew that making the baby go away was the only sure way to protect her father from the intense shame of a daughter's sin and a bastard grandchild. If Sarah had felt at odds with her family and had never really felt like a Boyd, her decision-making in 1920 proved that she shared their nature and temperament more than she may have ever realised. Following in the quick-thinking footsteps of her father, Sarah packed up her life and surrendered her fate to God and the sea.

Her departure from Scotland in 1920 was neither aspirational nor a romanticised adventure filled with promise. As the steamship powered away from her homeland, the dull drone of the engine grinding through the open water would have rung in her ears.

The two Sarah Boyds shared a further characteristic. While both women clearly had unsympathetic fathers, they were also motherless. According to Professor Andrew Blaikie at the School of Divinity, History and Philosophy at the University of Aberdeen, this is a highly significant fact that would have intensified the desperation of their situation as young unwed mothers. Using a hundred years of statistical evidence on illegitimacy, Blaikie developed an analytical device colourfully called the 'bastardy ratio'. This ratio identifies that Scotland had a more hospitable and accepting environment for bastardy, when compared to the rest of Britain, demonstrated through a low infant mortality rate in relative terms. However, the successful rearing of children born out of wedlock relied almost entirely on the presence of caring, supportive grandparents. Without such grandparents, illegitimate children had little hope. Neither Glasgow Sarah nor Paisley Sarah had this vital safety net to ensure a future for their children.

While the decision to leave may have felt to Paisley Sarah like an autonomous one, in reality it represented a single dot along an intergenerational timeline of carefully managed risk. The Boyds had always survived by running away. And now Sarah, with her father as a role model, was doing exactly the same thing. In seeking disconnection from her family, she had paradoxically achieved a deeper sense of connection. William had, in effect, taught her the very coping strategy that she was now using against him.

Sarah decided to travel as far from her father as possible. At the time, this was the voyage from Britain to New Zealand. Did Sarah know the level of risk involved? Did sea travel in itself represent an act of spiritual significance for her? In answer to both of these questions, the evidence points to yes.

There are few places that feel closer to godly omnipotence than the open sea. Sarah would have felt exposed to the heavens, with nothing between her sin and the sky. The lightning storms are dramatic and terrifying, the horizon seems endless, and the ocean is vast and powerful enough to swallow ships whole, with all souls on board. Is it possible that Sarah's shame was so great that she wanted to die and take her unborn child with her? If the baby perished while she gave birth on the open sea, it would be God's will, not hers. If the Lord in his wisdom chose to take her as well, there is little doubt that Sarah, a deeply religious woman, would have felt this was only what she deserved.

She may have thought that the child's death at sea would solve all of her problems. If God granted her mercy and allowed her to live, after a short sojourn she could return to Paisley and her old life. In time, perhaps she could even forget the terrible mistakes that had led to her predicament.

There is no doubt that Sarah knew the types of hazards involved in taking to the high seas while heavily pregnant. The journey to New Zealand included three harrowing ocean crossings and would take around thirty-five days. On its voyage from Sydney to London, just before Sarah's departure, the ship on which she sailed – the *Orvieto* – had one of the worst outbreaks of measles in the history of steamship travel. One third of passengers contracted the disease, and several children died on board.

Less than two weeks into the journey, Sarah gave birth at sea, just outside the port of Colombo, Ceylon (now Sri Lanka). She then gave the child, a boy, his second name – Orvieto. He would not be given his Christian name until several weeks after Sarah disembarked in Wellington. She needed time to create the facts that she would use to start her life there, and to sort these facts plausibly in a way that created two whole new people. Her son. And herself.

7

SUITOR

THE MOST SKILFUL SEAMSTRESSES KNOW HOW TO POSITION stitches closely together so there will be no seam visible between pieces of fabric. In this way, disconnected fragments can be sewn into something new.

Initially, at least, Wellington appeared to be a great place for Sarah to fashion a life for herself. The town had a large immigrant population, including a significant number of Scots. Sarah was not known to anyone and she could present a freshly pressed version of herself. She could weave any story she liked about her hurried departure from her homeland and about her son's father, so she decided to transform into a woman heroically coping with widowhood.

The first stitch in her new life was the Christian name of her son. She called him James Orvieto Boyd. But very soon afterwards, and for the rest of his life, he would be called by the nickname Jimmie.

As a textile labour market veteran, Sarah had skills to offer. And as a small country, New Zealand was keen to improve its textile export profile and gain a reputation as a wool product provider on the world stage.

Sarah had about ten years of factory experience in thread and textile manufacture. She also had impressive self-taught skills in small-scale customised seamstress work, which she had acquired from observing and helping her sisters in their dressmaking and drapery work. Another advantage that Sarah had over many other migrants was her high level of literacy in both reading and writing; she could do basic book work, read and take orders, and she understood how to record measurements.

Thanks to an active women's welfare and suffragist lobby, Wellington was a more progressive town than Paisley. There were burgeoning pockets of acceptance that women were capable of more than homemaking and child rearing. Wellington's newspaper, *The Dominion*, not only hired one of the youngest female journalists in New Zealand but also permitted her to write under her real name rather than a male pseudonym. While Iris Wilkinson's first column was targeted to children and focused on farm animals in *The Dominion*'s rural rag – the *New Zealand Farmer's Advocate* – she was offered a regular column 'Peeps at Parliament' to provide 'uniquely female perspectives' on parliamentary debate and political discourse.

In the wake of the war, single women became part of the social landscape of Wellington. Widows were nobly managing and running families single-handedly, socialising unchaperoned by men, and congregating not as wives but in order to advance their interests as women. Wellington was one of the first places in New Zealand to acknowledge that women of all classes could benefit from the provision of short-term and fee-for-service child care. The Women's Christian Temperance Union (WCTU) had its headquarters and a strong presence in Wellington, seeking to improve the lives of women across the city. Preschool centres were established with the help of volunteer labour.

However, it did not take long for Sarah to realise that her hopes for a new life would not materialise easily, even in woman-friendly Wellington.

Work was hard to come by. Although there were textile mills geared to woollen carpet and blanket manufacturing scattered across New Zealand, the Dominion was far from an industrial powerhouse like Britain. There was less work than in her native Scotland, and even less for a woman with a small child who couldn't work a fixed-hour roster.

As a fledgling nation keen to impress the Empire, New Zealand had been generous in its contribution to the war effort, and there were now many returned soldiers for the labour market to reabsorb. In a population of just over a million, 100 000 had served as combat, field or medical officers. Economic and social policy was geared towards taking care of the veterans, so in 1920 employment for women in the labour market was difficult to come by. Many women were displaced en masse in order for businesses to offer every able-bodied veteran the prospect of a job and a career. Women workers received less than half the pay rates of men. Sarah's financial position was even more precarious than it had been in Paisley – she was a fallen woman seeking economic stability in a nation gripped with grief for its fallen men.

In Wellington, the Women's National Reserve Residential Nursery (WNRRN) had just opened, an early incarnation of modern institutional child care. Were a woman in hospital with no relatives available to care for her children, the service could assist by providing care for weeks at a time. A nursery or day-care centre was also established so women could drop off children while they 'ran errands or went into town to shop for the day' – outside-the-house undertakings deemed most acceptable for women at the time. The crèche emerged from a grassroots initiative by the soldiers' and sailors' wives club and was focused on offering support to war-affected families.

However, institutions such as the WNRRN, which might have offered women like Sarah some real assistance in her struggle as a single immigrant mother, took an exclusive moral stand on who could access their services. The WNRRN did not want to develop a reputation as a sanctuary for wayward and immoral women. Though this was never stated in its charter, unmarried women were not permitted to purchase child-care services. The nursery operated on a sliding-scale fee structure designed to screen out unmarried women because the service required disclosure of the husband's income in order to determine the hourly amount payable. This was a clever way for the organisation to screen out people exactly like Sarah because unless mothers could be forthcoming with specific documentation relating to the father, and provide more than just a story, their applications for support were denied.

With Christmas approaching, Sarah came to the realisation that New Zealand could not deliver the 'milk and honey' prosperity that had been promised in the migration poster she had seen earlier that year in Paisley. New Zealand may have advertised for 'industrious Scottish men and women', but proof of good character was obviously required in order to achieve social mobility.

At the end of 1920, Sarah's savings ran out. Without the support of family, she had two choices: accept the help of established charities or try to make it solo. The knowledge that institutional help came at a high price that would be repaid over a lifetime was part of accepted social understanding. On a personal level as well, it is possible that Sarah's father, after his experiences with the workhouse, would have instilled in her a strong aversion to the acceptance of charity. It was a stigma that William had spent a lifetime trying to shake off.

In Wellington, the WCTU's welfare program offered refuge to 'fallen women', grouped with prostitutes as moral equivalents. Sarah could put food in her belly today and have a bed to sleep in tonight, but she would be labelled as morally irredeemable every day thereafter. She could be absorbed into the charity system and accept help, but with this she would forgo any hope of restoring her good character, dissolve any possibility of social mobility through marriage, and consign her baby to the lifelong shame of illegitimacy and moral corruption. Or, worse, Sarah risked losing Jimmie forever. Any self-respecting Christian charity could not be seen to condone wicked choices. Most institutions deemed the mothers unfit, incapable of making good moral decisions for themselves or their children, and either forced mothers to surrender their offspring or had them forcibly removed.

Sarah made her choice. She committed fully to a subterfuge that would permit her to maintain a facade of respectability, while living at variance with social and moral mores. Sarah had described her lover, John Aitken, as a bootmaker. He had been unwilling to meet his responsibilities as a father, and it had been Sarah and her son who bore the shame. Sarah's moral narrative gave the lothario bootmaker the boot, replaced him with a dutiful and honourable husband, then promptly and imaginatively killed him in a tragic bootmaking accident. To heighten her appearance of vulnerability and garner more sympathy, Sarah needed to chronicle the death of her entire family as well. Overnight she became a noble and struggling widow with no living family to assist. It was not a difficult narrative to retain. From Sarah's perspective, from a vantage point of absolute exile on the other side of the world, her family may as well have been dead.

Sarah, perhaps a little too optimistically, also committed to work her way out of her situation. She returned to her Free Church roots, drawing comfort from a Calvinist philosophy that toil renews and represents a divine endorsement that one is still in God's favour; where sin and desire are subjugated and replaced with a work ethic, this is restorative to the soul. Sarah abandoned the search for factory or rostered employment and resorted to consignment tailoring, sewing and repair work. For a woman seeking absolution through hard work and exhaustion, this was only limited by the quantity of work available. It could be done at any hour of the day or night in her boarding-house room, provided sufficient lighting was available. The factory whistle never blew. Her ability to work was governed only by the rhythm of a baby's sleep-and-feed cycle.

Sarah later described her occupation in this period as 'tailoress'. This suggests that the large bulk of her work would have included men's shirts, vests, trousers and collars. Unlike stitching women's garments of this period – which used gathering, pleating and hemming techniques to enhance the natural hang of the fabric – men's tailoring required precision of fit. It also required an eye for symmetry and the matching of patterns: herringbone, tweed, plaid, stripes and check. Collars and cuffs had to be expertly aligned. There was careful and exact measurement involved, and stitched sections required pressing with a hot iron in between sewing to ensure the material remained flat. It was highly skilled work, but as women's work it was defined as menial. Much as in modern outwork, Sarah would have received one of the lowest pay rates in the entire labour market.

For hours Sarah would be hunched in an upright sitting-room chair, the dim light of her boarding-house room cast across the fragments of fabric in her small hands. She worked as quickly as she could, taking advantage of the time available to her while her baby slept. Her livelihood relied on the completion of as many items as possible. Her stitches sutured the neatly pinned scraps of fabric together as perfectly as she could. If the work was poor quality or the fabric damaged in any way, Sarah would not be paid. She most likely did the bulk of her work late at night, when the boarding house was quiet. While she stitched silently, a tiny baby lay swaddled at her feet, sleeping like the dead in an open suitcase refashioned as a makeshift cradle.

To make it solo, Sarah needed to lie and lie well in order to gain any kind of employment. In December 1920, she met a mentor who would teach her how to do just that.

In recalling when and how they met, each woman remembered the details vividly, warmly and without hesitation. It was Hogmanay – the last day of 1920 – and they were at a New Year's Eve party in Wellington. They were both Scots. Their nostalgic recollections of their homeland carried the conversation along easily.

Both of them exchanged suitable lies, concocted to present an appropriate moral mask to the outside world.

'I'm married,' said Jean. 'My husband and I live in the suburbs of Wellington.'

'I am newly widowed. My husband, John Aitken, died in a bootmaking accident. I came to New Zealand to start a new life,' said Sarah, perhaps a little more rehearsed and stiffly than she would have liked. 'I am a seamstress and tailoress.'

'I've never been very good at sewing,' said Jean.

It did not take long for the facade between the women to fall away. It is unclear who spoke honestly to the other first, but what is certain is that the affection between the women was shared, and real. With each other, at least, and away from a morally disapproving world, the women could be themselves.

Jean was no seamstress and she knew little about fabric, but she was an expert in fabrication. Although she was married, she was disinterested in the upkeep of a good marriage as 1920 societal norms defined this to be. She had no interest in homemaking, was unapologetically fond of a drink, particularly gin, and she liked sex – just not with her own husband.

Sarah was fascinated. Jean was raven-haired and pretty, and she attracted the attention of men easily. She was everything that Sarah wasn't – defiant, and with an ability to engage in deceit guiltlessly, swiftly and easily. For Sarah, this was spellbinding. Jean had told a lie, and she had told it so long that her sins were closed seamlessly, the frayed edges hidden underneath her deep red fur-lined coat.

Jean adored Sarah and was deeply protective of her. Sarah was everything Jean was not – quietly spoken, gentle and trusting. When Jean discovered that Sarah had a small baby, she was unsurprised. Sarah seemed a natural mother – in contrast to Jean, who had not had children. 'I loved her immensely,' Jean once said of Sarah, like a child fondly remembering a much-loved pet.

A genuine connection quickly formed between the women, which included Jimmie at its very centre. He may not have had a father, but he was showered with affection by his two Scottish mothers. The intensity of the bond between them was revealed through Jean's own words; she rarely referred to Sarah by her first name, using the Scottish convention of 'Cissie' (or sister) instead. Jean was the only friend that Sarah made while living in New Zealand.

It was an unusual friendship between very different women. Each presented stylised masks of womanhood, and both were hardworking. Jean was a show pony and liked to attract attention. She frequented hotels and knew how to start a conversation with a man – and then very shortly afterwards be drinking with him, on his tab. Jean enjoyed the company of men more than women, something she admitted freely: 'I liked Cissie better than any other girl I ever met.' In contrast to Jean's show-pony antics, Sarah was a workhorse. She had a quiet, almost childlike voice. She projected the image of a dutiful, diligent 'good little woman' in low-heeled practical shoes and an oversized coat. The loyalty between the women, however, was unshakeable.

It was Jean who decided that Sarah needed a husband, and quickly. Jean assumed the role of match-maker with an enthusiasm that made it more akin to marriage-pimp. She focused on identifying suitable men for Sarah, then doing all she could to manage and oversee the negotiations to ensure a successful sale. Sarah needed economic stability, and the women agreed that marriage would be the only way for her to escape destitution.

Though the circumstances of the first meeting are not known, it was most certainly Jean who introduced Sarah to Edward Jackson. He was a ship's captain who frequented hotels in Wellington and was away for long stretches at sea. Little is known of the relationship. Indeed, Sarah's own words, constrained by the polite vernacular of the time, give no real insight as to whether she remained focused on marriage as an economic goal or had become swept up in a passionate affair. It was most likely a little of both. As Sarah described it, 'I became friendly with Mr Jackson. We walked out together.'

The affair lasted less than a year, after commencing sometime in 1922, and it was Jackson who ended it. There was no formality to this. Very soon after unceremoniously 'dropping anchor', Jackson cut Sarah adrift. He severed all contact with her and refused to acknowledge there had been any relationship at all. A short time later, he returned to the sea. Sarah had little recourse but to accept it, at least for the time being. She also had to accept the shame that came with the discovery that she was carrying an illegitimate child to a man she barely knew, for the second time in less than three years.

Old habits quickly returned. Just as she had in Paisley, Sarah spied a poster calling for immigrant labour. When delivering a consignment of completed clothing to her employer, she saw a poster advertising Australia as a destination of 'perpetual sunshine' with 'plenty of work'. There were children featured in the images as well. Australia seemed an ideal destination for a growing boy. It wasn't far away, and boats left frequently. Just as she had during her first pregnancy, she took to the ocean.

All at sea, Sarah was reborn for a second time. She was now Mrs Jackson, separated from her husband by the vastness of the ocean. Again, Sarah converted her shame into tragedy and thereby crafted a suitable moral narrative that was sustainable yet conveniently unverifiable. She was Mrs Aitken and then Mrs Jackson, without having ever been married. She killed one husband and lost another at sea. Though the narrative provided her with a practical and credible way to protect herself and her son, it must have felt like an open wound. In keeping with conventions of formality, she would have been referred to as Mrs Jackson on a daily basis and always introduced herself this way. This must have been a frequent reminder to her that while she had striven to achieve a common aspiration for women at the time – settlement and security through marriage, home and family – it remained beyond her grasp.

Sarah's exploits could not be dismissed as the follies of youth. When she boarded the steamship to Sydney, her life must have felt like a recurring bad dream. She had backed the wrong star-crossed Romeo not once but twice, and at twenty-seven would have been judged by many to be far too old to have not known better.

Sarah tried to contact Edward Jackson many times. She had a scribbled address on a scrap of paper that she carried with her, but nothing else. Her first letters to him pleaded for marriage. As the pregnancy progressed, and the burden of a second child loomed, Sarah's letters became more direct and pleaded for more tangible support. Did Edward have a childless sister or cousin who could perhaps take the baby and raise it as her own? If he could offer nothing else, she suggested, couldn't he provide money rather than see her and the baby starve?

Jackson's address was in a town called 'Akko', New Zealand – a place that both modern and historical records suggest has never existed. Akaroa, however, does exist: a harbour-side town on the South Island, consistent with the story provided by a mariner. Either Jackson deliberately gave Sarah a fake address, or Sarah recorded it incorrectly. If a fake address was supplied, the stunt is akin to what in modern-day slang is called the 'moth manoeuvre'. Using this slippery tactic, a 'player' appears to disclose all personal details to someone they meet at a club with whom they only want a one-night stand. The player even provides what appears to be a bona-fide business card with the name 'Nigel Moth'. To avoid the entanglements of a relationship, all the details are fake and, like a moth, by morning the smooth operator has gone.

Although Akaroa is frequented by seafarers, it has a very small permanent population and was colonised by an insular community of French immigrants. To this day it is considered a remote and somewhat isolated location, and it is not well known. In 1926, a few years after Sarah's time in New Zealand, a census identified only 124 permanent houses, owned largely by a closely connected community descended from the original French settlers. If Edward Jackson was indeed a Nigel Moth, Akaroa would have been an ideal residence for him, as its remoteness would have ensured Sarah could never have pursued him there to verify its authenticity.

The manner in which Sarah left Wellington reveals the true nature of the friendship between her and Jean. There was no tearful parting. Sarah boarded a ship in April very soon after her decision to leave. Jean did not say goodbye. She did not need to. She followed soon after, disembarking in Sydney a short two weeks later.

Mrs Jackson and Mrs Olliver did their best to create a little family home for Jimmie in two boarding-house rooms at the back of the Square and Compass Hotel. Sarah tried to find work but was even less successful than she had been in New Zealand. In desperation, she wrote to her family in Paisley for support. The letters were either not received or were not wanted, as there is no evidence of any reply. Jean continued to receive small amounts of financial support from her husband, who still lived in their marital home on suburban Cooper Street, Wellington, and with whom she continued to have regular correspondence.

The women loaned money to each other back and forth continuously, one always seeming to be in a state of debt to the other. Jean bought clothes for Jimmie. The women often shared a bed. If Jimmie was upset or unsettled, he would share it with them. Sarah and Jean also shared food, coats, gloves, stockings, handkerchiefs and undergarments. There were only two things the women never shared: booze, as

Sarah never drank; and hats. This fact, too, is reflective of their unique and fascinating friendship.

Jean had a fondness for the highly fashionable and tight-fitting French cloche, a bell-shaped hat with the brim turned back. It was a flirtatious and highly sexualised accessory. It curved around her face, framing it seductively, and accentuated popular make-up styles of the time: dark-stained lipsticks and strong sculpted eyebrows. Jean's hat also projected a subliminal sexual message, and not just because it emphasised her red pouting lips. The flapper look is sometimes described as androgynous or 'boyish' because the thin fitted dresses flatten the breasts and give the body a slick silhouette. However, it might be more accurate to say that the look is downright masculine. With the cloche hat atop, the flapper assumes the form of a long erect shaft topped with a bulbous end. Jean's look was provocative, outrageous and deeply erotic, and there was little more she could have done to advertise sex.

In contrast, Sarah's clothing reinforced her desire for shelter and her more reticent nature. She preferred the oversized hats that were lined, padded and pleated, pulled down to the eyes, with the brim curved to the shoulder. These were not hats for partying but for all-year-round practicality. In summer they provided shade – in winter, warmth. Sarah's hats projected anything but a sexually provocative silhouette, as their deeply domed shape typically transformed the wearer into a walking, talking lampshade stand.

By July 1923, Jean's concerns for Sarah began to grow. Jean may not have been able to read well, but she could certainly read the habits and vagaries of men. It became clear to her very early on that Sarah needed to abandon hope of resurrecting Jackson as either a lover or a husband capable of honouring his responsibilities as a father. Now in Sydney, Sarah continued to write to Jackson and still received no answer. Sarah needed to learn when to move on, said Jean knowingly. It was a skill that she had refined to an art form.

Though it was 1923 in the busy and hedonistic city of Sydney, for Jean and Sarah this was no jazz age. Jean may have enthusiastically embraced the consumption pattern and aesthetic of the flapper, but in reality her options for sexual and economic freedom were limited. Hedonists who were independently wealthy had the latitude to smoke, drink, party and indulge in extramarital sex with relatively few social and economic consequences that would have any real impact. For women without means, the exploration of jazz-age values came at a much higher cost. And the ability of married women like Jean to work was deeply constrained in many industries. She enjoyed the company of men, but this may have been an economic pursuit as much as a sexual one.

George Gore checked into the Square and Compass sometime around the middle of 1923. He was a labourer, an itinerant. The raven-haired woman caught his eye immediately, and it was not long before, as George described it, 'they became friendly' and began 'living in the hotel as man and wife'.

For Jean and Sarah, this offered advantages. Jean did not have to pay board. As the love affair continued, George began giving money directly to her, which she would share with Sarah. Jean dropped off and collected George's laundry – without telling him, she often included her own, Sarah's and Jimmie's laundry. Throughout this period, Jean's husband continued to send money from New Zealand, and the couple remained in contact.

Sarah was now in her second trimester and continuing, she believed fairly successfully, to hide her pregnancy under her overcoat and dropped-waist dresses. She had no work, and while she lived frugally, her savings were nearly gone. Just as she had in Wellington, Jean assigned herself the responsibility of finding an off-the-rack and ready-to-wear suitor for Sarah. The complications that Sarah faced, as a heavily pregnant woman seeking to court men, never occurred to the ever-optimistic Jean to be obstacles.

It was an afternoon sometime in August. Jean, Sarah and Jimmie were in the front lounge of the Square and Compass. This was a space where men and women mingled, and where local families – including very small children – came to socialise. Jean's striking grey eyes scanned the pool of men in the room, looking for targets. She immediately eliminated men talking to women or interacting with children, because she wanted a suitor for Sarah who was free of romantic or family entanglements. After closely watching the crowd for some time, she saw two men standing together, quietly talking and drinking. Without hesitating, she walked over and struck up a conversation. One was portly and with a swarthy complexion. The other was small, thin and had mousy brown–grey hair.

The swarthy man, Albert Pepper, was much younger and more outgoing than his companion, Joseph Shorrock, and it was Pepper who spoke to Jean first. She motioned to Sarah to follow her and join the conversation.

Jean was chatty, and she laughed easily. She seemed high-spirited – whether it was from the substantial quantities of gin that she threw back, or just her way of being, Pepper couldn't be sure. But he liked her.

Shorrock was quieter and more reserved. He had less to say. He found Jean's brash manner a little abrasive, and she knew it. To her delight, Shorrock seemed drawn to Sarah.

The four of them traded their war stories. Jean portrayed herself as a married woman, 'Mrs Gore', staying with her husband while he undertook some labouring work in the city. Mrs Jackson had a tragic backstory: widowed in her native Scotland while she was young, she had a small boy. She had travelled over to New Zealand to spend time with her close friend Jean.

Albert Pepper and Joseph Shorrock presented a moral narrative appropriate for men of good standing in the community. They were returned soldiers. Shorrock was a sapper. He had built bridges, trenches, tunnels and roads in Europe for the Allies during the war. He also had prospects – a farming property at a place called Kulnura. He owned an orchard. Sarah imagined a gracious property with fields, and Shorrock as an overseer, walking along rows of grand trees, watching the work of his pickers during harvest time. The image contrasted strongly with her dirty, noisy factory work. Life on an orchard seemed clean, quiet. It seemed a noble way to work.

Shorrock was frequently in Sydney on business, he said. Pepper had been coming to Sydney regularly as well, to attend medical and rehabilitation appointments for a war injury. Shorrock had made the offer for Pepper to stay with him on the farm, providing him with labouring work whenever he could. More than a year later, Pepper was still there. He had simply never moved out.

Shorrock made a special point of mentioning that Kulnura was a local Aboriginal word that translated to 'in sight of the sea'. He shared this information with the women pridefully, as if his orchard was a secret oasis that offered a rare tranquillity and beauty to be envied.

Things moved quickly. By the end of that week, the foursome had met almost every day at the hotel. Shorrock invited the women to Kulnura for a holiday, and the timing seemed ideal. George Gore was away on a labouring job for a few weeks. He had left cash for Jean's accommodation, and since an alternative place to stay was being offered, this meant the money could be spent on other things.

Sarah, meanwhile, was getting weary of staying at the hotel with Jimmie. There was a constant smell of alcohol, as the barrels were emptied and cleaned in the back alley just adjacent to the stairs leading up to the boarding-house rooms. It was a sickeningly sweet smell, and although Sarah no longer had morning sickness, it was particularly unpleasant for a teetotaller. The prospect of taking Jimmie somewhere new also excited her. While she and Jean had done their very best to create a home for him in the smoke-stained boarding house at the back of the pub, he was now almost three and needed space to run and explore. Most attractive of all, staying on a farm was free, and this alone would have been an offer difficult for Sarah to pass up.

Jean was delighted. This all seemed too good to be true. She had sized up not just one possible suitor for Sarah, but two. Surely one of them would represent a good fit. Jean had designed it all expertly. She had carefully taken the measurements. All Sarah needed to do now was stitch one of them up.

8

IN SIGHT OF THE SEA

Sarah, Jean, Joseph Shorrock and Albert Pepper boarded the Newcastle train at Central Station. They would disembark at Wyong, a few hours north of Sydney. From this smaller regional train station, Joseph said, they would take his car and drive inland to the orchard.

The mention of a car was significant and a detail that would not have been lost on either Jean or Sarah. Joseph owned both a farm and a private vehicle – this suggested some measure of financial stability, if not outright affluence.

Both women needed money, and their only sustainable income could be derived from their relationships with men: Jean's husband in New Zealand, and her makeshift husband, George Gore. Though her lawful marriage can't have been entirely happy, it must have on some level been amicable.

Should Jean have become financially desperate, she at least had the option of retreating to the New Zealand suburbs. Though she may have rejected the social conventions that came with marriage, it gave her access to two important things: money and moral legitimacy.

Sarah, on the other hand, had neither of these things. Without Jean's help, she would have been days away from homelessness. Her ability to work her way out of her situation was even further constrained than it had been in New Zealand. She was pregnant, and Jimmie was no longer a baby who could be parked in the corner of a tiny boarding-house room and left alone to sleep while she stitched. She had little prospect of attaining work at all with a rambunctious toddler and demanding newborn to manage.

With the passing of every day, Sarah was being whittled to the most basic of human needs. Inch by inch, she was a woman reduced. For three years she had sought the legitimacy of a marriage – the essential moral foundation for bringing up a child. But now this desire for respectability was over-shadowed by far more fundamental survival instincts. Sarah needed food, warmth and certainty, and the primal safety of shelter in which to birth a baby.

The group sat closely together on the train. The four adults chatted easily. Jimmie, an inquisitive toddler, fussed and wrestled to see outside. He crawled across the laps of the adults to stand on the seat and press his small hands against the window.

While Botany Bay and Circular Quay carve out the eastern perimeter of the city, the communities that sprout as the coast heads north are also shaped by what happens when the ocean meets the land. The estuary of the Hawkesbury is dramatic and eerie, created by a unique geological movement in which the sea literally rose to drown the land. Arboresque branches of river stretch as far as the eye can see, and lap at the edges of soft and undulating landmasses and islands. The scene transforms the train window into a camera shutter, with images worthy of a travel brochure appearing suddenly. Then the train rolls on, and the idyllic scene disappears, replaced with forest and scrub, cleared land for farming, and scattered housing.

The Hawkesbury railway closely hugs the coast of the eastern seaboard and carries travellers across the top of strange island-like land formations and stretches of open water. There is a stillness to the area that feels ancient and eternal. Only the sky is blue. The rest of the vista is all reptilian green. The Hawkesbury River stands still, the water tension barely broken except for the bump and roll of the odd boat, and with the silt beneath the surface as slimy and shiny as vaseline glass. The bends and curves in the land are deep, and the vegetation dense and primordial. Steep and rounded hills and islands resemble prehistoric dorsal fins, as if a giant sea serpent in retreat from the loneliness of the ocean has bedded down in the sheltered safety of the estuary.

Close to a century after Jean and Sarah travelled there, the isolation and seclusion of the Hawkesbury region is still apparent. The ancient landmasses continue to look immovable, and in many places remain untouched by modern civilisation. Those drawn to the area cherish privacy and are purposeful in their intention to achieve separatism from Sydney. While residents now need only to hop onto a highway in order to return to the mayhem of the city, in 1923 much of the area remained frontier land and the sense of remoteness was very real. For Sarah, the loneliness of the scenes framed by the train carriage window must have been haunting. Heavy with a broken heart and mourning the failed summer romance with her lover from the sea, she must have been filled with loss by the vastness of the water.

The Great Northern Railway to Newcastle represented a significant architectural achievement for New South Wales and, combined with the beautiful natural topography, the area drew a large number of sightseers in the 1920s. The group of five on the train would have looked just like any other family on holiday. Scottish accents, particularly Jean's booming voice, and Joseph's distinctive song-like Lancastrian accent filled the carriage. It was a scene from a painted post-card – two Scottish sisters, with their English husbands and a young son, taking in the beauty of Australia by rail.

After more than an hour on board, their ears adjusted to the rattle of the carriages. As the train pulled further away from the bustle of the city, the scene beyond the window became quieter, gentler. As the train stations became less frequent, and the jerking brake and lurching acceleration of the journey eased, the rhythm of the train rocked and comforted its cocooned passengers. Before long, Jimmie fell asleep. Fellow passengers who observed the small boy, dead to the world with his small body draped across Sarah's lap, his legs across Joseph's, assumed they saw a family. Sarah enjoyed the feeling of self-assurance and respectability that flooded her. For three years her husband had been the product of folklore, spun from the yearnings of her heart. A body of flesh and blood now sat beside her, and others were assuming him to be her husband. These would almost certainly have been powerful restorative emotions for a woman nearing thirty (considered almost to be middle aged) who had spent the better part of four years feeling discarded.

Sarah's imagination, laid waste by the failed designs of life as a bootmaker's and then mariner's wife, must have begun to populate with new fantasies inspired by the evocative scenes just beyond the train window. Joseph talked about the farm, and the seasonal demands of tending an orchard. There were locally raised cattle, and just out of sight there were allotments of fruit in the clearings beyond the forest. Joseph's talk of growing oats would have evoked images of the homeland to Sarah – oats had been a staple of her childhood and were almost synonymous with agriculture in Scotland. Some small spark of hope must have stirred within Sarah, fuelled by apparitions of orchard trees heavy with brightly coloured fruit, and by the blessed certainty of rain and sun and the abundance of harvest. This life was the product of celestial will, not the will of men. Life could be made real through the hard work of tilling and planting and service to the Lord. It was a philosophy that must have resonated deeply with Sarah's work ethic.

The dense forest, the deep water – this seemed a place barely inhabited. Did this represent the beginnings of a fresh start, somewhere to rebuild her life, revise history and create a place of acceptance for her son?

On reaching Wyong Station, Joseph said there was enough left of the day 'to take you all for a proper look round'. There was little of the fresh country air that the women would have expected, as the overwhelming smell of stockyards hung over the station and the town's main intersection. Joseph, his confidence seeming to grow as he stepped off the train into familiar territory, insisted they walk to take in the sights.

Joseph talked with great pride about the area. It was popular with tourists, he said. At Easter the lake and surrounding valley became flooded with holiday-makers from both Newcastle and Sydney who came to camp on bushland. The trains and ferries were often packed, he noted. He listed these facts pointedly, as if needing to affirm the unpolished agrarian character of the area as something that no reasonable person could not appreciate. Sarah was enamoured with the charm of the town, but even more enamoured with the man who seemed to be charmed by simplicity and unimpressed by the grandeur and bluster of the city.

Almost immediately Sarah felt a sense of place, more than she ever had in Sydney. It was quiet, and in the few women she saw in the streets, Sarah recognised herself. She looked every bit the farmer's wife in her matronly low-waisted dress, topped with her very functional overcoat. Her large hat, oversized and homely when compared to Jean's shallow-brimmed cap, shaded her from the relentless Australian sun. Sarah's durable boots, well-worn but carefully polished to conceal the scuffs, embodied the frugal and practical aesthetic of the town. They passed women in hand-knitted shawls, and in functional smocks and middies made pretty for a trip into town with crocheted yokes or embroidered collars. As a seamstress and tailoress, Sarah could identify with this way of thinking.

In contrast, Jean felt overdressed. Her shoes were designed to put on a show and not at all sensible for walking. Her slickly fitted shift and coat were more cocktail than country wear. The hardworking women of the land would have judged Jean immediately and unkindly as an outsider. She could certainly feel that she was turning heads – but on this day it was not in a way she appreciated. She felt gaudy, her desire for attention an affront to the bucolic sensibilities of a community both tightly knit and tightly knitted.

In the 1920s, like many rural towns in the postwar era, Wyong was defined by the duality of grief and renewal. The war memorial – constructed by a working bee of local veterans and the brothers and fathers of those who had not returned – stood in the very centre of town. To veterans like Joseph and Albert, it was a place of special significance. All five travellers stopped to pay their respects. The men stood quietly for several minutes, with no words passing between them. Eventually, the poignancy of the moment faded, and the group's conversation slowly returned to life going on around them.

Wyong was a proud little town with a sense of identity closely tied to Australia's developing national identity as a diverse and aspirational agricultural producer. At the time, Australian pastoralists were a strong and influential economic stakeholder, with vast tracts of land capable of grazing huge herds. They had the benefit of massive wealth behind them, and they were supported by the serfdom of Indigenous communities and the exploitation of unpaid Indigenous stock-workers. The efforts of Wyong farmers represented a very different type of farming ideal, one that was being actively encouraged by the state government. These were small-scale, trial-and-error business ventures propelled by hard work, Christian family values, and ingenuity. Frontline soldiers were signing up for a very different kind of gallantry as they pushed forward as frontline farmers in a patriotic charge to establish Australia as an economic powerhouse. Joseph's motivation to succeed as a grower was intense, redoubled by his position as both immigrant and returned soldier.

Wyong was keen to boast about its growing success in fruit production, and equally proud of its status as a haven for returned soldiers. As one news article at the time records:

For the important matter of settling returned soldiers and others who wish to take up splendid orchard and agricultural land, the large area in that sweep of country from Wyong

round to Gosford, between the ocean and the railway, occu-
pies pride of place compared to anywhere in the state.

Returned soldiers, eager to establish a tradition of family
farming, wanted their sons well equipped to run the enterprise. Joseph told Jean and Sarah with pride that the first-ever
farming school dedicated to the science and business of agriculture, Hawkesbury College, had been opened in the region
and that many sons of neighbours would attend. If he ever
had a son, Joseph noted, he would send him there.

Soldiers turned farming entrepreneurs, like Joseph, were
experimenting with small acre lots and new crop varieties.
They studied climate and the soil, and collected data on rain-
fall and fertiliser to understand the secrets of the earth and
harness all that it could yield. Local district farmers were keen
to establish themselves as masters of the land and astute agri-
culturalists at the forefront of an exciting national movement.
Like the miners on the western goldfields of New South Wales
eighty years before, and the cedar cutters of the Yarramalong
Valley nearby, the farmers of the Central Coast sought the
subjugation of the continent. From gold rush to grain rush,
men continued to prospect the land, seeking fortune through
what might be dug from it.

At the time, Australian town halls exhibited sporting
trophies and medals of achievement, alongside flattering
portraits of wealthy benefactors or the local mayor. Wyong
had these too, but the display cabinets of agricultural triumphs
including barley shaft and wheat stem dedications seemed

just as important as the portrait of King George V. A Wyong news correspondent of the time noted, 'District orchardists show commendable enterprise,' and with great pride reported that high-grade local produce was being shipped as far as Tasmania, rather than servicing just the Newcastle and Sydney markets. Oats close to 8 foot tall were grown less than 15 miles from Wyong, one local claimed. Others boasted that 6-foot-tall oats could be grown without the use of any manure but with superior knowledge of the soil profile, attention to its preparation and factoring in its drainage characteristics. The oats were on display, mounted on the assembly hall wall, the measurement chart laid out beside them to verify the local grower's claim.

The group returned to the train station, where the car was parked, and Joseph and Albert took their lady visitors and young Jimmie for a drive around the stockyards and the pony track. Wyong races were held regularly, and he and Albert often attended as they 'enjoyed a flutter', Joseph said. Jean's interest was piqued briefly before realising it was not a race day and that Joseph's idea of appropriate entertainment for women was a drive around a deserted racetrack. Sarah's only comment was that she did not really approve of gambling. This impressed Joseph – the races were not places for women, and Jean's persistent urging to attend the next track meeting seemed vulgar to him.

If the oats in the town hall and the lingering smell of cow dung in the air had not been enough to convince Jean that she had little affinity for country life, the scene as they approached Joseph's house must have deepened her resolve to return to the city at the nearest opportunity. The roads were rough. The descent into the property was slippery and narrow. Reflecting the rural sensibility of economics over aesthetics, the bulk of Joseph's efforts were clearly devoted to the care of the orchard and farm, not the facade of the home. Any additional income had obviously been ploughed back into the operation of the property. As a result, the homestead was run-down and unkempt. It was not the life of landed gentry that Jean had imagined.

Neither Sarah nor Jean could see, despite looking from various vantage points across the farm, how Kulnura was deserving of such a grand name. Contrary to what Joseph had claimed, there was no 'sight of the sea' to be had. Because of the way that banks of cloud roll in from the coast and across the mountain, the sea never featured as part of the view, even from the highest point. And Wyong, unlike places further south such as Berowra, isn't known for fresh movements of air as they sweep in from the sea. As Jean's experience in the town could attest, the area was not generally welcoming of those who blew in from the city and the coast.

As the two women stepped out of the car, they would have made further surprising discoveries about not just Wyong and its surrounds, but also about the uniqueness of south-eastern flora in Australia. In the 1920s the Central Coast was still densely covered in pilularis, a native eucalypt. Standing alone, it is a magnificent tower of a tree with an unusually dark jet-black trunk, ghostly white branches and soft phalange-like foliage that can vary from green to gun-grey. When grouped densely together in a forest, however, the pilularis is revealed to be a very different type of tree from the fresh-smelling birches and pines that the women would have encountered as girls in Scotland. Colonial botanist Joseph Maiden noted in one of the earliest forest flora surveys undertaken by a European that the region was soaked in the smell of onions turned sour due to the abundance of pilularis. Contemporary parlance being far less polite, the experience of walking through a pilularis forest today has been likened to a heady dose of cat's piss to the nostrils.

The uremic smell of the forest notwithstanding, Sarah and Jean enjoyed the first few days of their stay. The farm rested at the forest's edge and offered unique fauna and flora that must have seemed strange and wondrous to the women, and an inquisitive and excitable three-year-old boy. Families of kangaroos came close to Joseph's house in the early morning and at twilight, and they grazed silently while shrouded in a sea of low fog that hung heavy to the ground. With only their upper bodies, oversized ears and small paws visible as they hopped through the mist, to Scottish eyes the animals would have resembled mountain hares wading in the eerie mountain mist. Their slow, gentle movements would certainly have enchanted Sarah and Jimmie.

As Kulnura was a fruit-growing area, there were large numbers of possums. Their territorial arguments over fruit would have filled the night air as they hissed and growled with a ferocity that far outweighed their small size.

To Sarah, the experience may have had a feeling of Lewis Carroll's Wonderland about it. New Zealand's environment and climate would have, at times, reminded her of Scotland. The Australian forest, however, must have seemed curiouser and curiouser. Sarah was lost and preoccupied with a desperate yearning for home. Her life was populated by a strange cast of characters, and all the while she continued to chase something elusive, like a white rabbit that remained within her line of sight, but just beyond her reach.

The grandfatherly way in which Joseph doted on Jimmie was something that Sarah had not expected, and this made her feel more hopeful than she had in three years. Joseph was the first man to ever take an interest in her son. Jimmie was fascinated with the kindly older man and began following him around as he tended to the farm. Joseph seemed flattered that the boy had formed such a ready attachment to him; in return, he was especially kind to the boy. It saddened Joseph that Jimmie had no father. It also saddened Joseph that he had never had children himself.

The little boy seemed to be a natural farmer, Joseph noted. He was interested in the orange trees, the vegetable garden, and the comical chickens as they foraged and scratched in the yard. Sarah's lean income and the portability of her life meant that Jimmie had accumulated very few personal possessions and no toys to speak of. Joseph gave him a small hand pail and a trowel. Jimmie delighted in playing in the soft earth under the shade of a tree at the corner of the house. Sarah and Jean sat in small garden chairs and chatted.

Jean noted the ease with which Sarah and Joseph seemed to be building a relationship. It was Jean who had always used her siren-like qualities to lure men in the hope that Sarah might meet someone. But in this place, Sarah seemed to be doing very well on her own.

On the surface, Joseph and Sarah seemed well suited. Both were shy and naturally reserved, and there was a quiet chemistry between them that was undeniable. Joseph was fifteen years Sarah's senior, and Sarah seemed to like his gentle, kindly way of being.

The charm of the farm was absolutely lost on Jean. In less than two weeks she grew bored of oranges, dirt, sunshine and the lack of electricity. And it took far less than two weeks for Joseph to tire of Jean. Within the first few days it became clear to him that she knew little about cleaning and had minimal desire to learn. Her refusal to cook also irritated him. In slang of the time, she smoked like a chimney stack and drank like a fish. Considering the gendered social mores of the 1920s, the hypocrisy of his judgements would have entirely escaped him. While he may have disapproved of Jean's smoking, perceived her drinking as unseemly, and judged her inattention to cleaning and cooking as slovenly, he and Albert both smoked and drank heavily and did not afford a high priority to domestic niceties.

Very quickly Sarah fell into a living arrangement that was extremely common for married and unmarried women with children living within communities on or below the poverty line in Australia, right up until the 1960s. In return for board, she provided domestic services to a single, unmarried and older man. Joseph did not ask her for any money and often met small expenses that she had; in return, she was expected to work like a maid. For married women, this arrangement could offer some benefits because the family unit generally maintained an income stream through the husband's work while saving to purchase or rent their own accommodation. Unmarried women with children, however, were particularly vulnerable to the whims of their live-in landlords. But with the birth of Sarah's second baby close at hand, the arrangement at least offered her some form of stability for herself and her son, and given her financial position, she had little choice but to make the best of it.

Sarah found a mode of living on the farm that she understood. She enjoyed cleaning the house and restoring it to a sense of order. She washed and ironed for Joseph and Albert. With her tailoring skills she patched tears in their clothing and sewed loose buttons on shirts, and she cooked vegetables from the garden. Every day there was a demonstrable outcome from her efforts, something practical and real that felt comfortable to her.

Jean, on the other hand, found little to do and stayed only a fortnight. It was too far to walk anywhere, which meant she remained at the whims of Joseph and Albert to provide transport and entertainment. And George Gore was due to return to the Square and Compass, so she needed to resume her place as his proxy wife lest his attention and therefore money went elsewhere. She returned to Sydney alone. In her pocket she carried the very last coins that Sarah had to her name.

While the specifics of the plans made between Jean and Sarah remained between them alone, what is known is that they agreed to write to each other to ensure they didn't lose contact.

What is also known is that very soon after Jean's departure, the relationship between Joseph and Sarah became closer. What strengthened their bond is not entirely clear, as there are many possible reasons for this rapid shift.

Jean's absence may have put Joseph more at ease. He undoubtedly perceived the relationship between Sarah and Jean to be exploitative. Sarah, he believed, was being taken advantage of. 'I could not say the women were extremely fond of each other,' he is reported to have said.

The farmhouse itself may also have provided a place of sanctuary for Joseph and Sarah to speak more openly because it was safely removed from the judgements of wider society. Over the months that Sarah stayed there, Joseph received no visitors. Although Albert lived at the property, Joseph employed him as a farmhand and delegated a good deal of the most labour-intensive work to him. The long periods that Albert spent away from the farmhouse afforded Joseph and Sarah plenty of time alone.

In a state of desperation, Sarah may simply have adopted an all-or-nothing approach. Her baby was due in less than three months. She needed to determine quickly if Joseph could hear and accept what she herself believed to be the ugly truth of her life. This may have prompted a very rapid set of admissions from Sarah that was not typical of her behaviour to date.

It is not clear who shared their truth first. What is clear is that once the gates were opened, a flood of confessions poured out in a six-week period.

Joseph and Albert, like Sarah and Jean, maintained a projection of themselves that differed vastly from their interior reckonings of the world. Joseph was far from wealthy. He owned some land but not as much as he had led Sarah and Jean to believe. In truth, the farm didn't bring in nearly enough income to support him, even as a single man living as frugally as possible. He often tendered for small-scale road-surfacing and contracting work to the local council in order to maintain an income stream.

Despite Joseph's references to war service, he was no war hero. He had been one of the oldest recruits to ever sign up at Sydney's Moore Park Barracks. It appeared that his decision to join the war effort was the result of the well-considered judge-ments of a mature man of thirty-seven who had road-building skills much needed at the frontline. However, after only two weeks of training, Joseph bitterly regretted his decision to join up and managed this regret by simply running away. While desertion was not uncommon in World War I, and the records of Moore Park document that hundreds of men absconded, the records also document that a large number of them returned. Absconding for a night of drinking or womanising, or to attend to family businesses was a fairly common occurrence. Joseph, however, did not return, and after finally being located was forced to continue training on threat of court martial.

In the spirit of being honest, Joseph overshared Albert Pepper's indiscretions to Sarah as well. Albert was a deserter too, but of a different kind. Although he had seen out his full service in the armed forces honourably, his dishonourable behaviour on his return was more notable. While Albert entertained Jean and seemed eager to receive her attentions, he had deserted his legal wife and their dependent children in Adelaide. He had left them destitute and now seemed content to live permanently on the east coast with no plans to resume his life in South Australia.

Over the next six weeks, the relationship between Joseph and Sarah clearly deepened further. But Sarah's own account of the weeks preceding the arrival of her second child are unavailable to us. Her choice to maintain almost complete silence after her capture means that any insights into her state of mind can only be derived from second- and third-hand accounts of either conversations with her or observations of her behaviour.

Despite her pregnancy being well advanced, Sarah hardly showed. As Albert Pepper stated at one point when being interviewed by police: 'When Mrs Boyd first went up there [to the farm] it was not evident that she was pregnant.' She had gained little weight and was described by everyone who met her as 'frail'.

For six weeks, and despite ill health and the emotional burden of an unwanted pregnancy, Sarah did the only thing she knew how to do. She worked hard – cleaning, cooking, washing clothes with a boiler and hand wringing them dry.

Albert's accounts of Sarah also give some insight into her character. He lived and worked at the farm under a similar arrangement to Sarah and understood her position. 'I found her to be a fine sort of woman. A better woman in the house you could not wish for. She was a very quiet-living woman. She did not touch drink. She had very few belongings and she had absolutely no money whatsoever.'

Based on Joseph's and Albert's accounts, Sarah was very emotionally fragile in the weeks preceding the birth of her child. Both men witnessed her distress firsthand. When Joseph saw her unravelling, this seemed to strengthen his resolve to intervene. Each man recounted anecdotes showing that the reality of her predicament began to absolutely overwhelm her. She was often found uncontrollably sobbing.

'While she was with me she was not cheerful,' recalled Joseph. 'She seemed to be worrying and downhearted both before and after the birth of the child – particularly after the birth. Several times I walked in unexpected and found her crying. Sometimes she would be crying over the baby.'

Sarah continued to write to the baby's father, pleading for support. Joseph, responsible for posting the letters, secretly took note of the address.

'I posted a letter to Jackson to Akko, New Zealand, I concluded he was her husband,' Joseph later revealed. 'I posted a letter with my mail and after I found out how she stood I wrote again to this man but got no reply to either letter. The letters I wrote had not come back although I put my name and address on the outside of the envelope.

Apparently the man received them but did not feel inclined to help the woman in her trouble.'

Sarah found herself marooned. Having been tossed by the currents of the Atlantic and Indian oceans and the Tasman Sea, she had finally washed up on the shore of a broken-down homestead. Hope of rescue remained a distant and hazy point on the horizon. Was it creeping closer to offer deliverance, or was it disappearing into the distance? Was Joseph a confidant, an advocate and a defender, or none of these things? What did he want from her?

Sarah went into labour weeks earlier than she had expected. Like the labour itself, things moved quickly. Joseph began to assume a more directing role in Sarah's life. 'It was after the birth of the baby that I understood exactly the position she was in,' he said.

Joseph penned one last letter to the baby's father. If he would not honour his responsibilities and make arrangements to collect the child, she would be surrendered to a home. Joseph made arrangements for her to be photographed. Two copies of this picture were made, and a letter was sent to Captain Jackson with one enclosed as evidence that a baby girl had been born to him. In an act that can be interpreted as cruel and compassionate in equal measure, Joseph gave the other photo to Sarah. It would be a keepsake, he said, since after she had surrendered her daughter, she would most likely never see her again.

Joseph's use of the pronoun 'we' is profoundly telling in understanding the significance of the shift in his relationship with Sarah. In the analysis of all the primary and secondary source materials – transcripts, witness statements and newspaper reports – only one person in the constellation of people surrounding Sarah in 1923 used the term 'we' when describing their relationship to her. They may not have known each other very long but for Joseph at least, 'I' had become 'we'. However, this 'we' appeared to be conditional.

'Previously I thought she was married. After the child was born I had to discuss the thing with her and see how she stood. I found she was destitute and had these two kiddies and she had no work to go to. We decided to come down to Sydney and get the child placed in a Sydney home, after she had done that she was going to come back.'

A number of agreements were made between Sarah and Joseph. Sarah would return to Sydney for two weeks to make the necessary arrangements for the child. 'We agreed the child would be placed in a home.'

Joseph would care for Jimmie while Sarah was away.

Sarah would no longer contact Captain Jackson.

When she returned, Joseph said, they would begin to talk about the future in more concrete ways.

Albert Pepper, the observer closest to these discussions, and with nothing whatsoever to gain by offering his commentary, succinctly summed up Sarah's bleak and inescapable situation just after the baby was born.

'The holiday on the orchard was not going to last forever,' he said of her decision to return to Sydney.

9

WATER BABIES

'What do you see, my darling?' said the lady, and her eyes followed the baby's till she too caught sight of Tom, swimming about among the foam-beads below.

She gave a little shriek and start and then she said, quite quietly, 'Babies in the sea? Well, perhaps it is the happiest place for them' and waved her hand to Tom and cried, 'Wait a little, darling, only a little: and perhaps we shall go with you and be at rest.'

The Water-Babies: A Fairy Tale for a Land Baby, 1863,
Reverend Charles Kingsley

THE SUITCASE BABY WAS JUST ONE OF AN ENTIRE GENERATION of water babies born in Sydney in the 1920s. And this was not the first generation. Sightings of water babies had become commonplace in Port Jackson and the rivers and creeks on its outskirts. Spotted by sightseers at the Quay, water babies rolled along the sand, tossed by the sea as it rose and fell.

Like wader birds some of them clustered close to the water's edge on the shoreline at low tide. Others were gathered up in fishing nets or retrieved as fragments from the stomachs of captured sharks. The suitcase baby was only different to other water babies because her mother had been identified and trapped, and was now in captivity.

In 1897 in Rushcutters Bay, a water baby was washed ashore whole and perfect. In 1903 in Manly, one was seen floating like a misshapen balloon in the water, its skin tight with fluid. In the winter of 1904, two babies were spotted in the very middle of Sydney Harbour, and a third in Darling Harbour. From 1905 to 1909 in Balmain, Neutral Bay, Ultimo, Georges River and the Cooks River, locals reported sightings of water babies beneath the waves or bobbing just on the surface. One water baby, a particularly young hatchling, was found being gently carried atop the currents. She was lean, naked and draped in long strands of seaweed, like Botticelli's Venus reimagined as a baby floating in an open cardboard box instead of a clam shell. In 1910 at a La Perouse beach, partially buried in sand, a water baby was curled in the foetal position like a conch shell washed ashore. The face was hidden but the hair was visibly sticky with sea spray. In 1911, 1912 and 1913, newborn males were found floating peacefully in the harbour. In the gritty rabbit-warren suburb of working-class Balmain, a perfectly formed female water baby was found floating at dawn, alone and naked, just near the wharf. Her arms moved in the water with grace, as if gently caressed by the tides. Burly dock workers rubbed their eyes in disbelief, momentarily believing they had seen something angelic and divine, as if a cherub had fallen from the sky and was now swimming in the dirty water near Darling Street wharf.

In another incident, a small group of children in a rowing boat found what they initially thought to be a lost doll in the harbour because of the way it bobbed buoyantly in the water. The oldest girl of the party, realising with horror that it was not a child's toy but a bloated corpse, quickly took control. Showing incredible foresight for a young child, she snatched the baby from the water, wrapped it in newspaper and tried to shield her younger companions from the monstrosity. She then rowed the boat ashore and delegated the other children to find the nearest adult. She kept watch, patiently waiting with the water baby, until the water police arrived.

In Circular Quay, a body was scooped out of the water by police from the back of a boat. It included the legs and bottom half of the torso below the umbilicus. The police concluded that the top half had been eaten by a shark – alternative explanations seemed too gruesome to contemplate.

At Maroubra Beach, a fisherman hooked a water baby in the early morning. To his astonishment the baby was somehow still alive, though barely. He later swore he had seen it writhing, like a suffocating fish on land. When making his statement to the police the fisherman seemed spooked, as if mesmerised by the presence of something supernatural. He claimed to have also seen a woman in jet black walking the length of the beach soon after dawn. At first the police seemed eager to dismiss his ramblings as the tall tale of a fisherman. However, it was certainly a very real dead child they retrieved from the beach, and the unmistakable footprints of a woman's heeled boots were still visible in the sand until they disappeared behind the dunes.

On one occasion, the intent to release a water baby to the sea seemed evident but was unrealised. Rethinking their plans at the last moment, a person or persons unknown had left a newspaper-swaddled baby girl abandoned in the Sydney ferries terminal office, where she lay undiscovered for hours. Ink from the paper stained the baby's skin. The morning's news was emblazoned on her arms, as dark as the thick black stocking that had been knotted several times around her neck.

Was it possible to conclude that the majority of water babies had died by accident, or been stillborn and discarded to hide the shame of illegitimacy? The presence of white cords, black cords, household string, black stockings, white stockings, pyjama cords, lace – always around the neck – revealed a very different story. And if neck banding wasn't present on the water baby, other evidence made it clear the death was not accidental. A limb might be severed or partially severed, or a boot mark might be visible across the skull. In some cases, murder was as clear-cut as the child's severed throat.

Those keen to release water babies also used the opportunity afforded by the city's growing infrastructure. Manhole covers provided access to the sewerage systems, and cavernous stormwater drains provided habitats and shelters. One water baby was found in the well of an Ultimo sewer, another in the stormwater drain at Rushcutters Bay with white tape around the neck. Yet another was found in a Glebe drain, and a particularly small specimen in a Petersham sewer. Twin discoveries were made in the inner west of Sydney: two newborns were discovered on the same night in a Balmain sewer. Two men, bucketing nightsoil from back-lane dunnies in Leichhardt, found the bodies buried in human faeces as they emptied the night cart.

Water babies were also found on land. An unusual example, partially burned and one-legged, was found wrapped in a dishcloth and stuffed in a pillowslip as if it had been casually swung over a tramp's shoulder in a swag. The child's final resting place was the Moore Park tramway waiting room. Another was found in the bottom of a corn sack in a back lane of Redfern; this one was also charred.

The stories of water babies and other infanticides being shared across the city were folkloric, told and retold by clergyman and charity workers. Some defined the tragedy as entirely one of the soul, a sign that the city was being corrupted by the carnal depravity of unwed mothers. Others used tales of water babies to highlight the growing inequity and social injustice of life in Sydney. There was simply too much poverty while too little was being done to help the most desperate, some said.

A heartbreaking tale was shared by one priest. On the steps of his inner-city church early one morning, he had found a female baby. She was neatly dressed, as if for church, with a note pinned to her delicate layette. 'Heartbroken mother is driven to do this. For God's sake be good to her,' it said. The baby had died of exposure overnight due to unseasonably cold spring weather.

In a Castlereagh Street mission responsible for dispensing charity to the poorest in the inner city, a resident matron shared her own water baby tale. A young woman, unknown to anyone at the mission, strode through the door one day and handed the matron a suitcase. She boldly looked the matron in the eye with all the confidence of a good Samaritan nobly returning lost property. 'I just found it, will you look after it?' the young woman asked. The matron believed she had been handed a suitcase of second-hand clothes and so stacked it near a donation bin. She nodded politely at the woman who then promptly left. Later in the day, another charity worker opened the suitcase to sort the donated items. Inside was a dead baby with a drawstring pyjama cord tied tightly around its neck.

The authorities knew there was a problem, but measuring its scale was difficult. Infanticides were seen more as a civic than criminal problem, a scourge akin to rats – the kind of public health problem that administrators were reluctant to acknowledge because, as with rats or cockroaches in the street, it was assumed that for every one that was seen, there were probably twenty others.

In one of the only official surveys of infanticide in the early twentieth century the problem did appear to be significant. In December 1913, the unofficial count of baby cadavers (in less than two years) came to fifty-nine: on average, one specimen had been collected by authorities every fortnight for two years straight. It raised concerns. Sightings always exceeded collections. For those water babies spotted in bodies of water, by the time authorities arrived, the currents had often shifted the water baby further out to sea.

Busy train stations also served as a common place for the disposal of water babies in Sydney, particularly Redfern and Central. One was found riding the rails to the Southern Highlands and another in a passenger carriage on its way to Singleton.

Belmore Park adjacent to Central Station – which remains a grimy and poorly lit urban park that many avoid at night – was a gathering place for water babies between 1910 and 1915. These babies were simply left out in the open. In one instance, a vagrant wandering the park picked up a small parcel wrapped in brown paper. Given its weight and fullness, he assumed it to be a grocery parcel accidentally dropped by a housewife while hurrying to catch a train. He unwrapped it eagerly, expecting to find manna from heaven – grocery staples such as flour, salt, lard and meat. Instead he found identical twins.

In Ultimo, a sweet baby coated in powdered sugar was retrieved from a sugar sack left beside a tree in a park. At another park in Glebe, a baby cadaver lay face up. It was stripped naked with its eyes fixed open and unblinking towards the sun, as if positioned to receive a medicinal dosage of phototherapy to remedy jaundice.

Water babies also appeared to be perishing quickly and conveniently in transit. Commuters embarking a suburban train (which had departed Central Station only twenty minutes prior) found a newly dead baby on a seat in an empty carriage. The corpse and the seat beside it were still warm. There was evidence the child had fought hard to live – rolls and rolls of newspaper had been shoved in its mouth. When this hadn't worked, the child had been strangled. But neither method of choking had worked. The post-mortem determined death to have been caused by a bash to the head.

Several water babies were found bizarrely jammed under fences between houses in Waterloo. On vacant land in Rushcutters Bay, a baby's body was found fully dressed but soaking wet. Another was buried in the bottom of a chaff bag in a Paddington horse paddock. The horse's owner, who was found to have no knowledge of or connection to the dead child, had been feeding his animal from the chaff bag for weeks, completely unaware.

One water baby was found in an empty boarding-house room in Surry Hills; two more in Redfern. One was deep in a clothing hamper in Newtown, as if it had burrowed there and curled up to sleep. Another was hidden under a bed in Surry Hills. Yet another was buried behind the grate of a fire pit in a Petersham terrace, like a rat attracted to a warm site for its nest. And another water baby, like a tell-tale heart, lay concealed in a wall.

One water baby absolutely baffled police. It was found at the bottom of an 80-foot brick pit in Alexandria. Although it was soaking wet, there had been no rain for weeks before the discovery.

A single narrative is perhaps, above all others, emblematic of the response of Sydneysiders to the burgeoning population of water babies in the first few decades of the twentieth century. Early one morning, the owner of a bag store in Sussex Street found a baby drowned in the pan of the outhouse at the back of his property. The struggle of labour, birth and death had occurred only metres from his bedroom window, and he had not even noticed.

Water babies laid bare the most cruel and ironic of the hypocrisies of jazz-age Sydney. While sexual and economic freedoms could be explored by women, this also placed them in moral jeopardy. For unwed mothers, the stain on their reputations was permanent and the shame irrevocable.

Infanticide offered a solution. The unwanted child could be reborn as a water baby, and a stain could be lifted before it left a mark on a woman's life. Water babies were property transferred from the realm of the private to that of the public; they became a collective problem for everyone in the city. However, for this metamorphosis to be complete, both the mother and the child had to remain nameless.

The suitcase baby had been found, and so too had the women implicated in her murder. And what kind of women they were would matter far more to the outcome of their trial than any physical evidence relating to the circumstances of the baby's death.

10

FLAPPERS AND FLOPPERS

SARAH AND JEAN WERE IN DEEP WATER. ACCORDING TO NSW law in 1923, any verdict of murder required a sentence of death. But there was scope for the state to show leniency: the authority of the medical community said so, backed by the weight of more than a century of research into the physiology and pathology of women.

Medical practitioners of the day believed that women were vulnerable to the currents of their sexuality, with their madness comparable to tidal movements. Women, doctors argued, existed on a biological shoreline between sanity and insanity, their hormonal swells constantly tugging their feeble bodies out to sea while their mental stability sank rapidly beneath their feet like wet sand. As the president of the American Gynecological Society described it in 1900:

Many a young life is battered and forever crippled on the breakers of puberty; if it crosses these unharmed and is not dashed to pieces on the rock of childbirth, it may still ground on the ever-recurring shallows of menstruation, and lastly upon the final bar of the menopause ere protection is found in the unruffled waters of the harbor beyond reach of sexual storms.

Within the medical community, it was also widely accepted that while women did not usually kill as easily as men did, when in the grip of biological fevers, they could. Women killers therefore needed to be judged by a different standard; conventional legal notions of motive, particularly with regard to murder, needed to be adapted.

Today's medical community plays an important role during murder trials in providing evidence of mental impairment and insanity, and this was also true a century ago. In the 1920s, the body of work on female criminal behaviour as a medical condition was significant and provided Sarah's legal counsel with great scope to argue a compelling case for mercy.

In 1931, William Boyd (no relation to Sarah), medical superintendent of the Fife and Kincross District Asylum in Scotland, wrote a dissertation on the direct link between insanity and the presence of female reproductive organs. Published in the esteemed *British Medical Journal*, this dissertation was based on his practice in the field of psychiatry for women throughout the 1920s. While Dr Boyd's work was primarily concerned with the processes of the mind and mental illness, he highlighted that the practice of psychiatry with women patients specifically required what might be characterised as a 'hole-istic' approach.

Doctors today who describe themselves as holistic practitioners advocate for many contextual factors to be considered in the diagnosis and management of disease, including biological, environmental, mental and spiritual factors. In the 1920s, physicians advocated for a different kind of holism in their understanding of women patients. When it came to measuring the madness of women, it was not the metaphorical 'whole' but the literal 'hole' that was important. Interestingly, in developing evidence-based understandings of the madness of men, similar attention was not paid to the 'pole'.

If female body parts stretched to accommodate a reproductive process, madness would result – the only question was for how long. Pregnancy-induced insanity was easily observable, doctors argued. A stretching uterus could cause longings, neuroses, irritability and excitability, and lead the woman to desire absurd and extravagant tastes. Or a woman might irrationally refuse food altogether. Or, more irrationally still, a woman might come to dislike her husband or neglect her household duties.

Many facets of parturition insanity were noted by the medical community. Those women with an oversized vagina faced exhaustion, confusion or hallucinations. A floppy and cavernous vagina was a clear sign to doctors that the mind was struggling to maintain hold of sanity. Delirium, mania, excitement and 'noisy patient' syndrome were all observed in women sectioned to receive mental health care, and all considered to be the direct result of pregnancy, childbirth or both – and not the result of an underlying or pre-existing mental health disorder.

Similarly, doctors argued that lactational insanity could be observed and documented scientifically. Enlarging breasts could make a woman prone to melancholia, delirium and constipation.

Puerperal insanity could occur when the labia and vagina were shrinking after birth. This area of science was of particular interest to those medical practitioners studying infanticide and the physical preconditions that made mothers vulnerable to committing this act.

The conclusion seemed clear, the evidence overwhelming: women were unstable, the victims of their unfortunate and unpredictable reproductive physiology. Learned medical practitioners of the 1920s concluded that women were – to use a layman's term – crazy cunts. As a mother in the wake of recovery from childbirth, Sarah was viewed by contemporary doctors as more likely to kill and less likely to be cognisant of her actions.

In the 1920s and earlier, infanticide committed by mothers was an area of special interest for the British medico-legal community. While the *British Medical Journal* noted that the murder of babies by their mothers was both immoral and heinous, these sentiments were often quickly followed by 'but', 'however', 'on the other hand' or 'taking into consideration other factors'.

William Hunter, an eighteenth-century British doctor and legal commentator, did much to lay the foundations for the understandings of infanticide that would follow in the nineteenth and twentieth centuries. He argued the act could only be evaluated within its social and religious context. He believed that in most cases it was preferable to the alternative faced by fallen women: suicide. Hunter, who considered himself a strong advocate for women's rights, constructed his arguments through a uniquely historical method. Drawing on a hundred years of documented infanticides, Hunter claimed that most mothers who contemplated the deed had undoubtedly weighed up suicide as an alternative.

For English mothers throughout the eighteenth and into the nineteenth century, infanticide represented a much lesser sin than suicide. Up to the 1820s, a legal ruling of suicide culminated in the victim carrying the shame beyond death. Suicide victims were not buried in sacred ground and received no blessings from the Church. There is a widespread belief that a range of cruel and macabre community-level practices surrounded suicide burials which included the bodies being shovelled into unmarked graves at crossroads with a stake driven through them. All goods were forfeited to the state. The law requiring these sanctions was repealed by the *Burial of Suicide Act 1823*, but custom and practice that worked to ostracise the suicide victim and their family occurred in most Anglo-Christian communities well into the twentieth century. Infanticide at least offered the opportunity for redemption before the Lord; in contrast, suicide damned a woman for eternity.

To the medical community, mothers accused of infant-icide represented an opportunity to study female madness and a biological curiosity. Over seventy years, the *British Medical Journal* published reams of gynaecological studies that were then used to underpin legal arguments in defence of women accused of killing their children. William Acton, surgeon to the Islington Dispensary in Cavendish Square, argued in 1861 that 'shame, starvation, and a recklessness of consequences too often led . . . the unassisted mother of the bastard, to commit infanticide'. Acton proposed that hospitals could provide both a moral and economic solution to fallen women who had killed their children. The compassionate response, he stated, would be to offer them job opportunities in hospitals as human dairies: women who had committed infanticide because of immorality, destitution and shame could make amends for their sin by providing wet-nursing services for more-moral women. As Acton argued, a 'return to the paths of virtue, by becoming the wet-nurse to the child of one more fortunate' was a financially and morally optimal solution for unwed mothers. They could be shamed and marginalised for their behaviour, as they should be, but not so much that it produced a cycle of economic exclusion that would lead to further poor choices.

An intense reluctance to charge women who had committed incredibly heinous acts against children was well established by English case law. In 1877, a 41-year-old widow was discovered to have killed five illegitimate children over the course of twelve years. Their bodies were found mummified, stuffed in boxes around her home. Each body had a cord tied around the neck, and in one case the head had been severed. Coronial medical advice concluded there was no evidence for a murder charge to be laid. The definitive test for proof of life after birth could not be applied, doctors argued. In a post-mortem process the lungs were cut from the body and immersed in water to see if they floated, as evidence that they had drawn air after birth and the child had achieved 'independent existence'. Due to the corpses resembling pieces of dried fruit, medical examiners refused to offer an alternative explanation for death. The obvious evidence of strangulation and beheading did not enter into medical considerations. The widow received a custodial sentence of only fifteen months for concealment of the births.

In another case also from the late 1870s, a baby's body was uncovered in a single woman's bedroom, wrapped in an old skirt. The throat had been cut from the front, right around to the spine. The woman admitted the baby was hers but claimed the injury had occurred by accident – the baby's neck had become hooked in the latch of a door. When the defence proffered this explanation to the jury, coronial medical evidence shot it down. An assessment of the coagulation of blood around the wound identified that only a sharp cutting instrument could have caused it and that the pressure used must have been significant. The medical examiner identified that the jagged cuts on the umbilical cord bore an uncanny resemblance to the cut on the throat. It was most likely that the same knife had been used to make both wounds. The defence team then suggested an alternative theory that seemed even less plausible. In the mother's haste and having no skill in obstetrics, she had slipped and cut the baby's throat clean through when attempting to sever the umbilical cord. This theory was accepted by the jury, and they fully acquitted the mother.

A year before Sarah's trial, the *Infanticide Act 1922* was introduced in England. It was supported by a member of the House of Lords, Bertrand Dawson, who went on to become an influential physician to the British royal family and president of the Royal College of Physicians. A vocal and strident advocate for mothers who committed infanticide, Dawson would not ultimately see his version of the *Infanticide Act* realised until 1938, after fifteen years of political horsetrading. He triumphantly delivered the second reading speech of the final form of the Act, noting that

> under certain circumstances the killing of infants is provoked by illness and not always criminal intent . . . the subject matter of this bill belongs to the territory where law and medicine meet, and to some extent carries with it difficulties which attach to both.

He summarised the public sentiment which had surrounded infanticide for fifty years by saying that a 'horse sense' existed across the British Empire that compassion for mothers who kill was warranted; the only challenge lay in determining when to grant it.

In order to understand the legal interpretations that might be brought to bear about women who murdered babies in the 1920s, it is also necessary to look at the morass of medical understandings that had developed about women and birthing over a long period of time. Back in the mid-1800s, George King, a gynaecologist in Bath who considered himself a man of science and reason, had advocated for a more quantifiable approach to infanticide. King fancied himself a biologist in the mode of Charles Darwin. He collected and studied huge quantities of samples. Like Darwin, King collaborated and conferred with medical colleagues to test the soundness of his conclusions. But while Darwin studied the entire bird, King was interested in just one part of it – and the human 'bird' at that. The size of the vagina represented the baseline measure against which legally permissible infanticides should be assessed, King argued.

In an 1851 article, King shared his professional insights: 'We do not always find uniformity in the parturient passages of females; there is a vast difference in the capacity of the vagina and dimensions of the pelvis as well as in the size of the hand and arm.' King wanted his conclusions to change not just the way that medical practice occurred 'on' women but 'in' them as well. He argued that the measurement of a man's arms (including the amount of visible body hair on them) should be taken into consideration in the field of male midwifery and obstetrics. This had been an oversight in medical training and preparation to date, but his clear sense of determination, he said, had allowed him to gather new evidence. 'Whether a large hand or a small one will be best fitted for the purpose of operations in this diminished space we are not told, and we often meet with a very contracted vagina, and this is to be overcome by sheer force', he stated. King further noted that giving consideration to both the woman's vagina and the doctor's arm formed part of compassionate medical practice: 'the idea of an accoucheur with a tremendous hand and arm, to be in attendance on a delicate young girl, about sixteen or eighteen, with contraction of the vagina . . . is frightful'.

Vaginal capacity, he said, could explain many factors forming the preconditions for infanticide to occur.

> In some women we find the vagina large, loose, and flabby, and the outlet of the pelvis very large; such women will generally have very quick and easy labours, and we can be hardly ever in time to be present at the birth of the child . . . I have always thought that those unfortunate females who commit infanticide, or had been guilty of concealing the birth of their child, must belong to this class of women, having a large and well-formed pelvis, and a lax and capacious vagina, and consequently must have very easy and quick labours.

King's proposition also explained the discovery of newborn corpses in latrines – a frequent feature of documented child murder and those cases suspected to be murder. It did not happen, King claimed, because these women were seeking to disguise the evidence of an unwanted child. He posited what might be more crudely abbreviated as the 'loose flaps fast craps' theory. Having gone to the toilet to pass a motion, pregnant women with oversized vaginas and roomy pelvises, King argued, simply mistook the downward pressure of a baby for the engrossing pressure of a substantial stool:

> Such instances as these are numerous, and they most clearly show that women who have such quick and easy labours must have a large and well-formed pelvis, and the vagina and external parts must also be very relaxed, and easily dilated, which is a most satisfactory and convincing proof that during the act of parturition such women can have but little or no contracting or controlling power over the outlet, and this is, I believe, the cause of so many children suddenly passing through life into a fecal repository.

A floppy vagina was likely to expel a child at a moment's notice – in a privy, in a marketplace, or openly in the street during the course of a vigorous constitutional. A tight vagina, however, reflected a tight mind, finely honed senses and an ability to reflect. Women experiencing difficulty in childbirth because of a tighter flapped passage had time to think about their predicament, King claimed. In contrast, women who shot out babies like pellets from a gun were prone to the madness, shock and insanity that accompanies grievous acts against newborn children. King's dissertation was used to broadly inform Western thinking on infanticide cases because it spoke directly to the issues of motive, culpability and guilt. Those with vast vaginas and fast flaps could be gripped with urges both sudden and wicked. A rapid birth most certainly 'annihilated from the mind all recollections of the past, and it renders them incapable of thinking of the future', King surmised.

If it seems that these attitudes had been abandoned by the time of Sarah's trial, think again. As late as 1940, this way of thinking was factored into the defence of a woman who had drowned her child two weeks after the birth. Biological factors had shaped the woman's reasoning, a doctor stated at the trial, and caused an impairment so great that the court should consider her a victim rather than a perpetrator. In her medical examination, the woman was found to have a non-contracted uterus – or, in lay terms, a floppy uterus. To this day, an ongoing debate surrounds the type of delivery (vaginal or caesarean) and whether particular modes of birth increase the risk of post-partum depression.

In 1923, Sarah was well positioned to mount a legal defence capable of securing an acquittal. She was destitute, desperate, and carrying the shame of illegitimacy. She had no family support nor financial support. And while little is known of her medical examinations post-capture, she had experienced a short labour and had birthed the child quickly.

One British infanticide case bears an uncanny similarity to Sarah's and demonstrates that juries could present conflicted verdicts with regard to mothers who murder. A woman in her late twenties had a child to a man who deceived and deserted her. She hid the pregnancy, went into labour quickly and gave birth completely alone. Like Sarah, the woman had an older child from a previous indiscretion. Her second-born child was strangled when it was just over two weeks old and hidden in a box.

The accused woman was described as hardworking, thrifty and a good mother to her older child, just as Sarah had been. When the baby was observed by friends and other witnesses to be missing, the woman said she had left it with 'Mrs Johnson', who had agreed to care for it. Two medical witnesses – Dr Rutherford, a practitioner at a London asylum, and Dr Raglan Thomas, practising in Exeter – appeared for the defence. Both claimed that the woman showed no signs of insanity, but that she may have been insane at the time of the murder because of a range of environmental factors. There had been flooding in the local area when she had given birth. She had also experienced insomnia and headaches in the weeks leading up to delivery. This stress, the doctors argued, combined with the woman's dire financial straits may have caused temporary insanity. The jury acknowledged these piteous circumstances and were reluctant to return a verdict invoking the death penalty. The woman was found guilty by reasons of insanity and detained at Her Majesty's pleasure to receive mental health treatment. It was far from an acquittal but it provided scope for Sarah's defence. Many women who had killed in circumstances similar to Sarah's had received significantly reduced sentences in Broadmoor Hospital.

The increasingly influential and conjoined disciplines of psychiatry and gynaecology had a lot to say about the fleeting nature of criminal intent and women's biology. If some of this evidence could be incorporated into her defence, Sarah's level of responsibility for the crime would be diminished and so too her sentence. To achieve this outcome, she needed a legal defence capable of exploring and explaining how her degree of guilt could be reduced.

In developing a defence for Jean, the legal team had less medical evidence on which to draw. And society had come to firm conclusions about the type of woman that Jean was: a flapper. By late 1923, popular media had played an important role in shaping evaluations of these women.

Mothers murdered babies. But were fun-seeking girlfriends like Jean capable of committing or participating in a baby murder? The state was lost at sea with a limited compass of case law to get their bearings on this particular female form.

Contemporary rose-coloured interpretations of the 1920s depict the era as one that afforded social, economic and sexual freedom to women. Flappers, in particular, have become a glamorised archetype of this movement. They were pleasure seekers, flaunting conventions about drinking, smoking, marriage and sex. But they were also objects of ridicule and scorn because they participated in a range of behaviours of which society did not approve, not the least of which was sex outside of marriage. While the term 'flapper' described both a dress and dance style that assumed a flapping motion, innuendo pervaded the term's use. A flapper was a willing participant in promiscuous sex, and this implied it was not just her dress that flapped when she walked.

Flapper stories published alongside stories like that of the suitcase baby offered newspapers a win-win. Scandalous exploits of fashionably dressed young women provided escapism for some readers and the opportunity to pontificate on the moral degradation of society for others, and were pleasing to the press bottom line. Newspapers survived on selling advertising space, and an increasing amount of copy was devoted to the growing postwar market for women's fashion accessories, make-up and mass-produced clothing. Ads featuring the latest cloche hat, 'contouration treatment' or powder block make-up were invariably placed right next to articles about carefree and sexually adventurous young women: 'She wore a cheeky red lipstick, with a pretty pale face.' It was a seamless promotion of all the delights the city had to offer, from daytime shopping in fashionable department stores to cavorting in clubs and dance halls at night.

The community was fascinated with flappers, so newspapers exploited them. Gossipy scandals or humorous snippets about flappers were perfect filler. When bona-fide reports on flappers could not be generated, papers published short fiction, letters to the editor, and poetry on flappers to pad out Saturday and Sunday entertainment reading. Popular country poet Jim Bentley penned a dirty limerick-style ode that was published everywhere from the *Mudgee Guardian* to the city papers: 'I met a little flapper with her lipstick and her puff,' it began. Apparently if there was pleasure to be had, a flapper was up for it – and based on what the poet Artemus H implied, a flapper would be down for it as well: 'Down the street trips the winsome little flapper / Her tongue going strong like a church bell clapper,' he wrote in the *Truth* newspaper. Gruesome stories about child murder may have led to spikes in newspaper sales, but the regular publication of stories about flappers and the coarse innuendo surrounding their exploits helped to maintain stable circulation.

> My flapper
> Whene'er she trips down Swanston Street,
> My pretty flapper, slim and sweet
> With face demure and ankle neat,
> And costume dapper,
> With shortened skirts that swirl and swing,
> Red lips that smile and eyes that cling,
> She looks the very dearest thing –
> My flapper!
> Gone are the days we used to meet
> Gone too, the cakes she used to eat
> The chocolate boxes with those neat but costly wrappers,
> After the feast, the reckoning,
> That's how I know, past arguing,
> She really is the dearest thing
> In flappers!

American movies were a popular form of entertainment throughout Australia in the 1920s, and flappers commonly featured as characters. *The Affairs of Anatol* was particularly risqué for 1921, featuring chorus girls and extramarital affairs. *Daughters of Today* and *The Romantic Age* both attracted queues outside the Lyric Wintergarden Theatre and the Lyceum Theatre in Sydney. This gives some insight into the milieu of the flapper throughout the 1920s – movie-goers were mostly young women, and seeing the latest movie was as important as being seen. Flapper films are typically romantic spoofs and comedies with over-the-top zany plots. Although criminal activity is featured, it is portrayed as harmless, involving petty theft or scams designed to swindle wealthy hedonists. Flappers were frivolous pleasure seekers and sexual tricksters, but they were silly young women, and therefore not capable of malevolent criminal intent.

In *Daughters of Today* the central character, Mabel Vandergrift, is naughty but naive. It is a shock to the audience when she is ultimately charged with murder. Her make-up is heavy and overstated even by silent movie standards, and young female audiences emulated her style right down to the expert sculpting of her doll-like Cupid's bow lips. Movies like this sent a clear message to the public: Mabel wears make-up, Mabel makes out, Mabel makes good in the end. There is never a sliver of doubt within the film that she is absolutely incapable of the murder for which she is charged.

At the zenith of the flapper zeitgeist in the mid-1920s, newspapers also published poems as tributes to popular movies about women, sexual freedom, and the cultural phenomena and fashions that went with 'flapping'. An alphabet of the flapper was even published in newspapers Australia-wide a year and a half after the suitcase baby trial.

A stands for amours indulged in each day.

B for her bathing togs, gaudy and gay.

C stands for cocktails, for ladies who dare.

D for her dresses to make poor man stare.

E for the eye with which they give the wink.

F for the father of whom they never think.

G stands for gaiety so much desired.

H for the hats in which they are admired.

I for the impudence which they possess.

J stands for jazzing in scant evening dress.

K for the knitting that they never do.

L for the lingerie, rustling and new.

M stands for mother, best friend of their life.

N for the nerve that's as keen as a knife.

O stands for odours of perfume and scent.

P for the powders dabbed on with intent.

Q stands for questions, from parents a few.

R stands for replies that are not always true.

S stands for smoking, without which they'd fade.

T for the taxying, joy riding brigade.

U stands for ugly, they musn't be so.

V stands for vamping, the fine points they know.

W means willing to be loved all the time.

X for excelling some other girl's style.

Y stands for youth, meaning life, fun and joy.

Z is for zero, if they can't get a boy.

The flapper also garnered her fair share of moralistic scorn, and newspapers encouraged suburban housewives in particular to vent their anti-flapper frustrations. One letter to the editor – entitled 'The terrible trams: practices of passengers:

the jazzer and the flapper' – was published in a 1920 edition of the Perth *Sunday Times*:

> [P]erhaps the radiant specimen of the genus flapper deserves a place all to herself in this dissertation. Weighed down with about a ton, more or less, of powder and 'make up' with paint and lip salve to an alarming extent, she doesn't, except in exceedingly rare cases, resign her seat to the old or feeble. More often than not she is seated next to another of the same species, with whom she keeps up an animated conversation, the vapidity of which but adds to the agony of the unfortunate scrap hanger.

A credible and well-respected newspaper had devoted some of its front page to a housewife denouncing the selfishness of a whorish flapper who would not volunteer her seat to a hardworking mother with groceries.

Some conclusions were drawn about flappers by the general public. These young women were a scourge on public transport, and they were most certainly impolite and unashamedly immoral, but they were far from dangerous. They were scandalous, and they enjoyed deceiving men and disrespecting women of good standing, but they were not murderers.

Evidence from British legal cases suggests that flappers were more likely to be the victims than the perpetrators of crime. In one case, Ernest Rhodes, an eighteen-year-old valet, slit the throat of Grace Blackaller in a public street. In his confession Rhodes stated, 'Grace called me a poor fool. I had a fit of jealousy while kissing her good night and pulled out a razor which I drew slowly across her throat. She was always teasing me by nodding to other fellows.' Quick to affirm that flappers were pretty girls seduced by the excitement of the city but still in desperate need of a good mother's care, newspapers made certain to include the fact that Grace had run to her mother's flat in West Kensington desperately trying to seal her slit throat with the palm of her hand. Grace arrived just in time to die in her mother's arms.

Jean and Sarah presented the state of New South Wales with two very different dilemmas. According to medical evidence, Sarah had the capacity to kill because of hormonal swells and the physiology of pregnancy. Jean's situation, however, presented new criminal terrain. Women who acted as midwives to infanticide were almost always relatives of the mother and victim. In New South Wales, there had been a few examples of this. In 1889, Jane Culpitt had received a five-year sentence for helping her daughter kill her grandchild. Similarly, Mary Williams had received a ten-year sentence for assisting in the death of her grandchild. In 1867, Harriet Hannah Short had received a ten-year sentence for assisting a mother and father in killing their child, and she too had been related to the mother.

Jean's relationship with Sarah was different, and this was problematic. Jean was not related to Sarah. She was not a mother seeking to preserve the respectability of her family. Jean's role in an intimate murder like infanticide was less easily explained than Sarah's. Never before had the state had to judge a woman for her capacity to kill a baby for reasons of friendship alone.

It also raised a legal question that the state had never before had to answer. Was a flapper capable of murder?

11

HARD AND FAST

IN ITS FIRST HUNDRED AND FIFTY YEARS AS A BRITISH SETTLE-
ment, New South Wales had shown a willingness to kill
women, but only strategically. It did not like killing women
but it would if it had to. The death sentence had always been
passed on women with a sense of careful calculation and a
belief that it offered a powerful deterrent to curb emerging
criminal trends among women in the underclasses.

A detailed examination of sentencing records, undertaken
for this book, reveals that timing played a huge role in shaping
the state's dispensation of mercy to ladies regarding matters
of law and order. In Britain, judgements on infanticide came
down to a woman's reason for murder, but in New South
Wales Sarah's fate would also be shaped by when and how
she had committed the crime.

From the establishment of the first colony in 1788 to the abolition of the death penalty for murder in 1955, 3171 criminals were sentenced to death in New South Wales. Of these, almost one third were ultimately hanged. Legal and community views on the death penalty changed progressively over this same period. In the late 1700s in New South Wales, the death penalty could be applied to a much wider range of crimes than murder. By the 1950s capital punishment applied to a very narrow and specific range of offences.

What didn't change throughout this period, however, is the gendered pattern of criminal justice sentencing. Of the roughly three thousand people ever to be sentenced to death in New South Wales, only seventy-three were women. At first glance, this may not seem surprising – there is a higher incidence of violent crime among men, and there are far more men in prison today than women.

But when women criminals are considered as a subset of the NSW criminal population from 1788 to the 1950s, some insights on the judicial processes associated with women prisoners come starkly into view. Among the seventy-three women criminals sentenced to death, in only eleven cases (15 per cent) was the sentence ultimately carried out. In the overwhelming majority of cases, the rulings were commuted to sentences that did not mean life in prison. Women would formally receive a death sentence, but would typically serve ten, five or a few years with the stipulation of hard labour. For men sentenced to death, in over one third of cases the sentences were carried out.

Outwardly, the nineteenth- and early twentieth-century legal processes used to progress murder charges bear great resemblance to those currently in operation. Coronial inquests were held, charges were laid, a jury deliberated and a judge passed sentence – just as they do today. However, a century ago, mercy played a more conspicuous and political role in the machinations of this process, particularly regarding matters of women and punishment. For judges and juries alike, it was understood that women had a special entitlement to mercy, but this also afforded the executive the latitude to make an example of specific women criminals if it served the interests of the state.

Distinct patterns can be observed in the capital crimes committed by women in the early history of New South Wales. When women killed, husbands were by far the most common victims, with employers running a close second. Where theft or burglary was involved, it usually formed some part of a scheme for escape – a servant from a master, a wife from a controlling and abusive spouse. Women killed to gain control or liberation.

Distinct patterns can also be observed in the way the state passed the death penalty on women: a hard and fast rule always applied. As a new criminal trend emerged, the state reacted by taking a firm sentencing position. Unsavoury trends in female criminality were to be quashed quickly, before dangerous precedents were set. The custom and practice of leniency, which often formed the benchmark of judicial rulings in dealing with women (because they were perceived to be weaker and more fragile than men), could be and was put aside in New South Wales under certain circumstances.

Only one year into the establishment of the colony, Anne Davis received a death sentence for theft. She had initially been convicted in 1786 at London's Old Bailey for the theft of stockings and sentenced to seven years' transportation. She had arrived in 1788.

While capital and corporal punishment formed a common part of sentencing at the time, Anne was hardly a criminal mastermind, nor a violent or dangerous offender likely to compromise the security of the newly forming colony. On 14 November 1789, she robbed from a fellow convict and friend, Robert Sidaway. This amounted to crawling through a window, then falling over and spilling the household's water reserve across the floor before looking for something worthwhile to pinch. She took some clothing, a pipe and items small enough to stuff in a pocket. When Anne was captured, not far from the property, Sidaway identified the items in her possession as his.

For pioneers of a new colony very far from the Empire and supplies from home, resource management represented the highest priority. The colony's administrators were not overly concerned about murder and violence, but with the zero-sum dilemma of finite resources. As there was not enough to go around, thieves posed a great risk to the colony's operation. The newly forming settlement needed labour not larceny. Anne's crime was minor, rash and opportunistic, but the administrators perceived it as dangerous. It was behaviour that they wanted to discourage quickly, before the colony gained a reputation as a drunken, lawless outpost.

Anne was sentenced to death. She pleaded mercy, a stay of execution, claiming she was pregnant. This condition usually prompted immediate leniency. But the colony seemed determined to make an example of Anne. Due process was followed but carefully managed to ensure the result that the administrators wanted. The archaic ritual of a jury of matrons, in common usage in the fourteenth and fifteenth centuries, was resurrected to speed proceedings along. This amounted to little more than the on-the-spot rounding up of six older and very compliant women willing to eyeball the accused and reject her claim of pregnancy.

On 23 November 1789, nine days after she had committed the theft, Anne was publicly hanged. For making the unfortunate mistake of being the first woman thief of the colony, Anne received the most severe punishment and thereby served as a deterrent.

Interestingly, the executioner, James Freeman, would also suffer a particularly severe punishment that served an important purpose for the colony. James, who was himself a thief, and a more dangerous criminal than Anne, had been pardoned of his own hanging only to find himself appointed as the colony's executioner. It is argued by some historians that although James appeared to be a particularly skilled hangman who executed fifteen people, the execution of Anne Davis (his only female subject) led to his mental unravelling. After a week of drunkenness, he was found inebriated and delirious. There were rumours that Anne's death had turned his stomach. For his failure to affirm and reinforce the colony's position that Anne's execution had been both necessary and just, James himself received one hundred lashes.

Over the next twenty-five years many women would commit thefts similar to and in some cases much worse than Anne's, including Frances Morton, Elizabeth Roanes and Bridget Conoby. In accordance with prevailing ideas on sentencing, these women would also receive death sentences. However, none would be executed. Many were released after only a few years.

In 1799, Elizabeth Jones was the first woman to be sentenced to death and hanged for the crime of murder in the colony. So keen were administrators to increase their understanding about the types of females capable of committing murder that Elizabeth's body was handed over to the medical community for dissection and analysis.

The year 1808 saw the first recorded instance of a new type of crime among women. Mary Grady committed burglary of a wealthy home in Parramatta. This was not opportunistic but well coordinated and planned in advance. For her skilful execution of the crime and to ensure others were not encouraged to follow suit, Mary was, in turn, executed.

The next two executions of women also pertained to unique crimes, each dealing with a different type of conspiracy. Elizabeth Anderson was the first woman to be charged and executed for a conspiracy to murder. In 1816 she killed her husband and was seen to do this in an unusual way – by consorting and planning with two conspirators. After Elizabeth, it took almost ten years for the colony to execute another woman. In 1825, Eliza Campbell collaborated with four people to engineer the death of her employer. Female conspiracy, in particular, was a form of criminal enterprise the colony was keen to discourage.

Within the next twelve months, the colony faced a dilemma. A rocketing trend in highway robbery emerged. While many men were being charged with the crime, when the first woman was captured in a group of bushrangers, this presented a big problem. Florence Henley along with two male companions bashed and robbed the husband-and-wife innkeepers of the Bay Horse Inn. Florence went by the assumed name of Terry, and wore the clothes of a man. The reasons for this cannot be known. It may have formed part of a criminal disguise, or Florence may have identified as a transgender man.

The gang had developed an effective modus operandi: pick a remote location that offered time for them to commit the crime undisturbed. The Bay Horse Inn provided the perfect place. It was located on the Cowpasture Road into Sydney, roughly where modern-day Liverpool now sits.

The two highwaymen and Florence (aka Terry) were captured on the road well after the crime had been committed. All three were quickly found guilty and sentenced to death, but there was a catch. It happened to be the very same year in which Eliza Campbell had been executed. Reluctant to appear barbaric, the colony commuted Florence's sentence to life. The two male bushrangers, convicted for the very same crime, were promptly hanged.

The colony regretted its decision to not promptly deal with the problem of women and highway robbery. Less than a year later, in 1826, Bridget Fairless was captured, along with her bushranger lover, James. On this occasion the colony had little option but to hang her. They had not executed Florence, and female highway robbery had occurred again. It was a law-and-order oversight they were quick to correct. James and Bridget were hanged in a public execution. They were forced to walk under the gallows and paraded past their crudely made coffins, their arms pinioned behind them. This spectacle was seen by lawmakers as an important part of ensuring that copycat crimes were discouraged among women while assuaging public outrage over the crime. As one newspaper noted, 'During the time prescribed by law the bodies continued suspended at the sport of the winds.'

In keeping with mandatory sentencing provisions, many death sentences would be passed on women over the coming decades. However, it would take almost twenty years for another woman to be executed in New South Wales. Again, the death sentence was used to make an example of criminal trendsetters. From 1843 to 1860, four women were executed for killing their husbands: Lucretia Dunkley (1843), Mary Thornton (1844), Mary Ann Brownlow (1855) and Ellen Monks (1860). Mary Ann Brownlow had assisted in killing her daughter's husband rather than her own. Each execution was a deliberate action by the state to quash what it perceived to be a gendered trend.

The formal statement made by the presiding judge in Ellen Monks's case is long and detailed, and colourfully describes the frustration that was clearly pervading the colony. The sentencing runs for pages, and with excruciating attention to detail recalls the facts of the murder. Ellen had smashed her husband on the head and then barbecued him in the lounge-room fireplace while their children were sleeping in an adjoining bedroom. Even more chilling, she committed the act on All Hallows' Eve over the course of several hours – the thick black spirals of her cremating husband's smoke blanketed the neighbourhood. Throughout his statement, the judge notes Ellen's failure to exhibit 'female gentleness'. He describes a woman overrun with urges both 'fiendish' and 'devillish', and the document is peppered with woeful lamentations of 'O horrible!' The sentence of death, which was not overturned by appeal nor commuted, was delivered by a prominent judge whose name must have delighted state administrators of justice seeking to affirm the righteousness of legal rulings: Justice Wise.

While the death penalty continued to form part of the sentencing process for many female criminals, another execution would not be carried out on a woman in the state for close to thirty years. In 1888, Louisa Collins was hanged for being an exemplary and habitual poisoner, and retrospectively has been dubbed by some as the first female serial killer in Australia.

In seeking to understand how the state might have viewed Sarah's crime, it is important to look at what happened to other child killers during this period. In the years leading up to centenary celebrations in 1888, child neglect and infanticide were noted to be particular problems by the authorities, and widely acknowledged to be largely the result of widespread poverty and inequality. But the state had a problem: child murder – and more specifically infanticide – was not a 'new' crime. Documented cases could be traced back to the very inception of the colony and appeared to have always formed part of its social landscape. The state had long practised a high tolerance for the issue.

From the 1860s to the 1880s, only a handful of death sentences were given to women for infanticide, all of which were modified to reflect more compassionate sentencing. In court the women presented as broken or shattered, or sometimes seemingly unaware of their crimes. In 1869, Mary Holt received a sentence of five years for the murder of her newborn. In 1882, Mary Laye – after a particularly violent act of infanticide in which she had fractured the child's skull – received a death sentence commuted to ten years. In 1889, Amelia Culpitt received a five-year sentence for killing her three-week-old child. In each case and others from that time, the attitude and the demeanour of the women were assessed by the juries and judges in the formulation of verdicts and sentences. If a woman looked distressed in court, this was interpreted as remorse and a clear sign that piteous preconditions had prompted the act. If a woman looked confused in court, this was interpreted as mental dislocation, the biological madness resulting from pregnancy and motherhood.

For those women who were forced to serve life sentences in their entirety, the murders typically involved older children. These children had names, they had been christened, and the trial transcripts include detailed descriptions of their identities: everything from their personal and physical characteristics to their clothing. In 1871, Mary Jane Devlin killed her older child and received a death sentence, which was commuted to life. In 1872, Isabella O'Brien received and served a life sentence (commuted from death) for killing her son Daniel O'Brien by throwing him into a river in Wagga Wagga. Daniel was two years old, and newspapers published detailed descriptions of the nineteenth-century convention of dressing boys in highly feminised clothing, including his vivid red plaid frock, white cape, white flannel petticoat, pretty lace-up boots, and red and white socks.

One of the highest-profile infanticide crimes to occur in nineteenth-century New South Wales demonstrates the degree to which the legal system would afford leniency to women. John and Sarah Makin operated a discreet residential care service for unwed mothers and parents who wished to have their illegitimate children housed and nursed. For a fee, the Makins would take the child into their home and provide care on an ongoing basis, permitting the unwed mother to carry on life without bearing the shame. The practice was commonly known in the nineteenth century as 'baby farming', though it might be better described in modern parlance as 'factory farming' because the businesses typically operated on a high-intensity principle – lots of babies on small, cramped lots. John and Sarah lived in the inner-city slum of Erskineville and launched the enterprise after John suffered a workplace injury that left him unable to continue as a drayman.

While baby-farming models varied greatly, and in some cases parents engaged the services of a baby farmer knowing that it would lead to a child's murder, this was not the case with the Makins. They perfected a high-profit, high-turnover variation of the baby-farming model. The Makins preyed on and exploited those parents who loved their children and genuinely grieved the fact that social stigma denied them the right to raise their own offspring. The Makins offered parents peace of mind and a payment plan. They claimed to care for children in the long term, and carefully maintained a facade that the children were alive and doing well, often for years, all while continuing to take a monthly stipend from the parents.

In 1892, when the extent of their enterprise was discovered, more than a dozen baby corpses were found buried in back-yards or stuffed in drains where the Makins had been tenants across the inner city. While both of them were equally implic-ated in the crime, the wife served only eleven years and was mercy released. She lived long enough to become a great-grandmother, seeing out the rest of her days in the inner-city squalor of Marrickville. Her husband was hanged.

•

When Sarah Boyd was captured in 1923, the state had demonstrated a poor ability to locate, let alone capture, those responsible for infanticide. The babies were not named by their parents and were considered of such little value to society that police did not even apply the convention of christening them with a moniker of Jane or John Doe, only a filing number.

Of the few mothers apprehended for committing infanticide, the newspaper reports are sombre and succinct, and read like a casualty list from a war correspondence. The backdrop of tragedy is hidden behind a frugal retelling of the facts. The notations present an abbreviated form of loss.

FATALITIES

Blattman, 1w, male, weighted with stone in two feet of water; creek bed, Picton: Catherine, 25, unmarried.

Bruce, n/b, female, parcel of dirty clothing handed to a neighbour; Sydney: Ellen, u/k, domestic, unmarried.

Clancy, 12h, female, grass suffocation, exposure; Prince Park, Bathurst: Katherine, domestic, unmarried.

Cribb, n/b, male, suffocation, face crushed; bag, Muswellbrook watering hole: Gladys, 18, unmarried.

Davis, n/b, female, head wounds, means of death uncertain; cistern, Paddington: Minnie, 19, unmarried.

Deane, n/b, female, calico strangling; body wrapped, clothing hamper, Newtown: Edith, 18, unmarried.

Fox, newborn, u/k, sewerage submerged, possible suffocation; terrace, Petersham: Lena, 18, unmarried.

Groves, newborn, u/k, boot, eye & head injuries; Occidental Hotel, Bega: Sarah, 40, barmaid, unmarried.

Henderson, 2d, female, found after exposure; door step, St Johns Presbytery: Margaret, u/k, housewife.

Higgins, newborn, u/k, drowned, possible suffocation; water-hole, Coolah: Florence, 19, unmarried.

Hughes, n/b, female, burial, possible suffocation, bruising; backyard, Burwood: Ada Edith, 22, unmarried.

Hunter, u/k, male, neck strangulation by cord; discovered on bench, Hyde Park: Josephine, 18, unmarried.

Keogh, n/b, female, cut throat, discovered in drawer; Broken Hill: Maggie, hospital wardsmaid, unmarried.

Kramer, 7m, female, dropped, possible suffocation; discovered Albury Dam: Elsie, u/k, unmarried.

Layburn, n/b, female, death due to shock, incineration while alive; outhouse: Gladys, 25, unmarried.

Macdonald, u/k, exposure, possible suffocation, discovered Alexandria: Mary, u/k, unmarried.

Moran, 3m, female, cord around neck, suffocation; boarding house, Redfern: May, 19, unmarried.

Smith, u/k, female, throat cut, possible suffocation; discovered in Scarborough: Mary K, u/k, unmarried.

Stafford, u/k, u/k, drowned in river, possible suffocation; discovered in Eden: Harriet, u/k, unmarried.

Thompson, u/k, male, possible suffocation and exposure; Sydney park: Winifred Blanche, u/k, unmarried.

Wilkinson, n/b, male, dropped from significant height; wrapped parcel, Victoria Park: Mary, u/k, widow.

Woods, u/k, suffocation and drowning; river, discovered in inner city Redfern: Maud, 19, unmarried.

For a state wishing to pride itself on maintaining law and order, and for a city wishing to establish a reputation as a sophisticated metropolis, this was an especially shameful situation to be in. Sydney's daily newspapers were covered in the dead bodies of children – and many of these bodies were wrapped in newspapers reporting on the previous day's corpses.

Though the discovery of a suitcase baby, chaff-bag baby or water baby was a fairly routine occurrence, the actions of Sarah and Jean were indicative of a potentially new criminal trend. The two women were friends and they had colluded and conspired. This bespoke a fresh form of wickedness, and the news media relished the opportunity to characterise the state as threatened by a rising form of deviance and evil.

The capture of Sarah and Jean offered the state an opportunity as well as a dilemma. A high-profile inquest and criminal trial would allow New South Wales to reset the social and moral sanctions regarding infanticide. The state could establish a discernible legal course, and some hard-and-fast rules about child murder, while also quieting public indignation about the failure of law enforcement to address the shame of crimes against the most innocent. In setting these standards, both the proceedings of the suitcase baby inquest and the ensuing trial would be important.

How Sarah and Jean behaved during the course of these very public proceedings would prove to be very important indeed.

12

INQUEST NO. 482

After two and a half weeks of news stories about the suitcase baby murder, Sarah and Jean had attracted female groupies. While editorial attention had at first focused on wringing every last bit of morbid detail out of the act of murder, journalists now turned to the faces behind the crime.

Newspaper editors had effectively serialised the suitcase baby's death by providing daily updates that continually offered new angles. The grisly post-mortem results might be covered one day; a feature on the fashionable colour of Jean's shoes and her fur-collared coat might be printed the next. Death and sex sold newspapers, and this story had both in salacious spades. Editors were playing the role of conductors, orchestrating a sensational campaign around the two very different but equally intriguing female defendants.

The existence of the suitcase baby's silent fan club only became known to authorities in the early morning of Thursday, 6 December 1923. A small mob of women queued outside the entrance to the Coroner's Court. Beside them, a broad-shouldered woman stood alone in a brightly coloured floral hat that seemed more appropriate for a garden party than a gruesome inquest. She spoke to no one and assumed a seat towards the back of the courtroom.

Jean entered, led by an attendant. The first thing most people noticed about Jean was her hair, long and glossy like fossilised jet. Next – her eyes. They were an unusual grey, like charcoal granite. On this day she wore a blood-red hat, and she fussed with her hair throughout the proceedings. Removing her hat, she would shake out her hair, then fix it back into place before carefully replacing her hat. The act could well have been the result of anxiety; playing with her hair may have provided her with a distraction from the nervousness and fear of being in court. But the act could also have been interpreted as the coquettish display of a flirt. Jean was perceived as a flapper and she was studied as such, her every gesture construed as being heavy with sexual innuendo.

Sarah entered the room next. Every eye in the courtroom turned to watch her. She was quiet and homely, and at barely 5 feet (152 centimetres) tall she was tiny. She had large brown eyes and, perhaps due to her height, had developed the unusual habit of tilting her head upwards and to the side while she walked. As a result, she projected a strange air. She looked odd, different.

As the story had unfolded in newspapers, the headlines had gradually changed. The references to 'horror' and 'gruesome' had decreased and been replaced with descriptors like 'tragic', 'desperate' and 'pitiful'.

When she walked into the courtroom, Sarah's posture seemed to reflect the very portrait that journalists had painted of her. She was particularly fond of the low-waisted fashions that sat off the hip and finished at the ankle. This gave her an aura of childlike vulnerability. In keeping with trends of the time, Sarah wore a hat but pulled it low on her head – her dark doe eyes holding a static gaze from beneath an extraordinarily wide brim.

Sarah's steps were measured, and the controlled way she held her body suggested a desire for order. Her hair was always kept carefully pinned back, rolled along the sides of her head, and fastened in a knot at the top of her spine, in the style of a domestic. She loved the colour white and made almost every public appearance in her one 'good' outfit – a long white dress, turned grey and sewn from scratchy crepe.

Neither Jean nor Sarah had been able to properly clean their clothes for weeks. Sarah's dress now looked beggarly. This detail just intrigued the women spectators even more. An operatic scene was unfolding before them. A woman with the sorrowful aesthetic of a poor and dirty church mouse had found herself in indiscreet circumstances. She had sought refuge in the home of a man she barely knew (Shorrock) while giving birth to another man's child (Jackson), which she was now accused of murdering. Every woman in the crowd was fully apprised of the stories, having closely followed the newspaper accounts. They had come to see the next stage of this melodrama play out in real life.

There was no doubt that the unwed mother standing before them was a sinner. But was there something of the saint about her as well? Was it possible for a mother to be both self-sacrificing and murderous in precisely the same moment?

Journalists could not come to an agreement about Sarah's age, and this only added to the sense of mystery surrounding her. Some journalists reported her to be nineteen while others pegged her as thirty-nine. But Jean looked youthful – on this issue, journalists could agree.

Jean was in fact older. Some documentation notes her birth to be as early as 1891. Jean was also more vulnerable than she led others to believe. She was partially deaf, though it was a condition she rarely wished to admit to, given her vanity. Unlike Sarah, she favoured the busy chintz and boldly coloured geometric prints that were becoming increasingly popular as the decade unfolded. Jean's outfit was as filthy as Sarah's but it remained vibrant, with the pattern masking any stains. Jean wore heavy rouge and lipstick, dressed tight, and talked fast and loud, and her skirt finished at the knee.

The aesthetic contrast between the women could not have been more stark. Jean and Sarah offered something to every woman who indulged a psychoanalytic fantasy about a primal female archetype. For those who dreamed themselves to be a damsel in distress, there was Sarah. For those entertaining a racier and more adulterous imagination, there was Jean.

The suitcase baby murder allowed Sydney papers to indulge in imagery of both the housemaid and the harlot – all in the same story.

•

New South Wales coroners had a reputation for being bombastic and big-headed. Grim scenes of babies bobbing in harbour waters excited public interest and provided ideal terrain for coroners keen to showboat on the social policy concerns of the day. For over twenty years, coroners had been some of the most vocal political pundits on the issue of infanticide, and they often weighed in heavily when crises of motherhood and murder surfaced in their state.

In many ways, the interest of the coroner was not surprising. Infanticide impacted the coronial administration perhaps more than any other civic service provider because it played the role of intermediary. The Coroner's Office was responsible for the medical examination of bodies and for liaising with police for procedural record storage. Coronial staff also had to liaise with relatives (if any could be identified), the necropolis or both to ensure that the final dispatch of bodies occurred in accordance with sanitation ordinances. The police may have ensured that corpses arrived at the foot of the coroner, but it was the coroner's administration that took carriage of process and disposal. The coroner was also a key decision-maker because he made the final and most critical call when it came to establishing whether a murder or misadventure had occurred.

For a long time, the police chose not to play much of a role in investigating and managing the issue of infanticide. They had minimal involvement other than collecting the body and writing a cursory report. The matter was defined, at its core, as a social and economic problem more than a criminal one. While the coroner ruled in an overwhelming number of cases that the baby's death had been brought about deliberately, still the police argued that they had very little to contribute. Given the age of the victims and their lack of identifying features, there was usually scant evidence to collect and nothing on which a substantive case might be built. It was assumed that if a baby's death had been concealed, most likely so had the pregnancy. No amount of police investigation could solve the murder of a victim never even known to exist.

The prosecutions for child death that occurred in the fifty years leading up to the suitcase baby's discovery were vastly outnumbered by the bodies found. Motivated more by its budgetary interests than by compassion, the Coroner's Office took up the responsibility of reminding the collective consciousness that any dead babies in the street, whether wilfully killed or not, should be regarded as a problem in a society seeking to define itself as a progressive and civilised place to raise children. In 1887, the office had spearheaded the only state-level inquiry into infanticide.

Scarcely a week passes but that the records of the Coroner's Court show that young children have been found drowned, strangled or have died from exposure and in very few cases has anything been discovered leading to the identification of these 'poor waifs of humanity'. They just appear on the scene, and then by cruel, wicked and inhuman hands, life is taken from them.

In 1909, the ambitious and self-righteous Coroner James Murphy highlighted that the state had failed miserably to acknowledge, let alone address, the growing problem of infanticide facing the city. His strident statements demanded the redress of the social and economic conditions he outlined to be underpinning these deaths. Murphy argued that the problem of infanticide was a moral degeneration specific to the working class and went further by calling on the state to help deter child death. Put more simply, poor parents could be encouraged not to fall prey to the economic temptation to smother their children: bonuses should be paid to parents of larger families, and the introduction of a bachelor tax would also help, Murphy said.

By 1923, Coroner John Jamieson had taken the helm, and he too expressed concerns about the growing immorality of Sydney, although his focus was a little different from that of his predecessors. Jamieson sought to expose backyard abortionists. In this crusade, however, he had experienced a very bad couple of years.

He had a reputation for being tenacious and intimidating, a public figure not afraid to aggressively confront those who stood in his way. When overseeing an inquest, if he wanted answers and did not feel that witnesses were doing enough to provide them, he became ferocious. Then an inquest into a backyard abortion in 1921 weakened his resolve.

The mother had died of septicaemia after the poorly performed termination. In cases like this, Jamieson's usual approach was to use threats and intimidation to ensure witnesses answered every question to his satisfaction. But he met his match when he came face to face with Nina Webb, mother of the victim. While in court, Nina continually refused to disclose the name and address of the nurse who had performed the failed abortion. All police attempts to interrogate Nina had failed, but Jamieson believed the gravitas of the coronial courtroom and the menace of his personality would make her yield.

It did not. Rather than stating that she simply did not know anything about a 'certain procedure' her daughter had procured, Nina defiantly admitted that she had made a deathbed promise to her daughter to keep the abortionist's identity a secret. Her silence, she claimed, represented a code of honour that she would not break.

Nina's resistance infuriated Jamieson. He sentenced her to recurring bouts of gaol time. Each time she was released, he would ask if she was now prepared to offer up the information required. When she refused, back to gaol she was sent. Jamieson argued this would go on until she came to her senses and provided a name and an address beyond 'somewhere or other in Bondi'. Nina, a well-connected socialite, spent three weeks in Long Bay Gaol.

She emerged from prison determined to bring Jamieson down. Her articles about her experiences were published in the Sydney *Sunday Times*, and she ultimately counter-sued Jamieson for a thousand pounds, positing the convincing legal case that although she could be gaoled once for contempt of court, Jamieson was overstepping the law by re-sentencing her. The inquest became an embarrassment for the Coroner's Court, and Jamieson was publicly humiliated by the press.

On the morning of 6 December 1923, the official investigation of Sarah Boyd and Jean Olliver commenced at Inquest no. 482, but it was a very different, more tame and contrite Jamieson who assumed the coroner's seat in court.

The coroner was charged with the legal responsibility of exploring two key questions with regard to the suitcase baby. First, had a murder taken place? Second, was there sufficient evidence presented against either of the two women now seated in court to refer them for trial?

Stratford Sheldon, medical practitioner, described the conclusions of his post-mortem. He determined that the child's death had occurred unlawfully – suffocation being identified as the means of death. Jamieson's first question was answered before 10 a.m.

Eight witnesses spoke prior to Jean. They described the physical evidence collected by police: the suitcase and its contents. William Lodder and Eunice Clare, the Sunday school children, described their separate discoveries of the suitcase.

Violet Finney, wife of the proprietor of the laundry-receiving depot in Goulburn Street, identified the handkerchief as belonging to someone who claimed to be Mr Gore's wife, whom she in turn identified to be Jean Olliver, the woman in the chintzy dress.

George Gore's statement confirmed that the handkerchief with the heliotrope border belonged to his lover, Jean Olliver, 'the woman with the dark hair'. He also confirmed that the woman he was 'friendly with' and 'shared the same room' and lived with 'as man and wife' had called herself Jean Gore for a time, and that she was a close and almost inseparable friend of the woman he knew to be Cissie: the 'older woman in the court wearing white'.

Jamieson dated and signed off on the witness statements. He scrawled 'no questions' at the bottom of his notes.

Other witnesses then took the stand. These testimonies sketched out the months preceding the child's murder. Orchardist Joseph Shorrock established the fact that 'Mrs Jackson' (he pointed to the woman in white) had given birth to a baby girl on his farm. He had met Mrs Jackson a few months before, and she had been invited for a holiday but had stayed on at his residence. Shorrock also confirmed that Mrs Jackson and Sarah Boyd were the same person.

Amelia Townsend, Shorrock's neighbour at Mangrove Mountain, identified that the woman whom she knew as Mrs Jackson, with the white hat, had indeed had a baby. She had seen the woman with the baby and had checked in on her throughout the week after the birth. The baby had seemed well and healthy, she said.

Albert Pepper was given the opportunity to deliver a long and uninterrupted statement describing the desperate situation in which Sarah had been. She could not even afford a train ticket, he said. The father of the deceased child was not supporting her, he added. Pepper spoke warmly of Sarah. She had been a good mother, he said. He did not want to hurt her defence, he said. His testimony did not help either Sarah's or Jean's defence.

Pepper described the close relationship between the women. He noted that he had rarely seen them apart before Sarah stayed on at the farm. Sarah had told him that the baby would be handed over to a woman who would claim the state government five-pound bonus for formally registering the birth. This suggested that Sarah and Jean were close enough to conspire. It suggested that Sarah may have planned to kill her child long before she actually did it, because she had already developed an explanation for the child's disappearance.

After Pepper had given his statement, the coroner called a break for lunch. Some members of the public left the building, but the woman with the floral hat stayed in the corridor. She stood quietly alone, removed a small notebook from her handbag and could be seen scrawling in it. She filed back into the courtroom promptly.

The testimony of Maude Honeybone, the manager of the boarding house where the baby was murdered, also presented a conflicted portrait of Sarah as a mother. On one hand, Mrs Honeybone had observed Mrs Jackson to be a 'lovely mother' to her son, Jimmie; on the other, she had heard Mrs Jackson say something very disturbing to Mrs Wall, a fellow tenant of the Brighton Residential Boarding House. Mrs Honeybone was often in Mrs Jackson's room to check on her and the baby. Mrs Honeybone and Mrs Wall had both complimented the child by calling it a 'dear little lovely baby'. In reply, Mrs Jackson had said, 'People who don't want babies have them and people that want them don't have them.' After reporting this to the Coroner's Court, Mrs Honeybone quickly back-tracked and tried to dilute the damaging testimony. She had a great affection for Mrs Jackson, she said. Mrs Jackson had been a great mother to the baby, she added. 'I cannot say she was unkind to the child,' she finished hurriedly before being asked to leave the witness box.

Jamieson sat quietly listening to the evidence. He routinely signed his assent as each testimony was taken, sworn and verified. The formal remark of 'no questions' from the coroner was typed at the bottom of each transcript. He signed his name and pushed the paper to one side.

Coroner Jamieson's restrained oversight of Inquest no. 482 worked in Jean's favour.

When she stood to give evidence, she added much more detail than she had previously provided to police when being interviewed at No. 2 Station.

In this revised account, Jean said she had pleaded with Sarah on many occasions to give herself up to police. Jean claimed to have been so distressed by the sight of the baby's blackened face that she had drunk the rest of the 'baby's gin'. It was gin that Sarah had purchased to use when the baby seemed especially restless and would not sleep. She had encouraged Sarah to kneel and pray, in a back alley, as they hurried back from the Quay after the suitcase baby had been dumped. She urged Sarah to ask God's forgiveness for what she had done. Jean had only travelled to the Quay with Sarah to dispose of the body because she feared for her friend's safety – that she might 'do something to herself' if Jean did not escort her. This was a dramatic tale, heroically told. The public gallery sat on the very edge of their bench seats.

Sergeant Green and then Constable Sherringham took the witness box. They had a dim view of Jean's involvement. She had given them no indication whatsoever that she had tried to deter Sarah from committing this crime. There was no evidence for these claims, Green stated. Jean had also shown no indication that disposing of the body had been a hardship on her. She had not seemed distressed or confused when they interviewed her. Green said that in her original version of events, she had shown clear thinking and purpose. He stated that she had 'seemed to listen attentively' when the transcripts were read back to her. If Jean had been upset, this was certainly the first that Green was hearing of it, he said.

Jamieson again called a recess. It was now midafternoon. Many of the public spectators were housewives and were by this time hurrying home to await the return of children from school and to prepare the evening meal.

The woman with the floral hat did not leave. Her eyes had remained fixed on Sarah throughout the day. And her now lone presence was even more conspicuous.

A group of court attendants gathered quietly in the corridor, just out of sight of the coroner. In whispers, they exchanged theories about who the woman might be.

'She's not just a regular punter,' said one. 'She's older than a lot of the others.'

'Did you see it when the garden on her hat fell right forward at one point?' asked another.

'I know! She was actually crying.'

'Maybe it's Boyd's mother?' asked one.

'No way, I heard she's dead. Sherringham told me the family wants nothing to do with her.'

'Hardly surprising. Maybe garden hat is the other one's relative? The one who looks like a prostitute.'

'No way! Flowers is here for Boyd. You can tell by the way she watches her.'

When court resumed, Constable Sherringham's statement took up the rest of the day. He recounted in painstaking detail every step the police had taken in building their case. He noted to the coroner that Jean had behaved evasively when they met her at the Square and Compass. By her own admission, she was involved in the crime, and the handkerchief was hers, stated Sherringham.

Jamieson perfunctorily dated and signed each of the witness statements. He asked no questions.

Afterwards, he retired to chambers. For most of the following day he considered the evidence. On late Friday afternoon, as the coronial staff prepared to close for the weekend, Jamieson handed down his verdict.

Sarah Boyd (alias Mrs Jackson) would stand trial for murder. Jean Olliver (alias Mrs Gore) would stand trial for being an accessory – for aiding and abetting Sarah Boyd in commission and concealment of the murder of the child known as the suitcase baby.

Both women were refused bail. The coroner's decision signalled the end of their stay at Darlinghurst Gaol. They were transferred to Long Bay, to await trial.

At around 5.30 on that Friday afternoon, the prison shuttle service took its final journey for the week. On board were Jean and Sarah.

Although the natural environment of Long Bay is undeniably pretty, like some other ocean-side locations in Sydney it is not a place for the living but reserved especially for the exiled or the dead.

A little further north in Waverley, the beauty of the ocean view is undeniable. The cliff edge juts out over the Pacific, offering a dramatic vista of the sea and its curving horizon. But to see the ocean here, one must stand beside graveside monuments and mausoleums. The escarpment of Waverley is covered by a huge necropolis, and the view is peppered with crosses and the silhouettes of angels' wings in sharp relief against the vast blue sky.

South from Waverley, the coast has a long history as a sick bay. At Malabar Beach, local Aboriginal communities – vulnerable to the smallpox that came with European invaders – quarantined their infected. The natural sandstone grotto used by the people of the Eora nation as a quarantine site is still known locally as 'hospital cave'.

British settlers similarly designated coastal areas of Sydney to be places of exile for the incurable. Within walking distance from the hospital cave, they established Little Bay Hospital, which was used to confine patients with communicable diseases in the early twentieth century. The beachfront site was surrounded by locked gates and warning signs designed to turn away all visitors. Smallpox outbreaks, bubonic plague, tuberculosis, syphilis and leprosy have all been treated on the very shores of Botany Bay.

Bayside views of the coastline and water have little to do with Long Bay. While it was originally named for the expansive and picturesque length of land that creates the curve of the bay, 'long' is now synonymous with the length of time that most prisoners serve. In Sydney, 'Long Bay' is only ever used in reference to the gaol.

It was dusk as the prison tram pulled away from the Coroner's Court. The physical sensation of the ride must have held a very sad familiarity for the two women who were again bound for the Sydney coast. They were knee-to-knee passengers on a wooden bench riding the same model of tram that had carried them to Circular Quay. Although the carriages of the prison tram were custom fitted with caged compartments, the wheels squeaked along the tracks in the same way as those of a regular tram, so the rattling and jostling would have felt very much the same. On this night, however, the tram rolled eastward for a time, and then turned sharply southward from the shoreline and towards the imposing gothic archway of Long Bay.

The woman with the garden hat left the Coroner's Court and also took a tram. She travelled only a short distance, alighting in Redfern and walking the few minutes to her home in Pitt Street. She unlocked the door to her tiny terrace, swung her handbag from her forearm and dropped it to the floor impatiently. She sat at her bureau and began writing a letter, without even taking the time to remove her hat.

13

BOUNCING BABY

Not very much is known about the contents of the letter. It was addressed to the 'Prison Matron of Long Bay Gaol' and signed at the bottom by 'concerned citizen Mrs Annie Lee'. What is known – verified by several newspapers at the time – is that the letter prompted the beginnings of a friendship between Annie Lee and Sarah Boyd. Soon after it was sent, the same Mrs Lee of the striking floral hat began making visits to the prison. Journalists reported the delivery of meals including bread and stew, bacon and eggs, and pudding.

When Inquest no. 482 concluded in early December and the matter of the suitcase baby was referred to the Supreme Court, legal offices were winding down for the year. Sarah and Jean's trial was scheduled for the next available Supreme

Court sitting in late March 1924. This timeline posed problems for the state government.

In late 1923, forces both inside and outside the reigning Nationalist Party were placing pressure on Premier George Fuller. Historians have described Fuller as a politician of whom 'virtually no one had a bad word to say of him personally'. While a description like this might suggest a statesman with remarkable prowess as a communicator and conciliator, in Fuller's case it seems to have been a diplomatic way of characterising his lack of magnetism as a politician. Fuller was a key political figure during one of the most divisive and turbulent periods of NSW government. Despite the high political drama and leadership battles that characterised 1920s politics in the state, it is a remarkable feat indeed that Fuller remained 'solid to the point of dullness', in the words of political historian David Clune.

Newly appointed opposition leader and aspiring future premier Jack Lang was everything that Fuller was not. At a time when public oration could make or break a political career, Lang was the master of political speeches and had been nicknamed 'the human thunderclap'. He was bold, domineering and obnoxious, and he took a provocative stand on many social welfare reform issues. In 1923, Lang began to lambaste the Nationalists on many fronts, including law and order. Lang's Labor government could offer an alternative, he said, by addressing the poverty, desertion and destitution that led to crime. Sarah Boyd could be counted as one of the most needy in the state, and the association between destitution and crime was soon to be put in the spotlight at her trial.

Fuller was in trouble. He lacked the loud-mouth charisma of Lang and was encumbered with a very measured but ultimately dull attorney-general, Thomas Bavin. The past year had been exceptionally bad for Bavin, and issues of law and order had been at the very centre of a political scandal for him.

In May 1923, the murder of a small boy had occurred in suburban Arncliffe. Five-year-old Percival Carratt had been snatched off the street by Leonard Puddifoot, a young man of only seventeen. The Rockdale community was outraged that not only had a local boy been kidnapped, smothered and dumped in a deserted block of land near his own home, but that perverse and dark figures, their depravity beyond description, were lurking in the streets to steal the innocent.

Community leaders and journalists struggled to talk openly about the sexual dimensions of the crime. Puddifoot's florid descriptions in court of a little boy with 'golden flowing curls' whom he had 'mistaken for a pretty girl' alluded to sexual behaviours and desires deeply repressed by mainstream society. Unable to discuss these taboos, newspapers instead turned to dark mythical imagery, because this allowed terrorising elements of the story to be conveyed to the public while sidestepping direct references to Puddifoot's sexual interests. The *Evening News* dispensed with referring to Puddifoot as a young man at all, instead describing him as a 'human satyr'. In the minds of the public, he was no longer human but a hooved hybrid who had lustfully prowled the local government municipality of Rockdale.

In September, after the trial verdict, Puddifoot's story became a media firestorm for Attorney-General Bavin. A jury acquitted Puddifoot of murder: the teenager 'had not intended to kill the boy because the death had occurred by accidental asphyxiation'. The judge concurred and passed a three-year sentence for manslaughter.

All hell broke loose in Rockdale. Public meetings and rallies were held. Newspaper articles castigated Bavin and called for his resignation. Bavin, a competent and methodical legal practitioner outside of parliament, had no idea how to handle an angry mob. Using legal rationality, he attempted to quell dissent with comments about the need to 'place faith in the judiciary' and urged the public to understand that 'judges make difficult decisions for reasons which may not always be clear to the general public'. This did absolutely nothing to calm the widespread anger. Bavin was cornered in parliament and hosed with questions over the government's poor management of law and order, and its failure to protect the state's children.

When the suitcase baby murder occurred less than two months later, neither Premier Fuller nor Attorney-General Bavin could afford another public scandal over yet another child killing. Although the media continued to deliver mixed messages around the suitcase baby's killers, presenting them as figures of scorn on one hand, and sympathy on the other, one thing was clear: the public would be watching the trial with great interest.

In the case of Puddifoot, the time between his capture in May and his trial in September had proved critical, permitting the media to run wild with the story for a solid four months. Bavin had experienced significant political backlash over the verdict only because the public had come to understand the facts of the case so well. *The Sun* newspaper had then mounted a particularly vitriolic attack on Bavin and maintained a campaign calling for his resignation.

Just like Puddifoot's crime, the suitcase baby murder had been a high-profile news story from the moment it broke. Initially, it seemed, the capture of the suspects could be claimed as a victory for the government: the forces of law and order had worked skilfully and quickly. It appeared that the government was in a position where it could do something about the civic problem and public disgrace of infanticide. Individuals could finally be held to account for a crime that had too often remained faceless. However, the suitcase baby story had become morally complicated far sooner than anyone had expected.

If left to gather momentum in the media, the story put the government at risk. First, the crime had not involved elements too taboo to print. While newspapers generally censored explicit sexual details, they showed no hesitation in reporting on gore and death. With Puddifoot's crime, the papers had been forced to hold back for reasons of moral decorum, but they could revel in the details of the suitcase baby trial.

Historical research on media hyperbole in the English-speaking world of the nineteenth and early twentieth centuries suggests that the government's fears were justified. Public appetite for gruesome news stories was particularly intense at the time, with three facets of crime dominating newsprint. Infanticide sold newspapers. Murder really sold newspapers. Violent crime really, *really* sold newspapers. The suitcase baby trial embodied all three.

Second, the government's approach to law and order would again become front-page news. Fuller and Bavin could see it now: the media would delight in shaming their government yet again for failing to protect a child.

Third, Sarah's case raised social welfare complexities that the government was not yet ready to confront, and for which there were no easy answers. She was a poor, vulnerable woman who had been deserted by a scoundrel. Desperate and without any help, she had been pushed to commit murder.

Between the December inquest and the March trial, public interest was bound to escalate. Of the multiple spins and angles that could be taken by the media, none would benefit the incumbent government. The focus of the state executive quickly turned away from seeking a righteous outcome towards reaching a rapid one. Fuller and Bavin had only one option: bounce the suitcase baby along as quickly as possible before public interest in the case was piqued again. It was the hottest of political potatoes.

The premier and attorney-general no doubt held many discussions within parliamentary chambers regarding how best to minimise the political impact of the suitcase baby tragedy. However, it would be the actions of one woman on the prison frontline that would alleviate the brewing public relations disaster posed by the trial. Grace Braithwaite, head matron of the women's prison, would quite unwittingly help the government to contain the fallout.

Grace's approach to prison management was radical for the 1920s. She argued that the assessment and care of every woman prisoner was vital, and that prison work, prayer and rest routines should be organised with some regard for the prisoners' needs. Grace did not dismiss the need for rigid routines in prison, and she was not easy on inmates. However, she was prepared to work closely with individual prisoners to assess their situation and develop an understanding of how they could be rehabilitated. Her actions suggest a wholehearted belief that the state could work as a progressive and reformist force in women's lives and that this could be achieved without the heavy emphasis on shame that had historically charac-terised penitentiary time. Her maverick approach resembled a very early prototype of the one-on-one intensive casework that lies at the core of much modern-day social work.

The NSW prison system had been criticised by journalists before. Grace had taken the criticism personally. Only months prior to Sarah's arrest, Grace brought a personal libel suit against the *Daily Telegraph* seeking five thousand pounds in damages. The paper had implied that the women's prison was more focused on punishment than the compassionate rehabilitation of wayward women. Grace, although not mentioned by name, took the article very personally and insisted that the paper print a retraction.

When Sarah and Jean arrived at Long Bay, they presented a little differently from most Scottish women prisoners at the time. Impressions of prisoners were formed by prison staff very early, often on their first arrival. Scots, in particular, were viewed poorly. Found on the streets, often starving and homeless, the majority of women detained by police in the early to mid-1920s were Scottish and Irish migrants charged with vagrancy. When these women presented to serve time at Long Bay, they were often in a shambolic and sorrowful state, covered in filth with their hair matted and greasy. They were falling apart both metaphorically and literally. Many were missing teeth due to chronic gum disease and years of alcoholism, and their toes often protruded from the leather boots that decomposed around their feet.

Racism was endemic to Australian society in the early twentieth century, and the criminal justice system was no exception. In the 1920s, the Long Bay women's prison was akin to an expat outpost for Scottish and Irish women. As a result, prison officers saw the women as dim, indolent and recalcitrant, and perceived their ancestry as predisposing them to a kind of criminal idiocy.

Scottish women prisoners had a reputation for being loud and brash. They frequently entered custody inebriated and aggravated, and they were subjected to significant periods of isolation before they calmed to a point where officers believed they could mix with the prison population. Facing institutional racism from the prison guards, the women were assumed to be inferior on three counts: they were street gamin, Gaelic and girls. There was little understanding among the staff that alcoholism, aggravation and a profound lack of aspiration were the long-term outcomes of grinding poverty, not progeny.

Vagrancy and larceny were the two most common charges laid against women in the criminal justice system in 1923. Put another way, homelessness and abject poverty made women criminals.

Administrative protocol at Long Bay required a photograph to be taken of each prisoner on admission, irrespective of how serious their charge. These photographs were retained on the personal file of the inmate. Some, but far from all, of these records remain archived to this day.

Examining the photographs is akin to undertaking an archaeological dig. Each one is excavated from the gridded archives of the State Library. They are small enough to hold in one hand, and each represents a remnant of something bigger. The photograph is an individual artefact with shape and form that begins to tell its own story the longer it is studied. But unlike archaeologists who sift dirt from each discovery through a mesh-covered tray, the obvious layer of dirt on these women is an important part of their message from the past.

Each woman appears hauntingly sad. And while their faces are etched in emotional pain, they are also quite literally etched in poverty: the crevices in their skin are filled with dirt. The grease on their faces reflects the bright burst of light cast by the photographer's flash. In many of the images, the figures no longer look like women but instead characters from a distinctive technicolour fantasy – they have the metallic gloss of Tin Man from *The Wizard of Oz*.

When viewed together as a catalogue, historical photographs like these provide a vivid study of the socially and economically marginalised. They offer a poignant retrospective on the wretchedness of life for women living on the streets of Sydney at the time.

A qualitative analysis of the physical characteristics of Long Bay's migrant women prisoners reveals some clear patterns. Their bodies were typically small framed and remarkably short due to the stunting impacts of childhood malnutrition and lifelong poor health. One Scottish woman's prison file documents her height at just 3 feet 10 inches (117 centimetres). This fact is made even more notable considering height measurements of women prisoners were typically taken while they were still wearing heels.

While Jean was sober when admitted to Long Bay, she presented to staff in many respects as a typical Scot. She was mouthy. She cursed. She seemed to ignore some requests completely and was unafraid of punishment. Her behaviour was interpreted as defiant and oppositional.

Jean was resourceful and immediately looked for ways to improve her bargaining power in the system. She tried to sell her clothing. She requested permission to correspond with an inner-city moneylender so she could arrange to pawn her wedding ring and earrings. Such demanding behaviour would not have been well received by an institution that required demonstrable signs of contrition from its inmates.

The majority of Scottish women prisoners had been living on the streets directly prior to their admission. Outwardly, Sarah resembled these women. Her clothes were dirty and her skin was grimy with the filth of the city. In other key respects, however, she presented as a very different type of Scot from what prison authorities were accustomed. Sarah did not touch drink. She did not swear. She was meek and appeared generally unwilling to stand up for herself. From the moment she stepped foot in Long Bay, she displayed all the signs that prison staff associated with model prisoners. She was quiet and compliant. She submitted completely to the process and made no requests of the administration.

As matron, Grace took special interest in the highest-profile female suspect taken into custody in New South Wales that year. She was fascinated by the contradictions that Sarah represented.

Grace did not see in Sarah any of the exaggerated behaviours considered typical of madness by medical experts. Sarah wept in her cell and she was quiet, but she was not incoherent, nor prone to erratic rages or strange behaviour. Her demeanour was contained but not catatonic. When she could be engaged in conversation, she was lucid and her thoughts seemed well connected.

The letter Grace had received from Annie Lee must also have had some impact on her. Grace did not usually receive letters from the general public. Annie was not a relative of Sarah and had no personal connection to her. Yet here was a letter making a plea for the prison to show compassion for a woman accused of a crime worse than that committed by most of the men processed by the criminal justice system. Annie's dedication to regularly dropping food at the prison must also have piqued Grace's interest in Sarah.

While there is no direct documentation of the conversations between Grace and Sarah, indirect evidence suggests that they were significant to the outcome of the trial.

Since Sarah's confession to the police on the morning of her capture, she had volunteered no further information about the crime. She had chosen not to give evidence or add to her sworn statement at the inquest. Behind the walls of Long Bay, Sarah and Jean were separated. Sarah started speaking to Matron Grace. Through daily conversations, held over the course of a week, Sarah began to talk more openly about the killing of her daughter. Sarah received no visits from legal counsel to advise or assist her in the building of a credible defence. In the absence of this support, and without Jean as an emotional confidante, Sarah turned to Grace, who listened attentively, compassionately.

As a good public servant, she dutifully reported the content of these conversations to the police liaison representative for the case, Constable Sherringham, who fed the information directly to the Crown prosecutor, Mr Coyle.

Sarah admitted that the baby had been an inconvenience. She believed it should never have been born. She wanted to face the consequences of her actions by fully submitting to the legal process and judgement. If this was the case, Grace argued, then there was no point in dragging it out until March. Grace convinced Sarah that it would be best to request an earlier trial date.

Sarah admitted other things to Grace. Alone and in complete secrecy, Sarah had named her baby. It was something she had done in the quiet solitude of her own mind and not shared with anyone, even Jean.

This was a potentially damning piece of information for Sarah's defence. It implied much about her state of mind at the time of the baby's murder. Prosecutors could argue that naming a daughter and then killing her suggested that malice, not puerperal madness, had played a role in the crime.

While the executive applied pressure to the judiciary to move the trial date forward, it was in fact Sarah who requested an earlier date. Grace, as prison matron, had achieved what the executive could not, and she had done so with a speedy efficiency.

Legal teams were given a week to prepare their cases.

The suitcase baby transformed for a final time. As paperwork was prepared, the lawyers knew that it was not the death of a nameless child that would form the basis of their deliberations. The trial would address the murder of Josephine Boyd, and this is what the suitcase baby would henceforth be called. The prosecution would exploit her identity to great effect.

Some truths about what lay in Sarah's heart came more clearly into view. The orchardist was obviously much more than a friend to her. Despite her intense closeness to Jean, Sarah had not named her daughter after her. Nor had she named the child after her own mother, Jane, a Scottish family custom. Instead, Sarah had chosen the feminine form of Joseph. She had named her daughter after a man she had only known for a few months, who must nevertheless have represented the closest approximation to a father figure for her.

The timing of these events is also significant. Sarah had named Josephine not before the baby's death but after. She had strangled her daughter, then named her after the man who had made the progression of their romantic relationship conditional upon the child disappearing. Was the murder an act of love and the naming of the child an indication of a change of heart? Was Sarah seeking to bounce responsibility for what had occurred back to Joseph in a symbolic act of animosity or defiance? Did it suggest that killing her own child was a sacrifice that now filled her with bitterness and regret?

14

IN DECEMBER 1923

The trial was scheduled for a time of year in which Sydney picks up speed. A sense of acceleration can be felt across the city. In December, Sydney is charged with a unique energy that is not sensed at other times of the year, and in 1923 it was particularly so.

Within the first month of summer, the city heats quickly and with an intensity that can be breathtaking. In the 1920s Sydney was also growing rapidly, with suburban expansion pressing up against large tracts of dry bushland. New South Wales continued to grapple with profound drought, which had affected most of the state for over a year.

In 1923, the fear of bushfires even within the inner suburbs was particularly high. One newspaper headline captured the mood within Sydney: 'Bush Fire Peril', followed by 'any day may bring a bush fire ... townies travelling cannot be too careful'. Seasonal conditions throughout winter and spring meant that firefighters had been unable to undertake the controlled burn-off of bushland, traditionally done well before summer. The fear of a bushfire outbreak was so intense that even the use of small portable wax matches was banned until the fire season had passed.

In early December, a bushfire broke out in Blackheath in the Blue Mountains. Fear grew. By mid-December, areas in Katoomba and Leura also went up like tinder. The fire gathered momentum so quickly that locals, in sheer desperation, tried to contain the spread by stamping out flames with their feet.

As December rolled on, fear grew further. In Marrickville to the west, to the south-west in Rockdale and further north to Mosman, suburban fire crews were battling the unusual phenomenon of city bushland fires.

This was different from other years. In December 1923, Sydney sat right in the centre of a veritable ring of fire.

At pavement level in the central business district, the city hummed. The year was drawing to a close and the streets were filled with people. At some point in December, 'going into town' featured as part of the Christmas experience, not just for Sydney residents but for those from the country as well. The city transport system had been established with the intention of continually drawing and expelling crowds to the very centre of town with great efficiency and speed. Sydney trams had been designed to process crowds at the rate of a thousand head per minute, and Central Station was the largest passenger terminal in the British Empire at the time.

Even with the suburban expansion occurring to the west and south, the city remained the focal point for shopping in the 1920s. There were designated districts for furniture and upholstery through to large-scale department stores. The Palace Retail Emporium was the largest department store in the southern hemisphere, and it drew consumers and tourists from all over Australia.

Emporiums were not just places to shop but also to witness the latest technology firsthand, and this didn't only involve what was sold on a shelf. In December 1923 visitors came to the centre of Sydney to witness wonders of the modern world such as operational telephones, hydraulic lifts, pneumatic cash tubes and marble-topped soda fountains.

The Palace Emporium alone employed over three thousand people, and its ground space covered more than 3 acres (1.2 hectares). Its forty shop windows, spanning three corner blocks, were decorated for Christmas. Australian bush flowers and trees featured as a popular festive theme in shopfronts and as street decorations throughout the city.

Also in the lead-up to Christmas, church groups worked hard to elevate their social welfare profile. Community choirs carolled in the streets for donations to local charities. City church choirs performed Christmas oratorios, including Handel's *Messiah* at the Town Hall. City churches and charities held Christmas parties for poor families and children. Santa Claus made an appearance at the Sydney City Mission to hand out gifts to children and care packages to struggling families.

Jimmie, who was only three years old, had been placed in a local residential charity home not far from the centre of town. Joseph had initially resisted but had ultimately been forced by police to surrender Jimmie to Scarba Welfare House for Children – an institution for children up to the age of seven.

The majority of records relating to Scarba have been destroyed and any remaining records are tightly guarded by the Benevolent Society, even a century later. However, a picture of Jimmie's time at Scarba isn't difficult to glean.

At the Australian senate inquiry into institutional care held in 2005, thousands of public submissions were received and tens of thousands of pages of interview transcripts with ex-residents collated.

Ex-Scarba residents provided accounts of their time there in the 1920s, '30s and later. While every resident's road to Scarba was different, the tales contain a remarkable consistency. A wrenching sadness of separation from parents and birth family is described. An overarching charity mindset – bereft of any understanding of children's need for love and care – is evident. Adults describe their lifelong struggle to cope with the aftermath of what one witness describes as 'the survival of a brutal childhood': and it is not neglect or abuse by birth parents to which the witness refers, but the day-to-day practices of institutional care provided in the earliest stages of life. Scarba alumni attribute sixty-year battles with depression, drug addiction and alcoholism to their time there. They also identify that chronic insomnia, a lifelong distrust of others, strings of failed marriages and broken relationships with their own children are all results of their time in institutional care.

Many ex-Scarba residents are no longer alive or remain staunchly unwilling to tell their stories. At the 2005 inquiry, the children of ex-Scarba residents stepped forward to tell their stories and lift the veil of secrecy and shame that these experiences continue to cast today. These second-generation victims of Scarba talk candidly of the need for their own healing because their parents could not love them with their whole hearts. Their parents lived with prolonged mental illness and great emotional pain. Some were abusive. Some just remained emotionally distant for the rest of their lives. In the saddest stories provided to the inquiry, adult children talk of their ex-Scarba parents dying far too soon from alcoholism, drug addiction or suicide.

Jimmie's cohort at Scarba comprised children tainted by poverty or the shame of illegitimacy, or both. Scarba focused on an area of care desperately needed by the state. The organisation housed not only wards who would likely never be returned to their parents, but also those in need of temporary accommodation because their mothers were in hospital, gaol or psychiatric asylums.

In 1923, unfit parents were not just those with a propensity to abuse or neglect children. People who had children out of wedlock were considered unfit, as were many in poverty and those deemed to be morally unsuitable, criminally deviant, socially deficient or just downright irredeemable. Sarah would have been deemed the very worst category of parent, as she was a composite of all of these characteristics.

The vernacular and language used by the charity institutions reveal much about their attitude towards destitute children and their mothers. When Scarba first opened, about five years before Sarah's arrest, it had been named a Welfare House for Mothers and Children and described as a sanctuary for 'necessitous' mothers and babies.

Scarba was the brainchild of the Benevolent Society, which also ran a maternity hospital in inner-city Surry Hills. It was thought that Scarba could operate as an overflow facility by giving the most desperate women and their newborn babies somewhere to go immediately after discharge from hospital.

But very soon after its grand opening, mothers dropped out of the picture entirely, and Scarba reoriented its focus towards destitute children alone. Attitudes about child welfare in Australia in the 1920s, according to social historian Shurlee Swain, identified destitution 'as a moral rather than an economic or social problem and a fundamental aim of the child welfare system was to prevent this moral fault being passed on to the next generation'. Children were 'placed with' Scarba. The staff had no overarching imperative to care for, nurture or demonstrate compassion towards the children for whom they assumed custodial responsibility.

The origins of Scarba reflected core social norms about women and the work expected of them, particularly of migrant women, during this time. Moral matters took precedence over reform and intervention that might genuinely have empowered women to be economically independent; where programs to support 'fallen' women existed, they focused on opportunities to restore virtue rather than creating real job opportunities. Before Scarba had become a children's home, there had been very different plans for the site.

The state government had purchased Scarba directly from a prominent eastern suburbs council member and successful business broker, C. J. Loewenthal. It had been his very stately manor home, shared with his wife, Lottie, and their by-then grown children.

At the time, New South Wales had a significant labour shortage and was in desperate need of domestics in particular. The government had big plans for Scarba as a training institute for women servants, cleaners and cooks. Proper training would ensure the supply of better-quality domestic help for Sydney. Migrant women would have access to skill development and perhaps improved opportunities for stable employment (thereby decreasing the social and moral problems created by unemployment).

Soon after the NSW government acquired the property for well below market value, however, Scarba was very quickly leased to the Benevolent Society, with whom Lottie Loewenthal had close ties. The site would not be developed as a training institute but instead take the overflow of wards and fallen women that the state was not equipped to provide for. Reflecting the charity mindset of the time, the focus remained firmly on helping women to understand how desperately wrong their life choices had been, rather than on providing an institution that might actually help women escape from poverty.

If charity was what the Benevolent Society was selling, Scarba was the official showroom. As the jewel in the society's crown, Scarba formed the focal point of most charity functions, with ladies from Sydney's social elite populating the auxiliary and management committee. Scarba staff were instructed to keep the place scrupulously clean, as public viewings of the institution occurred often. The very early origins of Scarba's work focused on 'foundlings': those children left on doorsteps, orphaned or 'found' without any way of locating birth parents or family. Foundlings were the gold standard of currency in child welfare services. Biological parents, the source of the moral baggage and shame for the child, were completely absent. With foundlings, no parent had to be dealt with or hidden. Foundlings were clean slates and therefore could be more easily placed in a new situation with new parents and a new life.

The State Library photographic holdings on Scarba inadvertently disclose the hypocrisies of the social welfare system as Jimmie would have experienced it. The rooms were grand, hospital-grade clean. The crisp, ghostly white nurses' uniforms cut strikingly efficient silhouettes against the black and silvery grey interior shots of communal nurseries and rows of sleeping cots. What is most notable, however, is the absence of children from the photos. Demonstrable outcomes of good care came down to physical and visible things. Iron cots with bright white lead paint, solid glass nursing bottles, and sheets bleached and free of stains. Small lumps of babies were photographed, but being aired outside, lying in cots but not coddled or touched by staff. Given the clinical sterility of the setting at Scarba, even the cold embrace of a child is hard to imagine.

Other photographs show crowds on the large Scarba estate, with the social elite in their finery. The grand beauty of the two-storey mansion features prominently.

All charitable institutions in the city and surrounding suburbs held annual Christmas parties. Scarba took this to the next level. The Benevolent Society skilfully orchestrated a Christmas campaign that was statewide, instituting a system of town and suburb endowments. Regional areas had fewer social welfare options for children, and Sydney remained the hub of institutional care. Local regions paid an annual stipend to cover the sponsorship of a 'cot for a year', which was typically paid to Scarba in December. When a child was removed from a family in Orange or Port Macquarie, and no place could be found locally, these regions would therefore be assured that a place would always be available.

Grand garden parties were held outside on the lawns to take advantage of the warm December weather. The gardens were meticulously maintained by a full-time groundskeeper to complement the grandeur of the mansion. Christmas fundraisers provided opportunities for female socialites to showcase their musical talents and dramatic accomplishments, and have their tireless humanitarian efforts in the name of Christian charity celebrated by newspapers. Coloured lights were hung in the trees, and the Scarba Ladies' Auxiliary organised sandwiches for guests and potential sponsors.

Jimmie's life that December would have been surrounded by the distress and disruption typical of group homes. Children would have come and gone. Many children would have cried themselves to sleep. It is hard to imagine that Jimmie would have been any different. Within a couple of months he had lost every key attachment figure in his life. In October, he had lost Jean when she had left the farm to return to Sydney. In mid-November, he had lost Sarah when she had been arrested on the morning of his third birthday.

Jimmie had also attached strongly to Joseph. The serene environment of the orchard and the stability provided by the constant rhythm of farm life would have been a far cry from the noisy boarding houses and hotels that had characterised Sarah's and Jimmie's life. At the orchard, Jimmie had his own room and his own bed. When he was taken to Scarba, he left behind the longest period of safety and security that he had ever known.

•

Sarah, alone in a Long Bay remand cell, must have ruminated on the bitter ironies of her experience as a mother. She had done the unthinkable by taking the moral leap of sacrificing one child to spare the other, and it had directly resulted in her loss of both.

In December 1923, the city of Sydney not only hummed with the energy of upcoming holidays and fears over bushfires, it also sparked with a dangerous kind of energy for the legal establishment. The first wave of feminism was in full swing. Having achieved the right to vote in 1902, women were starting to flex their muscles as citizens. In 1918, the right to stand as a member of parliament was achieved. By the early 1920s, attention had turned very determinedly towards matters of law and order and gender equity. And by the end of 1923, at the same time as the suitcase baby trial, several important campaigns for local women's groups were building momentum. This heightened the attention surrounding women's issues in court, and also heightened the level of establishment resistance to the concerns raised by feminist groups.

Two weeks before Sarah and Jean's trial, representatives of the Women Justices' Association, National Council of Women, National Women's Club, Women's Work Union, and the Soldiers' Wives and Mothers Association met in down-town Sydney. In the meeting hall of the avant-garde Culwulla Chambers, adjacent to the very law courts to which femin-ists were directing their protests, women debated issues of equality. A resolution was voted on and passed by a majority: a deputation of women would make a formal representation to the justice minister to demand the right for women to serve on juries. The campaign sought to legitimise the role of women as participants in legal decision-making, in a direct and unprecedented way.

The rationale offered by feminist lobby groups for women's right to serve on juries reflects the conflicted values held about women, even by women themselves. Rather than campaigning that women deserved the right to participate more fully in the deliverance of law and order because they were equal to men, their arguments suggested the exact opposite: women were inherently different from men, and that was why they needed a public voice. Feminist rationales for fairness reflected prevailing views about women and were imbued with biological determinism. Women, they argued, had the intellectual characteristics and inherent aptitude for compassion necessary to strengthen the capacity for justice. Only women jurors could offer 'deeper insights into some of the matters that come before the law courts'.

They identified two key problems and inequities with the current criminal justice system. First, men were receiving light sentences, ranging from only a few months to a few years, for their crimes against women. 'A man should not be allowed to ruin the lives of little girls and then be sentenced to two years' imprisonment,' said one woman campaigner.

Second, male jurors were making decisions on issues – particularly with regard to divorce – that they could not possibly comprehend because they were not women. In this context, women's groups argued, the only way to achieve fairness was via a gender-balanced jury system. As one campaigner argued, 'only women could understand sometimes what constituted cruelty on the part of a man'.

Within their first twenty-four hours on remand in Long Bay, Sarah and Jean saw firsthand what the criminal justice system could do to women. In the prison entry books, Sarah's and Jean's names are closely followed by the name Mary Walloff.

Mary had been found at Watsons Bay by the police. After escaping from a mental asylum a few days earlier, she had wandered from the city all the way to the notoriously dangerous cliff edge of The Gap. For reasons not entirely clear, Mary was sent to Long Bay after she was found, rather than returned to the asylum. Mary's history was well known to authorities: she had tried to kill herself twice before, first by drinking the disinfectant Lysol, then by choking herself with shoelaces. Police charged her with vagrancy.

Mary was transferred to Long Bay in the afternoon. The night warder locked the prisoners in at 5 p.m. and went off shift. The day shift warders did not arrive until the next morning.

Mary's act of insurgency was a conflicted one, embodying both defiance and surrender, achieved with a small leap of faith from a cell stool. She took her prison-issue stockings, swung them over an electric light bracket suspended from the seven-foot-high ceiling of the remand cell, and hung herself. Whether Sarah or Jean in the adjacent cells heard anything of the woman's final struggle for life is unknown. What is certain is that all of the remand prisoners became intimately familiar with the mechanics of Mary's death. As the two women warders unlocked each of the remand cells, one called loudly to the other, 'No. 47 has hanged herself.' There was no sense of urgency or fright in her voice as it echoed back and forth across the stone walls. The two warders then discussed the discovery with a routine matter-of-factness that must have seemed truly chilling to any prisoners in earshot: 'she seemed normal' and 'she ate her food all right'.

Journalists were equally dispassionate about Mary's situation. They reported her death as the inevitable outcome for a madwoman, rather than the result of a system unwilling to recognise that she had needed mental health treatment. One title simply said: 'Succeeded at last. Woman suicides in Gaol'.

Mary's death was tragic, and even more so because it could have been prevented. On the same afternoon that she was found wandering at The Gap, a group of twenty women calling themselves the Lunacy Reform League had taken a list of demands to the health minister. Though Mary's case did not prompt their visit with him, the issues they raised eerily foreshadowed key frontline responses that might have prevented her death. They argued that patients in mental asylums required more thorough assessment and should be afforded the opportunity to complain about mistreatment. The league also argued that those within the criminal justice system, particularly women, should be entitled to better mental health assessments provided by external and impartial psychiatric specialists and not just prison doctors.

Mary had role-modelled a dramatic way for Sarah and Jean to avoid their day of reckoning in court. This would have further confirmed to the two women how very grave their position was. They were charged with a capital offence that carried a mandatory sentence of hanging if they were found guilty. Mary had taken this step herself, and she had only been facing the minor charge of vagrancy.

While the forces of law were objecting to the increased involvement of women in public affairs, so too were the forces of order. In the second week of December, the Australian Public Service Federation endorsed the principle of equal pay for equal work for women. Three days later, the chief commissioner of the NSW police went rogue. The police force could not accept the decision, he said. The women employed by the force would have to go, and this included the only two women police officers, not long after their very high-profile appointment.

Colloquially called 'social workers in uniform', the state's first women police officers represented something of a public curiosity. Their assignments, postings and careers were closely followed by the media. The academic Leigh Straw notes in her biography of Sydney crime figure Kate Leigh that percep-tions of the police force in the city had reached an all-time low by the 1920s. The appointment of Lillian Armfield and Maude Rhodes to the force was an attempt to improve its public image by expanding the range of issues with which frontline officers could deal. Female police officers, it was believed, were more capable of managing and processing women criminals, which relieved male officers of potentially embarrassing situations like raiding brothels full of half-naked women. Women were also perceived to have a stronger innate capacity for dealing sensitively with children. Armfield and Rhodes could be rostered anywhere in the state, at any time, to handle matters relating to women and children in the criminal justice system.

One of the two, Lillian Armfield, had been assigned to work closely with Sarah and Jean during their period on remand.

December 1923 also saw a significant and vocal pushback about the poor conduct of women when in court. In the same week as the suitcase baby trial, a number of judges grumbled, very publicly, about the increased amount of interest that women were showing in legal proceedings. Lower-level courthouse staff had been put on notice to heed the 'display' of women.

The way women dressed in court was not only noticed but also garrulously disapproved of by one District Court judge, Justice Curlewis, in particular. The week before Sarah and Jean's trial, he had commented on the standard of female dress in court: 'the uglier they are and the more unbecoming, the more fashionable they are supposed to be. Ladies do not want to be comfortable, they do not want to look nice. They just want to be fashionable.'

In the very same week as Sarah and Jean's trial, the intense interest of Sydney women in another case upset both a judge and the senior Crown prosecutor. Two Sydney men had been arrested in the inner-city suburb of Tempe, and one – a local butcher, Reginald Ide – faced trial on a charge of rape. Using a horse-drawn sulky like the 1920s equivalent of a 'fuck truck', the men had been cruising around Tempe, looking for young girls to abduct and rape. The rapists, both of whom were in their early twenties and one of whom was newly married, lured the girls with the promise of a 'late-night ride'.

One twelve-year-old accepted the offer. She was taken to an isolated grove and brutally raped.

Tempe is an older suburb between the city to the north and Botany Bay to the south; part industrial and part rural, it embodied the duality of Sydney at the time. On one hand, Sydney was growing rapidly, a furnace for industrial development and urban expansion. On the other, it was still barely a city, on the cusp of frontier lawlessness and bordered by bushland that lay beyond the power of civic police. Tempe's shale quarries and factories sat beside raw and wild undeveloped land and pockets of orchards. Dense forest hung over the Cooks River and lapped at the surface of the water as the dark river wound its way through the suburb.

The women of Sydney had become fascinated with the capture of Reginald Ide, who was believed to have terrorised women and girls in the Tempe area for some time. The case had all the core elements of a terrifying urban legend for young girls: stranger danger, vulnerable virgins, predatory men, abduction and paedophilia. Through media reports designed to instil fear in the community – including 'Another Infant Assaulted' and 'Sexual Offences Butcher Remanded' – women had followed the case closely and attended court to see the rapist with their own eyes. While it is not known how many women turned up, the crowd must have been large because it was sufficient to attract the notice of both the presiding judge and Crown Prosecutor Coyle.

Justice Beeby ensured that it was entered into the public record of the trial that he was thoroughly disgusted with the women of Sydney for their obsessional interest in the case. 'Sticky beaks,' he called them. 'I cannot understand why women attend court when these cases are being heard ... The details are not for any woman to hear.'

It was a view that Coyle shared, as he too voiced his disapproval in court. 'It is a pity there is not a law to prevent women with prurient minds from attending court on such occasions,' he noted. None of the women seated in the public gallery took the very large hint. They simply refused to budge. It was only after direction by Justice Beeby that court officials leaned in and spoke to the women, out of earshot of the journalists in the press gallery. Shortly afterwards, and looking ashamed and embarrassed, a large number of women left the public gallery.

•

Sarah and Jean's trial was to begin the next day, 20 December. The prospect of the death sentence loomed, as did the prospect of a very long time in prison. While the women prepared to fight for their lives in court and struggled to come to terms with the enormity of what they had done, the sombre atmosphere of the prison momentarily lightened.

Even Long Bay's managers had become charged with the festive energy rippling across the city. The usual rules regarding visitation had eased slightly in December, and inmates with local family were permitted to see children and loved ones more freely. Preparations began for a series of Christmas concerts to be held within the usually sad prison walls. Excited discussions of carolling and sing-alongs among the other prisoners must have seemed jarringly at odds with the dark predicament in which Sarah and Jean found themselves.

A movie and sing-along night was scheduled for the eve of their trial. The prison chapel was converted into a makeshift cinema with a piano moved in to accompany the silent movie.

The evening opened with 'The Bonnie Banks o' Loch Lomond' and rolled from one Scottish folksong to the next. For Sarah and Jean all of this could only have served to intensify the loneliness of two migrant women a very long way from home. While the majority of prisoners sang along whole-heartedly with 'You'll take the high road and I'll take the low road, and I'll be in Scotland afore ye', it is hard to imagine Sarah and Jean capable of participating. The last tune, 'Annie Laurie', was so well received among the Scottish prisoners that they clapped and cheered for an encore. The final lines of the old folksong must have cut Sarah and Jean deeply. Hundreds of voices heartily and perhaps wishfully singing 'I'd lay me doon and dee' must have been almost impossible for the two women to bear. As the song ended, the prisoners stood and gave a round of thunderous applause. Some wiped their eyes, tears streaming down their faces. Others leaned against the prisoners beside them, taking comfort in the companionship of women who shared their loneliness and sense of loss. The applause slowly subsided. The pianist and lead singer took a long bow. Then the pianist resumed her seat to accompany a newly released movie.

Hearts Aflame is romantic pathos of the highest order. Against all odds, a hunky outdoorsman and a headstrong woman fall in love. The dramatic and rugged backdrop of the British Canadian frontier conveys the passion of their love story. In the end, a raging forest fire almost kills the heroine.

The mournful Scottish singing and the plot of the movie must have taken Sarah's sorrow to an even more bitter low. However determinedly she had left Scotland, her escape had not delivered the freedom nor happiness she had hoped for. The wish that she had never left in the first place must have been intense, and a creeping sense of longing for her homeland must have surfaced in the prison chapel that night.

When Joseph had paid the fare and put Sarah on the train to find a situation for her baby in Sydney, he had placed her in an unwinnable position. It could have produced no other result than her emotional unravelling.

It is unclear whether Joseph and Sarah were willing to commence a physical love affair while she was carrying another man's child and in the late stages of a pregnancy. The promise of an affair commencing after Sarah had given birth, however, was very real. Joseph offered the stability that neither the flighty young bootmaker nor the salty sea dog had been able to provide.

Joseph was psychological dynamite to Sarah, with Freudian and Jungian overtones. To Sarah, who was hauling a tonne of unresolved baggage because of her father, Joseph offered a Jungian 'Electra' focus. He was close to her father in age, but simultaneously assumed the role of father with Sarah's son. Joseph appeared to provide approval of Sarah that would have satisfied a yearning within her for approval from her father. Unlike her father and brothers, Joseph did not outright reject her for the moral missteps of her past. He promised acceptance and love, though it was not unconditional: he was willing to father another man's child, but his limit appeared to be one and it had to be a son.

Sarah knew what a heart aflame felt like because she had experienced both the passion of an illicit affair and the aftermath of love burned out. She did not have just one but three lost loves to lament: John Aitken, Edward Jackson and Joseph Shorrock. While it is unclear who had lit the match to spark the attachment in each case, it is certain that love had razed Sarah's life to the ground and she now stood amid the ashes.

15

THE TRIAL

THE SIZE OF THE LOUD AND RESTLESS CROWD FORMING OUTSIDE the courthouse on Thursday morning, 20 December, suggested that an early trial date may not have been the tactical media victory the government had hoped for. Interest in the trial had waxed not waned. It also seemed that the women of Sydney had done little to heed the warnings and threats of judges for them to stay away from the law courts.

At the inquest proceedings a small crowd had surfaced, but that had been nothing at all like this. Large numbers of well-dressed women were alighting from trams in Taylor Square. Others had walked down Oxford Street from the railway stations. It was an unusual sight for Darlinghurst, an area known more for its prowling underclasses than promenading middle classes. Not only the morbidly curious had gathered;

women were coming from all over Sydney to witness the moral fabric of society tearing. Monied and working-class matriarchs were sharing tram seats to visit the sacred site of the city's fallen, Darlinghurst Courthouse. This venue could not have been more appropriate.

The inner-eastern suburb of Darlinghurst was, in the 1920s, ground zero for Sydney sin. It had a dangerous reputation as a town on the border between the gritty city and the growing affluence of suburbs further east.

A century before, the area had looked very different indeed. Dotted with large home estates, windmills and fields, Darlinghurst had resembled the English countryside. In the 1830s, clusters of housing sprouted on higher ground. A village high street hugged the water line down below. Darlinghurst's topography and its proximity to the centre of Sydney made it a desirable place to live because it offered multiple vantage points of the city and its progress.

Expansion of the city, and the need for a high-security and more modern post-convict gaol complex, changed the area. Darlinghurst Gaol was built over the course of twenty years, during which residents decanted from the innermost city in patterns that would define the character of Darlinghurst for the next hundred and fifty years. Monied residents, concerned by the prospect of having inmates for neighbours, settled further east and closer to the water. For those Sydneysiders without the luxury of choice, Darlinghurst became home.

Economic recessions – and there were many over the century – also had a role to play in building Darlinghurst's profile as a place of misery. Itinerant and transient workers, many of them migrants, flooded towards the centre of Sydney in search of opportunities. What they found were crowded conditions, sporadic and unstable economic growth and decline, and a day-to-day reality of tramping between sites to eke out day-labouring work as the city slowly expanded. Darlinghurst increasingly became the catchment area for those caught in a cycle of subsistence. Many had enough money to get by, but not enough to move somewhere else and make a better life. Older homes were gradually replaced with boarding houses and saloons to accommodate the growing itinerant population.

By the early twentieth century, Darlinghurst had the highest-density accommodation in the state, sheltering the city's lowest-income residents. While every migrant may have felt their misery to be uniquely their own, they shared some common misfortunes. Their dreams of prosperity had been replaced with the realities of survival in a city where migrant labour was needed, but the migrants themselves were certainly not welcomed nor wanted.

The Darlinghurst of the early 1920s was a mecca of migrant misery, and two women were emblematic of this tragedy. Sarah and Jean were new arrivals, just like many of the workers in the area surrounding the courthouse. Their heritage was a fact that newspapers never failed to overlook. They had come to the country and committed murder. Sarah's dead child had become a cause célèbre for the hundreds of anonymous water babies plucked from drains, harbours and rivers across the state. It was no wonder the suitcase baby tragedy had captured the attention of the public, particularly women.

Court was scheduled to begin promptly at 9 a.m. Ushers needed to manage the sizeable crowd and have the public gallery seated in an orderly fashion. Just after 8 a.m. the dispersed crowd began to herd, converging slowly but determinedly towards the entrance. A queue was forming at the large and very imposing wooden door.

Frontline court staff were on high alert. The judiciary had made it clear that they were displeased with the spectacle of women in court, so ushers were closely scrutinising how the public gallery would look from the perspective of the judge.

The hot December morning would also have worried staff. Darlinghurst Courthouse was notorious for its poor ventilation and stuffy rooms. Staff and prisoners had long complained about the heat that became trapped within the gaol complex and adjoining courtrooms and offices on summer days. Now staff feared that on this humid and heavy day, a suffocating courtroom and the distressing events to be discussed would be a dangerous cocktail. The sight of bumbling staff as they struggled to scoop overwrought women from the floor after mass faintings would be grist for the media mill. It was the kind of press that the administrators of Darlinghurst Gaol were keen to avoid.

A court official opened the wooden door; a middle-aged man with an oily slick of hair, he slipped greasily out of the courthouse to speak to the crowd. He wore a heavy suit that, even at that time of the morning, was proving to be a poor choice for a summer day. An officious and effective clerk, he assumed a no-nonsense tone. He would need to turn people away, but he did not lack compassion. He wanted to ensure that those there to support Jean and Sarah would be able to attend. 'Any family or friends of the two accused, please step forward to be seated.'

Silence.

'The court will be unable to accommodate all of you. I suggest to you that due to the unsavoury nature of the events to be considered by the court that many of you will, with all likelihood, find these proceedings quite distressing. I suggest that those of you easily prone to fainting or feelings of light-headedness would be best to leave now.'

The mob stood firm. Some of these spectators had travelled a long way in order to attend, their voices could be heard to mutter. One woman called out, 'My mother and I have travelled all the way from the Central Coast'. Another group, members of the Women's Christian Temperance Union in Katoomba, said they had 'come down from the Blue Mountains'.

One woman spontaneously stepped forward as unofficial spokesperson for the crowd. She had the appearance of a tincture bottle: wide and short-necked, concentrated and intense. With a stern jaw jutting from beneath her broad-brimmed hat, she stood toe to toe with the clerk. She argued firmly that it was her right as a member of the public and a woman to observe the proceedings. The crowd was quiet, free riding on her determination and confidence.

'And what is your name?' asked the clerk, attempting to intimidate her.

'Mrs Annie Lee,' she replied curtly and threw back an intimidating stare. Her feet held firm to the stony path. Mrs Lee would not back down. She projected a serious bearing at odds with her comically oversized green hat, covered in mismatched fabric flowers.

Court staff caucused quickly. Should they continue to argue it out with the crowd? Should they simply surrender and allow the large group of women inside? It was not just the judge they were worried about. The suitcase baby trial was one of the highest-profile cases the Supreme Court had faced that year, and Coyle would be handling it for the Crown. It was the same Coyle who had voiced his disdain towards the women in attendance at Reginald Ide's trial that very week.

The staff weighed their alternatives. At this time of year, so close to Christmas, a delayed start could be catastrophic for scheduling. It would anger those in charge because it could have flow-on effects for every case scheduled to be heard in the final few days of sitting.

The staff decided to surrender. To the surprise of the entire crowd, it was the male official who took a step back.

The doors opened like floodgates and a sea of large hats surged forward in waves of wild colours. Their brims knocked together as the women jostled down the corridor towards the courtroom. The public gallery benches filled quickly. Staff took the unusual step of permitting some women to assume seats reserved for the press. Staff then did what they could to accommodate the rest of the women by scavenging chairs from the back chambers.

Despite the staff's best efforts, the mayhem created by seating the crowd had significantly delayed the start of proceedings.

The courtroom was divided in half by a low polished wooden banister and a large wooden arch. As is still the case with many modern courtrooms in Australia, there was little to physically separate the public and press galleries from officials of the court. While all of the spectators were women, the rest of the room was dominated by men.

The figures of Corringham (defence representing Sarah), Clancy (defence representing Jean) and Crown Prosecutor Coyle assembled along the bar table facing the bench. They attracted every eye in the public and press galleries. Outside of court and in civilian clothes, the men looked nothing alike, but in their customary white wigs, black robes, high-buttoned waistcoats and pleated wide-legged trousers, they were doppelgangers. To the two women accused, who had no familiarity with legal proceedings whatsoever, it would have been an intimidating scene. Distinguishing between their own counsel and the Crown would have been far from easy.

All were told to rise. Justice Gordon entered the room looking stern indeed: this was a serious capital case, and there had been a tardy and unprofessional start to proceedings. He had also only just recovered from a particularly bad case of influenza in the months preceding the case, and this no doubt was contributing to his ill temper. His high, domed forehead wrinkled, and he snuffled in irritation and combed his pronounced walrus moustache fastidiously with his fingers. Gordon had a reputation for pomposity, and as he assumed his seat he grumbled for the jury to be led in without delay.

Twelve jurors filed into the room. They had been selected for their respectability, fair-mindedness, and capacity for objectivity in assessing the facts and evidence in the determination of guilt or innocence. The legal fraternity of the time considered one gender to hold the monopoly on these capabilities. The jury was composed of men, all suited, all old and all Christian.

The layout of the courtroom offered a clear and unobstructed sight of both Sarah and Jean from any vantage point.

Everything about Sarah suggested resignation and surrender. Her movements were careful and silent and slow. She kept her head bowed. Despite the humidity, she was wearing a long and heavy brown coat. As it fell open, a tired and stained white dress could be glimpsed. Her only concession to the fashion of the day was a white straw hat with a thick silk band, which looked new and had possibly been given to her by Annie Lee. Her hair was tied neatly into a bun at the base of her skull. Her face was weathered and ruddy.

While the public had mainly come to see Sarah, Jean offered a scene too delectable to ignore in such a solemn setting. She had dressed as if ready for an evening at a bar, not for her day of judgement *by* the bar. Her tight-fitting shift finished cheekily above the knee and was a deep taupe that journalists reported as 'heavy mole', in keeping with fashion terminology. With a low-cut neckline and a dramatically thick fur collar, the ensemble imitated the heavily stylised opulence not of old money but of the new-money gangster molls of Darlinghurst and Surry Hills. Jean's scarlet hat with an emerald trim made a striking statement; it was covered in a decorative brocade that newspaper artists took great pains to recreate in their sketches. Jean's bold red lipstick was a deep shade known on the street as ox blood. It was popular with local harlots because it could be used to create a well-defined Cupid's bow.

The only other woman there in an official capacity was Lillian Armfield. As she was one of the only two women police officers in the state, her services were in high demand. Only the previous week she had been close to losing her job, but after a series of blustering threats, the police commissioner had ultimately backed down.

Lillian Armfield had not been hired just because she was intelligent and capable of the psychosocial demands of policing, but also because she was wide shouldered and strong. At the time, a burly frame was considered a prerequisite for employment in the police force. Seated in the courtroom together, the three women must have been a striking sight. Next to Sarah and Jean, Armfield epitomised the image of a strong protector. At 5 feet and 8 inches (172 centimetres) and over 175 pounds (80 kilograms), she was significantly taller and heavier set than Sarah and Jean, who were remarkably tiny framed, each standing at a little over 5 feet (152 centimetres).

Armfield's presence indicated that the state was very much aware that the suitcase baby trial was a public event, meaning that damage control measures were necessary. It is significant that one of only two policewomen had been deployed to liaise with Sarah and Jean, and the positioning of the three women within the court suggests a highly orchestrated public relations stunt. On one hand, the justice system had to be seen to mete out punishment to criminals. On the other hand, because the accused were women, the system had to show an extended capacity for compassion. Armfield's presence sent a message to the general public: we, the state, are fully committed to the delivery of justice, but we are not heartless. Whatever verdict was reached, the state did not want to face the accusation that the system hadn't treated these two women fairly. Lillian was seated like a tower of strength between them, as if providing a shoulder to comfort each tiny woman.

Opening statements were not made until almost eleven o'clock. The Crown's case was methodical, focused heavily on chronology and not psychology. It shrewdly avoided issues that were likely to create moral complications for the jury. Eleven witnesses were called, including the police, one medical professional, and everyone whom Sarah and Jean had counted as friends during their short time in Sydney.

The Crown sought to establish four fundamentals:

I.   The suitcase baby had been murdered.
II. Sarah was the suitcase baby's mother.

III. An act far more depraved than mere infanticide had taken place.

IV. There had been a single killer (this would reduce the complexity of the crime for the benefit of the jury).

To prove that the baby had been murdered, the Crown called Dr Stratford Sheldon to the witness stand. The prosecution directed the jury's attention to two key exhibits: the string tied around the child's neck, and the handkerchief removed from her mouth and throat.

'Dr Sheldon, please describe to the jury your post-mortem findings regarding the body of Josephine Boyd,' Coyle requested.

'There was an ordinary Turkish towel around the body. There was a piece of string tied tightly around the neck with a firm knot [string tendered and marked Exhibit A]. The mouth was stuffed with a small muslin handkerchief with a heliotrope border. That is the handkerchief produced [handkerchief tendered and marked Exhibit B].' Sheldon noted that one or the combination of both items could have caused death.

Three witnesses then established that Sarah was the baby's mother: Joseph Shorrock, Albert Pepper and Shorrock's neighbour, Amelia Townsend, who had been called to check on Sarah after the birth. Each confirmed that Sarah had delivered a healthy baby in late October.

In order to establish the third fundamental – that the crime was more depraved than mere infanticide – Coyle went in hard by redefining the nature of the crime from the outset of the court proceedings. He did this by drawing attention to the fact that the so-called suitcase baby was not an anonymous victim at all, but a child with a name. This immediately separated and distinguished the murder from other infanticides, affirming the pure criminality of Sarah's act of violence. She hadn't smothered her baby in a fit of pique. The murder had not occurred in the dramatic and emotionally overwrought moments during or just after labour that doctors throughout the Western world argued could make the sanest of women go mad. The delusions and hysteria that can accompany birth were not to blame here, asserted Coyle. Josephine had been killed weeks after her birth. Her death had been planned and evidence of the murder surrendered to the ocean.

This approach was later driven home by Justice Gordon in his summing-up, just before the jury filed out of the room to make their deliberations. Gordon used the name Josephine repeatedly in the final summation, reinforcing to the jury that she had been a child with an emerging identity and not a newborn who had been done away with only moments after delivery.

From the outset, the Crown had also focused on Sarah's clear motive for murder. The first witness important to this line of argument was Albert Pepper. He was perceived by the police as a knockabout and a bit of a no-hoper, and had only been included on the witness list because he provided a timeline for Sarah's movements in the week leading up to Josephine's murder. In court, Pepper not only identified Sarah as the woman who had given birth to a baby at the farm, but also said that he had seen her in Sydney with a baby before 15 November and then without the baby shortly after. It was a detail he had not mentioned to the police before.

His testimony presented both the prosecution and the defence with a number of compelling possibilities. The Crown used his statements to cast Sarah as a liar: she had exhibited deceitful behaviour and had been purposeful in her intent to kill. She was certainly not a mother in the throes of madness or distress, the prosecution claimed.

'Between 10 and 15 of November I saw her periodically,' Pepper said. 'Boyd told me the sister of the father of the child was ill and that another woman would take the child over until the sister could take it. When I saw her, she did not always have the child with her but whenever I saw it, the child was well and Boyd herself was very well, only she seemed terribly worried about the child.'

Clancy, one of the defence counsels, stood to ask Pepper about his relationship with Sarah. Pepper did his best to leave the jury with a good impression of Sarah. She was a respectable woman who had faced very hard times, he said. He reinforced this by consistently referring to her not as Sarah, nor by the alias she had used while living in Sydney, but as Mrs Boyd. Pepper repeated the tenor of the testimony he had provided during the inquest proceedings. He commented on her good habits, her Christian values and her dislike for alcohol. He worried for her. She had no money, and very few belongings at all. He also liked Sarah, and saw her as a generous spirit, this much was clear.

'The last few shillings she had she gave to Olliver to go to Sydney . . . She was not paid any wages by Shorrock and myself. I saw her other child, a little boy . . . She thought the world of that boy and he was well looked after.'

Pepper then provided an opportunity for the defence. His comments could act as a catalyst for a line of argument about the desperation of Sarah's circumstances. 'She had only been in New South Wales a few months, I believe. So far as I could tell, she had no knowledge of what was available in the state so far as homes for children were concerned. She knew nothing at all about the state or homes where children could be placed or that kindly hearted people would adopt children.'

Pepper was right. As a new migrant, Sarah had little knowledge of Sydney, its geography, or its network of welfare and benevolent societies. Nor did she have any knowledge of the local reputation held by these agencies. The institutional care sector was fragmented, difficult to navigate and almost inscrutable from the outside because so many organisations were privately run.

The Catholic Church was the biggest provider of social welfare for mothers and children in need of aid, but this would have been little use to Sarah as a Free Church Scot. A key focus of Catholic welfare was the care and very discreet adoption of illegitimate children born in families within the Catholic laity. St Anthony's in Petersham, for example, hid 'girl mothers' during a pregnancy and then quickly adopted the child out afterwards. For well-connected Catholic families with an unmarried and pregnant daughter the service was absolutely crucial to maintaining the ongoing respectability of the entire family. Similarly, St Margaret's Home for Unwed Mothers in Surry Hills focused on 'shelter and care for unmarried girls of the comparatively respectable class'.

Had Sarah sought help, she would have found few options available to her. She was Presbyterian, not from a well-connected family, and nudging thirty. While there were Presbyterian homes for abandoned and destitute children in Sydney at the time, with the exception of Burnside at Parramatta, they were for the most part fledgling organisations.

Joseph Shorrock took the stand. His evidence spoke to Sarah's state of mind prior to Josephine's murder. She was frail and unstable, he said. But would the jury see this fragility as part of a mental instability that absolved her of responsibility? Had she been desperate and depressed or desperate and depraved?

'It was my house she was staying at on the orchard,' Shorrock said. 'I found Boyd to be a good little woman around the house, tidy and clean. Her manners were all right and she never had a drink although there was always a drop in the place if she had wanted it. While she was with me she was not cheerful. She seemed to be worrying and downhearted both before and after the birth of the child – particularly after the birth. Several times I walked in unexpected and found her crying. Sometimes she would be crying over the baby. She was very fond of the little boy and treated him well.'

'How would you describe the relationship between the two women?' asked Coyle.

Shorrock made his disapproval perfectly clear. 'The only money Boyd had she gave to Olliver . . . When she went to Sydney I gave her what money I had. She said she had expected to get the money Olliver owed her, which would enable her to carry on in Sydney and pay her board until she could get a job.

'Their relationship were nothing extraordinary but just in the way of friendship. There was sufficient friendship apparently for Boyd to lend Olliver her last money.'

It was at this point that Jean's behaviour began to change. She appeared to become disoriented. Was this genuine confusion or a performance? She got out of her seat and began heading for the exit, bold as brass. When stopped by a court official, she looked at Justice Gordon with a bewildered and pleading expression and asked, 'Is it over and can we leave now? Is it time for us to be released?'

In contrast with Sarah's stolid demeanour, Jean was animated and nervous. Because she was partially deaf, she found conversation difficult to follow when it echoed in a large chamber such as the courtroom. Her confusion was often mistaken for distress and nervous agitation, and she overcompensated by talking loudly because she found it difficult to judge an appropriate pitch. Whether at a bar or in court, Jean's presence filled a room, and this made Sarah seem all the more cold to a jury looking for any sign of the overwrought emotions associated with the frailty of womanhood. Sarah gave the jury, the judge and the crowds absolutely nothing.

Every other witness, including the police officers, provided a vastly different picture from Joseph's of the friendship between Jean and Sarah. Maude Honeybone's testimony, in particular, framed the image of the two women. She had also spoken at the inquest. As the boarding-house manager, she had observed the two women closely.

Mrs Honeybone described Jean as a loyal friend who protected and cared for Sarah. 'They were together all the time . . . and it was Jean who returned Sarah's key when she left . . . as far as I could judge they were close friends I should say.'

Mrs Honeybone's portrait of Sarah was less flattering. She repeated the testimony she had provided at the inquest. 'The last time I saw her was on the afternoon of 15 November. I live on the premises . . . Mrs Jackson said, yes people have babies who do not want them, while people who do want babies cannot have them.'

These were visceral and embittered words. The statement hung in the air. Real damage had been done to Sarah's character. Whether it was the very serious atmosphere of the courtroom, or the intense gaze of the Crown prosecutor, Mrs Honeybone seemed hesitant to speak. 'That is all that was said,' she said, with a sense of hesitation in her voice, shortly followed by, 'The woman herself did not appear very strong when I first saw her.'

The Crown now turned its attention to Jean. The morning's proceedings had focused closely on Sarah's character, and her conversations and actions leading up to the murder. As the afternoon approached, Jean was drawn more clearly into view for the jury.

The turning point came when Jean's lover, George Gore, took the stand. An audible gasp came from the public gallery. Jean was married. This was not the behaviour of a good Christian woman at all, despite what Jean claimed about her fondness for prayer.

Gore tried hard to minimise his involvement in the case. He immediately distanced himself from Sarah. 'I knew her by the name of Cissie. I did not know her surname nor anything about her.' It was an unlikely claim, given that Jean and Sarah seemed inseparable, yet it remained unchallenged in court.

Gore also now sought to distance himself from Jean and minimise his relationship with her. Sentiment in the room regarding Jean changed after this. She was immoral and immodest, and she looked like a flapper – however, at thirty-two she was also nearing middle age, and her attempts to fit into a youth subculture now seemed sad, desperate and pathetic. While society may have somewhat tolerated if not approved of young women flouting conventions, bad behaviour remained deeply disapproved of in older women. Jean no longer looked like a slip of a thing searching for a joy ride: she now seemed like an old fool.

'I knew Mrs Olliver there, I became quite friendly with her. She used to do my laundry for me,' said George. Everyone in the court knew what 'friendly' meant, and suddenly 'laundry' became something far dirtier than a pile of soiled under-garments. A few women could be heard to giggle quietly. Justice Gordon looked in the direction of the public gallery with great disapproval.

'I saw Boyd on the night of the fifteenth, she was at the Square and Compass and stayed there for that night.' Gore knew this, he said, because he had been passed out drunk on the boarding-house-room floor, while Jean and Sarah shared the bed.

On the issue of whether or not there had been a single killer, Jean did most of the heavy lifting for the prosecution. She was helped in no small measure by the directions that Justice Gordon gave to the jury – and also by the testimony provided by ambitious young Constable Sherringham.

The constable's testimony about Sarah was damning. With Detective Alchin no longer involved in the investigation, Sherringham referred to his findings regarding motive. For the jury, Sherringham read the statement prepared by Alchin, which described his car trip back to Sydney with Sarah after her capture at Wyong. 'Why did you do it?' Alchin had asked of Sarah, who had replied, 'I was in the room and I did not get any word from the father. I had written him a couple of letters and he had not replied.'

Sherringham was eager to defend Alchin's need to take leave because of the vicarious trauma associated with partici-pating in the investigation. 'Alchin conducted the questioning. The story of her life and sufferings did not affect him so much that he was not able to give evidence at the Coroner's Court. He left on holidays.' Sherringham had done what he could to preserve the reputation of a fellow officer for whom he had great respect.

Sherringham had conducted background checks on Boyd and Olliver on 17 December 1923. These too were submitted to court.

'Boyd arrived in Sydney from New Zealand about 1 April last and has lived in various places about the city and suburbs since then. So far as can be ascertained, prior to the offence she is now charged with, Boyd conducted herself fairly well.'

Sherringham's profile of Jean was rather more colourful. 'Olliver arrived in Sydney from New Zealand about the middle of April last and has lived at several boarding hotels and boarding houses in the city and has visited relatives in the country. She appears to have been drinking very heavily and leading a very immoral life.'

Ironically, the commentaries surrounding Jean as someone of little virtue only seemed to help her case. She was painted as a flapper. She gallivanted around town with George Gore, the furthest thing from the acceptable behaviour of a 32-year-old married woman. They went to the races to gamble. Jean drank and smoked to excess. Gore was often found passed out from inebriation in the public bar. Even more shocking, Jean and George lived together openly, in a city hotel, while her husband remained in New Zealand.

Yet while the police believed Jean to be completely immoral, they also perceived her to be foolish and incapable of murder.

Sherringham's testimony was elegant and efficient. He made his own views on the subject of Jean's guilt clear. He did not believe Jean to be a murderer, but he did think she had assisted Sarah in cleaning up her crime. 'It was quite clear to me that she was shielding Boyd.'

A skilful legal professional would have been able to harness all of the testimonies that described Sarah's sadness, suffering and shame, and then used them effectively to mount a defence that her judgement had been impaired at the time of Josephine's death. Infanticide cases in England had shown this to be possible – women had been released.

Although legal historians have noted that New South Wales had historically exhibited the 'ingenuity and determination of doctors, judges and juries in avoiding murder convictions for women suspected of killing their newborn infants', no such ingenuity was employed by the state on Sarah's behalf. The approach taken by Coyle is difficult to interpret. Mark Tedeschi QC has written extensively on criminal trials in the state and notes that Coyle was known for his compassion towards women prisoners, having demonstrated this in his dealings with high-profile prisoner Eugenia Falleni in the early 1920s.

Coyle approached the suitcase baby trial as a lawyer doggedly determined to get to the truth as he perceived it to be. It is paradoxical that the prosecution's open approach to interviewing witnesses significantly broadened the scope for the defence to develop and flesh out an insanity plea for Sarah. But although there was immense potential for Corringham to advocate for leniency on Sarah's behalf, this was left unexplored. She was a good mother – her loving treatment of Jimmie was evidence of that. Good mothers only kill when disturbed in the mind. Instead, Sarah's lawyer offered no defence whatsoever, and no exculpatory evidence of any kind was provided for the jury to consider.

The fact that Sarah refused to speak or give evidence at trial would not, in all likelihood, have undermined Corringham's ability to mount a defence. In 1923, the body of cases on puerperal fever to emerge from England shows that the accused did not need to give evidence in order for a viable and cogent defence narrative to be formed. When it came to matters of maternal insanity, this was an issue best left to doctors to explain.

Corringham could have framed a set of arguments to demonstrate that shame and desperation had driven the killing. Or medical evidence could have been compiled to demonstrate that Sarah's female physiology and psychology had, in momentary madness, made her a murderer. Corringham used neither option. No verbatim transcript of his representation on Sarah's behalf exists because none was presented in court. Sarah had entirely surrendered to the process – so too, it seemed, had her defence team.

Initially, at least, elements of Jean's written confession and her description of what had happened on the day of Josephine's murder were consistent with the Crown's single-killer theory. Jean described walking into the room. She claimed that Josephine was lying face up on Sarah's lap, the baby's head on Sarah's knees. It confirmed the broad mechanics of the murder as described by Dr Sheldon, because it suggested that Sarah could simply reach forward and strangle her daughter.

Other elements of Jean's description were not consistent with the theory that Sarah had undertaken the murder alone and without assistance. One of the murder weapons – the heliotrope handkerchief – was identified as Jean's.

If a string had been used to strangle Josephine, it was highly likely that two hands would have been needed to tighten it across the baby's neck. Yet the handkerchief had simultaneously been pushed with force down the throat. The coroner himself had stated that the two methods had clearly been employed at the same time. This suggested that two pairs of hands had worked in concert to commit murder.

Jean's testimony shows inconsistencies – unexplored in the trial – that suggest she may have been in the room when Josephine was murdered.

Jean claimed that on her return to the room, Sarah had already killed Josephine, and the baby's face was wrapped in a towel. She also claimed that she knew without doubt the child was dead because its face was black: 'I opened the door and I saw Cissie with a towel around her baby's face and all its face black.' Although Turkish towels are more lightweight than regular bath towels, they are not transparent. How could Jean have known immediately on first sight, as she claimed, that the child's face was black when it was completely obscured by a towel?

Jean and Sarah had spent much of the day of the murder alone together. Joseph Shorrock was at the orchard with

Jimmie. George Gore was at work. Jean claimed that on this day she had convinced Sarah to give up entirely on Jackson, and she admitted that this conversation had immediately preceded Josephine's death. Jean and Sarah could easily have spent the day talking through the options for Josephine's murder and the disposal of her body, in light of the letter that Jean claimed to have received from New Zealand that morning. 'I got a letter from home saying Cissie was not wanted, and Cissie saw my letter. I showed the letter to her and it said her boy was happy and did not want her.'

This raised more strong possibilities for Sarah's defence that were left unexplored. Jean may have actively participated in the murder, and if it could have been established that she had incited the crime and that Sarah's mind had been frail, the jury could have perceived Sarah's level of guilt as lessened and Jean's level of participation as heightened. This could all have dramatically improved Sarah's chances for a reduced sentence or even her release.

When the two women had huddled together at the police station, they had seemed completely loyal to each other in every respect – except one. Sarah had always maintained that Jean had been in the room when Josephine was killed. At the police station, Sarah and Jean gave their statements, then Sarah's was read aloud and Jean challenged it: 'I was not in the room, Cissie, when you killed the baby.' Sarah replied, 'Oh yes you were, Jean.'

While Sarah had told many lies in her life, everything about her behaviour leading up to the trial suggests that she had openly admitted to the police what she had done. It is unlikely that Sarah would have challenged Jean, and insisted that Jean admit she was in the room with her as well, unless Jean had been actively involved in the murder.

Other pieces of evidence that were dismissed as irrelevant by police raise vexing questions about Sarah's intent to kill. Was it something that she had maintained as a dark desire even before Josephine's birth?

When Josephine's body was found, it was dressed in a baby corset, commonly known as a binder: a short flannel shirt and a napkin. The warm spring climate of Sydney would have made the choice of a lightweight garment a sensible one for a caring mother. The use of a binder, however, is a little more intriguing. Binders restricted a baby's intake of air every time it drew breath. In the nineteenth century, the binder would have been unremarkable: baby corsets were seen as a preventive health apparatus because it was believed they could reduce the risk of umbilical infection and the possibility of colic and gas.

By the 1920s, the fashions and customs of mothercraft were undergoing rapid change and binders were far less common. They remained popular among those nannies and mothers who wished to contain noise, because they worked like a volume control on the human voice. The tighter the binder, the more constricted the diaphragm, and so the child's cries would quieten. On one hand, the use of a binder might suggest a mother with very old-fashioned notions of child care; on the other, it might suggest a mother on the brink of nervous collapse, desperate to muffle the screech of a demanding baby.

The police observation that Jean was fond of 'drinking the baby's gin' also raises questions. That Sarah used gin frequently to put Josephine to sleep is undisputed. Was her measure of gin, however, in keeping with dosages considered reasonable and helpful as a sleep aid at the time? Or was the gin dispensed with a generosity that suggested she was trying to overdose the baby?

All of these complexities were left unexplored at trial. Instead, a single line is typed by the court transcriber: 'No evidence is offered for the accused Boyd.'

Jean spoke in her own defence: 'Accused Olliver elects to give sworn evidence.'

'My name is Jean Olliver. I am a married woman and my husband is at present in New Zealand. I have known Boyd for three years this New Year's Eve . . . my feelings towards her were that I loved her immensely and her little boy also.

'On 15 November I was with her all day and I went home with her to her room. I think it was just after six o'clock in the evening. I remained in the room for a while with her and she was undressing her baby and giving it a drink. While she was undressing her baby I went across to the people's palace to see if there was an answer to my cablegram to my husband. I had cabled him saying I was coming home. From there I went back. I went into a tea room first and made a purchase there and then I went straight back to Cissie in the residential in Pitt Street. I was away not more than ten minutes . . . the door was shut but not locked.'

Jean claimed she left again in terror. And by the time she returned, Sarah had already put Josephine in the suitcase. 'I was in an awful state. It was like a nightmare to me.'

At this point, Jean's confidence in court grew. She told a more embellished and coherent story that cast her as a hero. She travelled on the ferry with Sarah because she feared her friend 'like someone gone mad' might kill herself as well. 'I only went over the harbour because I thought Cissie might throw herself in.'

Jean also described events in a more exaggerated way than she had in prior interviews by police or during the inquest. Jean had advocated on Sarah's behalf to the Lord, she said. She had tried to encourage Sarah to go to the police. In a back alley, somewhere between George Street and their arrival at the Quay, dead baby in suitcase in hand, Jean had fallen to her knees and pulled Sarah to the ground with her. 'I pray to God he will forgive you,' she said to Sarah. 'If you like, we will go straight to the police now.'

Jean also claimed that she had offered to take Josephine to New Zealand. She claimed to have bought several items for the baby that very afternoon, so that Sarah could take her out more in public. None of these items was found in the suitcase when it was discovered, despite the fact that it had contained every piece of evidence pertaining to the baby's existence.

The Crown prosecutor responded to Jean's testimony by saying, 'You have added a good deal of evidence.'

Jean's next statement was undoubtedly true. 'I had no one to assist me with my evidence.'

'The next morning,' said Coyle, 'after you were taken into custody, you told lies about everything when seen by the police.'

'Yes,' replied Jean.

'Did you say one word about going into a dark lane and telling her you hoped God would forgive her?'

'No.'

'You had been forgetting about God a bit before, hadn't you?'

'But it happened, we both prayed together,' she said.

A major question for the jury to consider was – had they killed together?

16

THE VERDICT

AT 4 P.M. JUSTICE GORDON BEGAN SUMMING UP FOR THE JURY. In giving instructions to the twelve men it seemed, at least initially, that he was directing them to consider the role of each woman in the act of murdering Josephine.

'Gentlemen of the jury, the two prisoners Sarah Boyd and Jean Olliver are charged before you upon one indictment, but the charge made against each woman is absolutely distinct.

'The evidence is uncontradicted, there is no statement to the contrary or anything else that this child, Josephine Boyd, who lost its life after three weeks being in this world by having a handkerchief stuffed down its throat or string being put round its neck, was up till that time a healthy child with every prospect of living to a good old age.

'As the Crown prosecutor has perfectly fairly told you, it is incumbent on the Crown to prove exactly what they charge, and if the facts of the case were equally consistent with the killing having taken place in the absence of Olliver or having been done in her presence, then the jury should convict her of murder. In order to be guilty of the murder of Boyd's child, she must either be present when the murder took place or she must have been an accessory before the murder – that is inciting Boyd to kill.'

However, Justice Gordon's comments then rapidly narrowed. He made it clear that in the case of a newborn baby's murder, motive can only have one point of origin: the mother.

'Take Boyd's own statement uncontradicted which was made and which was admitted at the invitation of – or certainly without any objection after they were invited to raise any objection – on the part of her counsel. That statement is in evidence and can be perused by you in the jury room. You will read that statement when considering the question of whether or not you see any reason to doubt the fact that it was Boyd who killed her child on that day. You will ask yourself what other hand could have put the handkerchief in its mouth or put the string around the child's neck. Who had any object?

'The sole evidence before you is that the cause of the death of that child of three weeks – the illegitimate child of Sarah Boyd – was suffocation from one or other of those two causes. The whole of the evidence – certainly the evidence given by Jean Olliver – distinctly proves that the hands which put that handkerchief down the child's throat and which tied that string around the child's neck were those of its mother – Sarah Boyd.'

In his assessment of Jean, Justice Gordon offered some very clear directions to the jury about both her role in the crime and how they should measure the immorality of her actions on 15 November 1923.

'She did what may be meritorious in one sense of the word but which none the less comes within the definition of being an accessory after the fact to the murder. When she finds that Boyd will not give herself up – according to her own evidence – she goes with her with the dead body of the child in order to throw it overboard and conceal it. In addition to that she helped to bring to her friend the block of wood required for the purpose of concealing that dead body by being put in the suitcase . . . of course if you and I were asked ought a friend to stick to a friend even to the extent of committing a crime, we might say yes outside a court, but when we are administering justice we have got to administer it according to the law.'

With regard to Sarah, Gordon did the work for the jury. He posed the necessary questions and then answered them.

'You have it from Mr Gore that on the Thursday afternoon, 15 November, he saw Sarah Boyd and Jean Olliver and they told him that they had met a woman who was willing to take charge of the child and that they were going to take the child over to the woman. That is a most material matter. It was all lies as far as we can see. There is no evidence of a woman who was going to take charge of the child. But there is evidence that the child's life was taken and after the child was killed by the mother what were her actions? Were they the actions of a person who had no recognition of what she had done?'

In response to his own question, Gordon said there was no scope for an insanity defence to be considered. Instead, Sarah's actions suggested that she had been 'perfecting the design of her crime'. Her behaviour in the weeks leading up to Josephine's murder should be interpreted, he said, as that of someone exhibiting the signs of malevolent intent. Sarah had not taken any steps to register Josephine's birth, despite the fact that she would have received a five-pound baby bonus. She had lied about the placement of the baby. The judge's summation was clear: Sarah had lied and lied and lied, and this was a clear indication of planning to commit the act.

Gordon performed one critically important task for the jury. He eased any burden they may have felt in putting a woman to death. Should they return a verdict of guilty on Sarah, this carried a mandatory sentence of hanging. But this, Gordon reminded them, was beyond the parameters of their responsibility, or his. 'It was distressing for all concerned to have to deal with Boyd . . . it is a painful matter for both you and me . . . but it is a matter you and I have nothing to do with. That lies in the hands of the executive . . .

'This is a place not for sympathy but evidence,' said Justice Gordon firmly.

It is impossible to assess the merits of Corringham's legal representation of Sarah's defence. This is not because a century of evolving social norms means that a fair critique of 1920s values cannot be made in the twenty-first century. It is just simply not possible to assess something that does not exist. Only in his closing arguments did Corringham allude to the suggestion that Sarah might be suffering the effects of what he broadly called insanity. He established no evidentiary links to this claim, and he did not highlight nor medically corroborate the convincing witness statements made by Shorrock, Pepper and others describing Sarah's distress prior to Josephine's murder.

Justice Gordon gave not just legal direction, but emotional direction to the jury as well. 'This case is very painful. I do not suppose that any of us have the slightest pleasure or feel anything but the greatest pain in seeing two women, whether their lives have been strictly moral or not, in such a position as this . . . but our judgement must not be disturbed by sympathy to disregard the facts.

'Some suggestion has been made to you without a scintilla of evidence that if Boyd did it she was not responsible for her actions. I know of no evidence to support that. The whole of the evidence shows perfectly rational consistent conduct on behalf of Boyd on that day, but it is a matter for you. Where is there any evidence which would justify you in saying that if it was the hand of Sarah Boyd which killed her illegitimate child, she was not responsible for her action because she could not support the child without aid from its father? Everybody is supposed to be sane until something to the contrary is proved.'

At 4.18 p.m., the jury retired. An hour and a half later, at 5.50, they returned. 'We find the accused, Sarah Boyd, guilty of murder with a recommendation to mercy.' They added, 'We find the accused Jean Olliver guilty of being an accessory with the strongest recommendation to mercy as we are of the opinion that she was the victim of circumstances and she was led into it by her close friendship to Boyd.'

Before passing sentence, Justice Gordon asked if Jean had any final words to say. Mr Clancy, her counsel, then rose for almost the first time during the trial. He said he wanted to read a letter sent by Jean's husband from New Zealand. It would speak of her good character, said Clancy.

The judge refused to have the letter read. 'The least said about her husband the better, in view of the evidence here, I think.'

To Jean, Gordon said the following: 'You, carried away as the jury have mercifully said by your friendship let yourself to try and help her to escape from the consequences of her wicked act. The jury have recommended you to the very strongest mercy on the ground that they are of the opinion that you were carried away by your great friendship for Sarah Boyd in doing what you did. I accept that view; if I did not, I would punish you severely but I think the jury are quite as competent and more so in their united wisdom than I am to draw the conclusion that that was why you let yourself to do what was wrong. As a matter of fact the statute provides the punishment for being an accessory after the fact is penal servitude for life. That, however, would be a case of far different circumstances to this one. I intend to give the fullest consideration to the jury's recommendation and pass a far lighter sentence than I would have passed if it had not been for the recommendation of the jury.'

Gordon passed a sentence of twelve months' imprisonment on Jean. Journalists provide the only source of information on the demeanour of the women in court at that moment. While there are conflicting reports, with some newspapers reporting Jean to be more emotional than Sarah, and others claiming the reverse to be true, the majority report that Jean's behaviour was calm at the time of sentencing.

Gordon passed the official sentence of death on Sarah. Unlike his relatively kind comments on Jean, he had very little to say about Sarah.

'It is very distressing to everybody concerned in the administration of justice in the court to have to deal with your case. The verdict which the jury returned is the only possible one open to reasonable men on the evidence . . . The result as far as I am concerned is automatic.' The judge then pronounced the death sentence with the disclaimer: 'in all human probability the extreme sentence will not be carried out, although it is entirely in the hands of the executive and I have nothing whatever to do with it'.

Sarah and Jean were sent back to Long Bay, arriving there at around seven on the evening of 20 December 1923.

17

SUITCASE

FOR THREE GENERATIONS, A SUITCASE HELD MEANING. FOR William and Jane, it was a capsule of promise. They carried it across the Atlantic as they settled their young family in New England and then carried it home again to Scotland. For Sarah, the suitcase held promise too. From the lightest to the darkest imaginings possible, it carried her hopes for a new life and held her shameful secrets.

When Sarah arrived at Long Bay, for the first time in three years she was truly alone. As a death-row prisoner she was separated from Jean permanently. She had lost her son. And daughter. And Joseph. She had been stripped clean of the few possessions she had. Her suitcase incinerated, she was now empty-handed.

She was shown to a single cell in an isolated part of the prison. The death-row cells were larger and filled with more light and air than any others. Different routines also applied to those awaiting the gallows. They were offered food and drink frequently. But prison authorities recorded that Sarah ate very little. The prison doctor monitored her closely.

On 15 January 1924, Sarah's defence team made a number of public statements about a possible appeal. Corringham gave interviews with the Sydney press, and the stories received national media exposure. At the Court of Criminal Appeal they would seek a complete reversal of Sarah's conviction and sentence, they said, and triumphantly achieve her immediate and unconditional release. Her lawyers were casting her as a damsel in distress whom they would seek to rescue. Given the inadequate and incompetent defence they had mounted, this was big talk indeed.

The media campaign continued for another few days. By Friday, 18 January, the newspapers were saturated with stories of the woman on death row. Journalists posed questions of the NSW government. Was it conceivable that the state would carry out the death sentence and thereby make a vulnerable woman suffer further? Would Sarah receive a reprieve? If so, when? Could the defence counsel masterfully secure the exoneration of a woman who it now appeared had not had an entirely fair trial?

Two key lobby groups – the Lunacy Reform League and the Howard League for Penal Reform – stepped forward to advocate in support of Sarah's release. The local chapter of the Howard League, a Britain-based charity that had success-fully achieved social justice prison reform in England, began agitating on Sarah's behalf. They moved forward with the strategy that should have been used at trial: they would compile a viable and medically bona-fide set of findings about motherhood and madness. They approached doctors, including both provocative and prestigious practitioners. With the assistance of the Lunacy Reform League, a contingent of experts specialising exclusively in women's health was iden-tified and indicated their willingness to offer statements of support. They were all doctors situated within Sydney's elite medical precinct in Macquarie Street and not far from the other key decision-makers of the state – the law courts and parliament.

Macquarie Street was a hub of medical practices that offered a range of legal and not-so-legal therapies. Since the rebuilding of Sydney Hospital in the late nineteenth century medical practitioners had bought up property clustered around the hospital entrance and up and down the length of the street. The precinct had become a densely packed network of private consulting rooms for doctors who considered themselves the best in the state. By 1928, more than 260 doctors were located in the hospital precinct alone. They included mental health specialists, self-proclaimed women's health experts, heart and orthopaedic specialists, and even those doctors prepared to offer discreet terminations.

In other words, Macquarie Street was populated with doctors who were willing to take radical steps, not always legal, if the medical matter was one in which they held deep convictions.

One of these doctors wrote provocative articles on women's health using an alias. His newspaper articles criticised the medical fraternity for their overuse of surgical intervention when treating women's gynaecological concerns. To protect his reputation as a prominent Sydney surgeon, he assumed the pseudonym 'the Family Doctor', as his views were not always well received by his peers.

Another Macquarie Street doctor, Terrence Green, offered services to unmarried women like Sarah. Appalled by the stories he had heard about the barbaric practices of back-yard abortionists in nearby Surry Hills, he stepped in to do something about it. For a fee, he referred women to an ordinary house in Bondi that he had remodelled to be a make-shift abortion clinic complete with a resident nurse. Only a few weeks after Sarah's trial, this high-profile surgeon was charged with the murder of a young mother, Elsie Burke, whose circumstances were remarkably similar to what Sarah's had been. Elsie had one illegitimate son who was three years old when she became pregnant, again out of wedlock. In desperation she sought the services of Dr Green. But a short time after her termination, Elsie died rapidly and very pain-fully of septicaemia. It was suspected that a contaminated hook had been used and had punctured the uterus. A rapid infection, almost impossible to treat, had ensued.

No records are available to identify the doctors who were approached to support Sarah's appeal. The Howard League inferred to the press that medical support for Sarah was unanimous. They also claimed that all of the doctors they had consulted expressed surprise that the issue of insanity hadn't been raised at trial, because it represented an obvious and viable line of defence. In early January, with the support of doctors keen to preserve their anonymity, the league made representations to the Minister for Justice seeking to have Sarah properly assessed for an insanity plea.

In making their case, the doctors advocated for the use of diagnostic tools that had been employed to scaffold medically verified insanity defences throughout 1922 and 1923. A team of two to three doctors would require unrestricted access to Sarah in order to assess her capacity for impulse control. These assessments would need to occur over at least a week and be undertaken without the involvement of medical prison staff.

The media storm that had been created by the suitcase baby story in November and December was building once again, much to the government's frustration. The state acted quickly. After four days of newspaper stories about the preparation of an appeal, a special meeting of Cabinet was arranged. On 22 January, a formal statement was made to the press. The government, showing infinite mercy (so said the papers) had commuted Sarah's death sentence to life in prison.

Whether the legal plans to mount an appeal for Sarah had been genuine, or simply a ploy to force the hand of government, is unclear. What is clear is that after 22 January, these plans stopped dead.

Sarah's commutation had been swiftly and smoothly achieved. It was a remarkable feat by the government, given the high profile of the case. The authorities were satisfied: an example had been set, and the perpetrator of a heinous crime captured and sentenced. The state had also not wanted a public backlash about a woman being sent to the gallows. Both public relations goals had eventually been achieved by commutation of Sarah's sentence to life.

•

Each admission to Long Bay commenced with the opening of an entry file. Over time, this grew to provide an abridged history of life behind bars for the individual. The files not only detail convictions and sentences but also capture personal statistics, including hair and eye colour. Whether a prisoner could read or write was recorded. Occupation, religion, and any distinguishing marks through which identification might be verified (significant scars, marks, moles, tattoos, missing fingers) were also recorded. These details were particularly important in the event of prison deaths, enabling staff to quickly identify a prisoner's body.

Sarah's entry file differs from those of her Scottish peers in almost every respect imaginable. While only 5 feet (152 centimetres) tall, Sarah was a veritable giant compared to other Scottish migrants. Mary Foster, for example, was a hard-drinking recidivist who spent many years in and out of prison in the lead-up to Sarah's incarceration. Ellen French was a Glaswegian girl with a criminal history that in the most optimistic retelling could still only be described as a sorrowful tale of petty crime. Both women were less than 4 feet (122 centimetres) tall in their stockings.

Sarah may have been much taller than her counterparts, but her prison record was significantly shorter. The records provide vivid histories of the vicious cycle of capture, charge, convict and release that was common for women prisoners. Pages of handwritten script accompany prisoners' profiles, including long entries with history repeating itself, often for years. All of the offences reflect the impacts of social marginalisation and poverty. The crimes of vagrancy, drunk and disorderly behaviour, stealing, larceny, theft from a dwelling, and indecent language appear often. For some prisoners, reoffending was so endemic that processing staff simply resorted to using the convention of the ditto mark (") down the length of the column titled 'offence'. In contrast, Sarah's file contains just a single note: 'Murder'.

The sentencing documentation also highlights how easily these cycles were created. Migrant women turned thief because of little-to-no opportunities for work. Once a woman thief was captured, the state calculated the value of the goods stolen. This debt was then repaid to the state by the prisoner in the form of hard labour during time served. Once the prisoner was released, the cycle would start all over again, and for some women it was lifelong. One Scottish prisoner's file, that of Nellie Scott, is hefty indeed. Her records of charges, sentences and time served run to forty-three entries. The frustration of administrative staff must have been the topic of much office conversation. Maintenance of Nellie's file alone would have required engineering innovations in the gluing, folding and sealing of additional pages to the heavily bound leather book – and this process did not end because of her successful rehabilitation but because of her death.

On 4 February 1924, Sarah formally received word that her sentence had been commuted to life. She signed the official entry book at Long Bay that legally acknowledged her acceptance and comprehension of the letter's contents. But whether she fully understood the meaning of her commutation is unclear. Prison staff reported that she was disoriented, confused and detached. Although Grace Braithwaite, the prison matron, described Sarah's mental state to be lucid before the trial, it now bordered on catatonic.

As Sarah commenced serving her life sentence, child welfare authorities began planning for Jimmie's future. No one in Sarah's family offered to make the journey to Sydney to claim the little boy, who had remained at Scarba. The group home met a niche area of demand in the social welfare system because it provided temporary care, particularly for the children of impoverished mothers in hospital, gaol or mental asylums. Keeping beds available for this purpose was important: Jimmie could not stay at Scarba forever.

The morning of Sarah's arrest had been the starting point for a cascade of failed decision-making that would define Jimmie's life for the next four years.

The fact that Sarah was taken into police custody on the morning of Jimmie's third birthday is a matter passed over by all recorded accounts of the suitcase baby story. While a little boy losing his mother on his birthday might seem a sad postscript to the tragedy, vignettes of far greater hardship were to follow for Jimmie Boyd.

In 1923, the needs of the child were narrowly defined by society, and even more narrowly defined by the state. Researchers have identified the 1920s as the era of 'scientific child care' because feed, sleep and toilet routines were considered paramount in the healthy development of the child. For small children in statutory care, the greatest focus was placed on their physical needs, delivered via a highly disciplined and morally righteous regime with a strict routine. As the Australian Catholic University academic Nell Musgrove wrote of Australian institutional child care in the early to mid-twentieth century: 'Children, and their bodies, were objects to be managed rather than loved.'

Toys, for example, were considered by some key policymakers to be an indulgence to which poor children were not entitled. The NSW Minister for Health argued that toy drives for poor children at Christmas should be abolished, and citizens should be encouraged to donate only milk and oranges.

It is not that Jimmie's needs were overlooked by the state, but rather that the emotional comforts of a small child were viewed as the very lowest priority. There was no theoretical framework yet established through which decision-makers might consider and factor in the emotional and psychosocial needs of children into care planning. This is most clearly illustrated by the state's decision to remove Jimmie from the farm at Kulnura.

Joseph Shorrock pleaded with the authorities for Jimmie to remain there. He asked if it was possible for him to adopt the boy. The child welfare department returned a firm and unequivocal answer of *NO*.

Shorrock communicated, in his own stoic and unpretentious way, that he had developed a fatherly love for the boy and had the financial resources and capability to care for him. 'I took a fancy to him and offered to take him and look after him but the detectives would not allow him to stay with me on account of me not being married,' he said in a formal statement. For the state, one goal assumed priority over all others when it came to the placement and care of children like Jimmie: moral redemption for their mothers' sins. Shorrock was not considered to be an appropriate alternative carer for Jimmie because as an unmarried man he was seen as incapable of providing a respectable upbringing.

Authorities were weighing options regarding Jimmie's placement and care. 'Herding children together' in group homes was increasingly being deemed unsafe, not because of the psychological damage caused to children by these arrangements, but because of the physical health risks these institutions posed. Epidemics could quickly spread in a communal environment. For those too young to be apprenticed and too old to be adopted, foster care was becoming more widespread. This form of care was also far more cost effective for the state, particularly when compared with other residential forms of care that had fixed infrastructure, staffing and monitoring costs. And foster care offered many working-class families the opportunity to achieve greater economic security during hard times. Foster-care benefits provided an additional (if paltry) income stream, and foster children were expected to contribute to the economy of the home in which they resided: work was often a requirement even among those who were very young.

Sarah had shared her name with a woman in Scotland whose life had followed an eerily similar trajectory to hers – and in 1924 in New South Wales, two little boys, almost identical in age and both called James Boyd, were subsumed into state care. One was taken to Scarba. The other died from the neglect and abuse he experienced as a result of his time as a 'boardie'. It seemed that Scarba, at least temporarily, had spared Jimmie an even worse fate.

Just as it had been for Sarah and her parents, the suitcase was an object of great meaning for her children. For Josephine, it was something eternal, a sarcophagus. For Jimmie, the suitcase would come to mean something else entirely. It would offer the surety of an object of attachment. It would be his only anchor to his past.

The symbolism of the suitcase is meaningful for many people who have experienced the child welfare system firsthand. It is referenced as a powerful object in their oral histories. The very presence of a suitcase summons and conveys a sense of loss.

Contemporary frontline community service workers often speak of the emotional baggage that children carry with them from prior experiences of separation, trauma or neglect. Children bring these burdens, like an invisible suitcase, into foster care. But the mythology of the suitcase in child protection is grounded in an attachment to the object itself.

Children typically enter statutory care with very few personal belongings. In their qualitative accounts, people who lived through the boarding-out system (the earliest incarnation of foster care) have described their visceral childhood reactions to the suitcase, and the place it held in their lives and psyches. For these 'boardies', as they are sometimes called, the suitcase became a powerful totem because it contained the only tangible emotional archive of their lives: toys, blankets, hand-me-downs from siblings, fragments of a birth parent's clothing – or, the most precious of all, photographs.

Some boardies – those who experienced multiple placements or maintained a fervent belief that they would one day return to their birth parents – report living out of their suitcase, even after they had found a settled placement with a foster family. This finely attuned sense of 'suitcase safety' can last for months or even years: for some children, the suitcase is who they truly are, because it contains the last remnants of their life before state care, perhaps including the only tactile memento of a mother or father now shrouded in a blanket of secrecy.

At Scarba, Jimmie was stripped of his possessions and supplied with clothing and a small suitcase in readiness for his departure from the institution.

It is possible that he was even stripped of his religion. This is an intervention that, possibly more than anything else, would have scarred Sarah deeply. Religion remained a connection not just to her God, but also her homeland. Scarba prided itself on its facilitation of fair and progressive social welfare to all children regardless of their denomination. This was indeed radical for the time, as most residential care institutions for children operated under highly exclusive models and provided services only to families within their own religious auspice. In the case of foundlings or those children with particularly shameful pasts, Scarba helped to make them reborn in the eyes of a morally righteous community. With a view to fairness, Scarba arbitrarily assigned a denomination to a child, in rotation, with every fourth child being designated a Roman Catholic.

Residential care institutions operated like moral laundries. Children, much like pieces of soiled clothing, were scrubbed and disinfected. They did not stay long, but were processed quickly for dispatch when clean, pressed and free from stains. Some institutions even dispensed with using children's names and instead assigned them with a number, akin to a laundry code. This, it was believed, would help to create a clear break from a child's dirty past. It must be noted, however, that there is no known evidence of this being practised at Scarba, but it was commonly done in some other residential care facilities.

Scarba would wipe Jimmie clean of his mother's sin, and set him on the road to a new life, suitcase in hand.

18

DOING TIME

THERE IS ONE FEATURE OF PRISON LIFE THAT APPEARS UNIVERSAL, shared even by those incarcerated by vastly different penal institutions operating centuries apart. Inmates report that both the objective physical measurement and metaphysical experience of time become altered. Units of time – days and weeks, minutes and hours – assume new meanings when they occur behind prison walls. Time becomes a philosophical undertaking for those on the inside. This held true for Sarah and Jean.

Nineteen twenty-four would be the beginning of the end of their friendship. Jean had taken the measure of this relationship. In her own words, Jean said that the three years of her life with Sarah had redefined how she felt about women. She loved Sarah immensely. To her, their friendship possessed an eternal quality. It was special, Jean said. Meanwhile, on Sarah's thoughts of Jean, little direct light can be shed. Her words were never captured in a way that permits proper retrospective study, unfettered by the views of others. On many occasions and about many things, Sarah had very little to say.

After their entry to prison, the paths of the two women diverged. Prison authorities immediately separated them because they belonged to different cohorts. Age, cultural group or religion were not considered relevant to the establishment of functioning prison communities and inmate rostering. Neither the existing friendship between the women, nor their shared ethnicity, were taken into account. One criterion above all others shaped the placement of women in Long Bay's wings: time to be served. Jean was housed with short-stay prisoners, Sarah with other lifers. Though they would no doubt have occasionally crossed paths during their daily work routines, rosters sought to separate the hardened from the petty, and by conscious design the prison would have afforded little opportunity for the women to spend time together.

Perhaps it was this lack of an ability to talk, share and support each other that severed their friendship. Perhaps it was also the distortion of prison time that created a chasm between the women that could not be bridged. Jean's finite sentence would have assumed a feeling of infinity as time crept at an excruciatingly slow speed towards her release. For Sarah, it is likely that time lost all meaning and became incomprehensible.

As Sarah and Jean commenced their sentences, Jimmie began to serve time in the boarding-out system. With no relatives willing to care for him, the paperwork necessary to make him a long-term ward of the state was prepared.

Sarah and Jean shared their time at Long Bay with Sydney's criminal royalty: women whose lives were also altered by the vortex of prison time. Matilda 'Tilly' Devine, known for her swaggering personality on the streets, and her dramatic performances in court, was a much more subdued figure in Long Bay. Prison records show, limited as they are, no evidence of Tilly being anything other than a compliant model prisoner during her regular rotation of short sentences.

Whereas prison life severed the friendship between Sarah and Jean, it created a lasting friendship between two very infamous Long Bayers of the 1920s and '30s. Eugenia Falleni was impoverished, a rape victim and an Italian immigrant with very poor English literacy. Eugenia was also born a woman but sought to live much of her life as family man Harry Crawford, having married twice as a male. Dorothy Mort was affluent, an educated North Shorer who had married well and lived as a housewife with children in the suburbs. Eugenia, living as Harry, was serving a life sentence for killing his first wife, Annie Birkett. Dorothy had shot her lover, a young doctor, after he attempted to break off their affair. Both serving life, Eugenia/Harry and Dorothy formed a strong bond that would ultimately help to secure Eugenia's release, because of the connections and significant resources of Dorothy's family.

There is no doubt that Jean and Sarah had very different prison experiences. In some ways, the relative brevity of Jean's sentence made it more difficult for her to settle into the routines of prison life. She had never shown an inclination towards any of the pursuits that were encouraged. Reforming women involved developing skills that were considered accomplishments for women in the early twentieth century. Unlike the men's prison, the women's prided itself on offering activities that provided scope for rehabilitating and re-socialising women to be compliant and suitable for private domestic service, as Sydney was experiencing a significant shortage of domestic labour. But it was not a reform program that had much to offer Jean. She could not and did not want to sew and had no interest in handicrafts. She disliked cleaning and cooking, a fact that had been observed by Joseph Shorrock.

Sarah would have been better off. Prisoners were required to sew their own clothes and even their own bed linen. Sarah would have found herself in a leadership role, as the prison expected skilled inmates to mentor and train others. And there was a library – Sarah was able to read and could access a large number of donated books. For women who could not read, there were programs to lift basic literacy levels.

In a perverse way, Sarah's time in prison may have been the only period in her life in which she felt rewarded and valued for her skills. Though there is no doubt that Long Bay was a place of hardship and punishment, there is also evidence that a degree of compassion was shown towards its inmates, at least by some staff members. There was a recognition by frontline workers that many women criminals were victims as much as perpetrators. Women were redeemable because they were women, or so argued Matron Grace. Sarah's commitment to prayer and her attendance at church services, every Sunday morning and night, would also have been looked on favourably by authorities.

First bell rang at 4.30 a.m. Women prisoners rose and immediately commenced their assigned cleaning regimes, which were defined with a Fordist precision. They were expected to clean and polish every part of the prison from the floor to the ceiling. One woman prisoner might be assigned the job of polishing banisters. Another would scrub the floor, counting the precise number of tiles she was required to clean. In one newspaper's account of the prison during the time of Braithwaite's administration, Sydney Hospital was reputed to be dirtier than the women's prison. The matron placed great emphasis on the cleansing of the soul by literal scrubbing.

Second bell rang at 6 a.m. for breakfast. A third bell for lunch. And so the prison day would roll on. Bells for prayer and for supper, and ten-minute warning bells before lights out marked the passage of time for women inside.

Outside the prison walls, despite her strong work ethic, Sarah had struggled to manage the responsibilities of motherhood because the social stigma of illegitimacy had prevented her from getting work. Inside the prison walls, a community of women who lived at variance with social norms created a more accepting atmosphere. Many inmates were single mothers. Matron Grace felt a special compassion for prisoners with children and had a reputation for showing kindness towards them, and Sarah's Calvinism had currency because she was perceived by those in authority as dutiful, contrite and compliant.

The prison also offered comfort. Unlike many of the male prisoners, women at Long Bay were not confined to cells. Sarah was able to see the sun on a daily basis. In fact, the women typically spent a lot of time outside.

Government policy emphasised that prisoners should not be indulged, and so the prison was not awash with funds. Prisoners took on a variety of roles in order to keep the place running. Laundry work, cooking, needlework, gardening and spinning were all common jobs. All socks and stockings, slips and undergarments were knitted by the prisoners. The prisoners tended to an ornamental garden, an extensive vegetable garden, and an outdoor summerhouse that permitted the cultivation of ferns. The extensive grounds and pleasant coastal weather meant plenty of rain and warm days, and this meant that fruit and vegetables could be grown without a high degree of skill. The women kept chickens and operated an incubator to hatch the chicks, and an aviary was onsite as well.

A large community of feral cats lived in and around the prison, attracted by the vermin that nested in the food scraps. The cats fascinated Sarah, and it was not uncommon for her to wake in the morning and find a cat inside her cell. One cat was particularly adept at legging it when warders were heard to approach and then returning when the coast was clear, and the animal became a companion for Sarah during her time in prison – she told a journalist that she often shared her meals with a black cat.

In a rudimentary way, the organisation of the prison mimicked the therapeutic models used at modern psychiatric facilities in which patients suffering similar conditions are grouped together. The treatment of Dorothy Mort – Eugenia's friend and a high-profile lifer like Sarah – demonstrates the system's flexibility to accommodate the mental health needs of women and the underlying desire for rehabilitation as well as penance. While newspapers at the time suggested that Dorothy's social status and affluence made her incarceration easier, other evidence attests to the character of Matron Grace, who placed a value on the psychological healing of women. Inmates were encouraged to engage in tasks considered wholesome, but there was also some regard given to the interests of the women themselves in developing a program of activities.

Dorothy was a wealthy woman, but she was also a very disturbed one. Grace permitted Dorothy to maintain the library and live within a private section of the prison hospital. Dorothy was a highly skilled and prolific embroiderer, and she was allowed to decorate the walls with specimens of her needlework. One woman released from Long Bay reported that inmates often referred to a section of the prison as 'Mort's quarters' or the 'Mort Wing' because there was so much needlework on display.

There is further evidence to suggest that the women's prison, at least under the leadership of Matron Grace, showed significant compassion for inmates – a compassion that was clearly not limited to those who were connected to influential families. In her biography of the infamous baby farmer Sarah Makin, Annie Cossins reveals that Grace showed particular kindness to her. As Cossins describes it, the Makins were 'wretchedly poor' and would have had no way to influence prison management in order to improve Sarah Makin's living conditions. New South Wales records still retain the letter that the former baby farmer sent to Grace after her release, and its sentiments seem intensely personal:

> Dear Matron
> Just a few lines to express my very deep gratitude to you, the Governor and the staff connected, for the many kindnesses I received while with you. My life being such a very sad one, you did all you possibly could to brighten it. May God keep you and every blessing that can be sent to one, who always did her best to brighten the life of others. Dear Mrs Braithwaite I shall never forget while it is God's wish to spare me, to be truly thankful to the Minister of Justice, also the Comptroller General and the Deputy Comptroller for all they have done for me . . .

But while Grace obviously did her best to treat the prisoners well, there were harsh and undeniable realities to contend with. The order books for Long Bay give insight into day-to-day life inside the gaol: a sense of industry, self-sufficiency and cleanliness defined the work regime, and this is reflected in the order registers. Calico and soap were the largest monthly orders. Mutton, tea, oats and flour were staples, supplemented by the fruit, vegetables and eggs produced on the premises. Sugar, salt, butter and cheese were luxuries that rarely feature in the register of larder items ordered.

Sarah slowly settled into a routine that, though not happy, provided comfort and certainty. In contrast, Jean's eye remained firmly fixed on returning to the life she'd had before she met Sarah.

Jean's name appears in the register of letters and parcels for Long Bay. Her husband, the only person who had come forward in her defence at trial (through the letters that the judge had refused to read), continued to write to her. She reciprocated with a renewed enthusiasm for both him and the institution of marriage. In the months leading up to her release, Jean requested permission from prison management to write to the pawn broker in the city to whom she had pawned, among other things, her wedding ring and some earrings. She would need them when released from prison, she said.

19

STRANGERS IN A STRANGE LAND

SARAH BOYD'S LIFE HAD BEEN A BATTLEGROUND BEFORE. IN 1923, in the room of a boarding house, she had battled her own maternal demons and lost. In 1927, Sarah would again find herself at the centre of a battle, this time over the sanctity of motherhood itself.

To understand how 1927 became such a turning point in Sarah's life, it is necessary to understand what was happening outside the prison walls, inside the state government offices of Macquarie Street and on the floor of the NSW parliament.

In 1923, the NSW government had successfully passed the *Child Welfare Act*, which among other things abolished the Children's Relief Board, created the Department of Child Welfare, and made provision for the first legal adoptions in the state. Prior to this time, child welfare had been a legal and administrative mess.

Children who had been boarded out were often neglected and abused by foster parents. The system had a high level of control over the removal of children, while low levels of scrutiny were brought to bear on the situations in which they were placed. The foster-care stories were horrifying, even by 1920s standards. Some children said they had been beaten by their carers. Other children reported unfair and cruel treatment. One young girl said she had been given only maggoty meat and weevily porridge, while her foster family ate well. Some foster parents stole anything of value from their foster children in the first few weeks of placement, distributed the booty to their biological children, and then simply handed the foster children back to the department, complaining that they had been 'badly behaved and unruly'. One child in foster care said he had never owned a pair of shoes and was made to work outdoors in the freezing cold. In many cases, foster parents appeared to be worse than the birth parents who had been deemed unfit by authorities.

The administrative system supporting children was also failing miserably. It provided a range of indirect incentives that all but encouraged foster parents to put foster children to work. Foster parents who received support payments for assuming the 'burden' of a child were often underpaid or not paid at all, sometimes waiting months for reimbursement due to clerical errors. At the same time, the numbers of children being removed from birth families and boarded out continued to grow, and this compounded the administrative failures of the system.

The *Child Welfare Act 1923* would help create cultural change on adoption more rapidly than anyone expected. It properly came into effect in April 1925, just before the Lang Labor government took power in June 1925. The legislation was wholeheartedly embraced by comptrollers of the child welfare system and frontline workers alike.

Boardies had historically been viewed as tainted. They were either stained by the sins of their parents or bore the long-term impacts of destitution. Poorly fed and poorly educated children were often smaller due to malnutrition and had extremely low levels of literacy.

The Act encouraged a shift in community attitudes towards boardies. Adoption became a noble act, one of good Christian charity. It also provided a way to resolve other taboos surrounding family life, and in a manner that left the dignity of the infertile intact. Childless couples could now be made 'whole', and children who were otherwise condemned to bear the shame of their parents' indiscretions could be made 'new'. Or so it was believed.

A type of pragmatism about procreation began to emerge in the community. News media were complicit and willing partners in the process of encouraging this cultural change. Newspapers began publishing articles about 'blue-eyed orphans' being adopted by 'joyful couples'. Boardies – once considered dirty, uncultured, and the product of morally corrupt and possibly criminal underclass parents – were now seen as vulnerable and in need of help.

In the 1920s, a popular syndicated children's columnist called 'Poppy Penmore' featured in city and regional press. Poppy wrote treacly moralistic tales about grateful children, happy families and fairies at the bottom of gardens. Through December 1924 to February 1925, Poppy's column included a sickeningly sweet tale that bore an uncanny resemblance to Hans Christian Andersen's mid-nineteenth-century story of 'The Little Match Girl'.

There had been several versions of this story adapted and shared with different audiences in different cultural contexts. In one retelling, the young girl is homeless. In another tale she has a home but fears returning to it because of a brutal father. In all retellings, the match girl is motherless. Though a pauper, she is virtuous, never stealing or begging – rather, she nobly commits to the clearly futile pursuit of selling single matches to those passing in the street. The story culminates in hypothermia-induced hallucinations in which she is warm and loved again by the only woman who ever cared for her, Grandma. The girl lights the few matches she has left, one by one, then dies in a delusion of ecstasy in the gutter. Despite a final scene of the girl's ascent to heaven, the story is anything but a happy holiday page-turner.

In the 1925 Poppy Penmore version, the basic story is harnessed to great effect to 'sell' adoption to the general public. A couple who happen to be on their way home from their child's funeral come across a homeless orphan. The little girl, Lucky Lalla, is brought into a 'cosy and tastefully furnished home' on Christmas Eve to 'partake of a substantial but daintily served supper'. The waif is the perfect grief remedy and fits perfectly into the dead daughter's bed. Lalla ends up opening the deceased girl's Christmas presents. These events are applauded by the story as a healthy and functional response to grief. Lalla also shows abundant gratitude in the act of being a dead child's replacement.

Poppy's story is a triumph in adoption propaganda. God did not see fit to bestow fertility on all women, and in some cases he called children home too early to heaven, but legislation could now correct all of this. God made mothers, but so too, it seemed, could the state.

An international conference on child safety and security, the very first of its kind, pronounced 1925 as an earth-shattering epoch of child welfare. New South Wales social workers keen to offer better opportunities for children were quick to jump on the bandwagon to 'save' those lost to poverty and immorality. In the mid-1920s, the rescue mentality that still pervades child protection first emerged. While no doubt some children were taken away from parents because of abuse or neglect, the notion of removing children from 'moral danger' shaped much frontline practice.

The adoption platform was one area of policy on which the conservatives and Labor could agree. Adoption rates skyrocketed almost immediately from a handful of private informal arrangements to a mass movement of children out of state care: between April and November 1925, nine hundred boardies were legally adopted. The system was designed to ensure that these children would never see their biological families again.

Mrs McWilliam was one of thousands of Sydney residents who applied to become a foster carer in 1925. She was a widow in her fifties, with four grown children who had married and moved out to raise families of their own. Being a good Christian woman, Mrs McWilliam was keen to make a charitable sacrifice by opening her large empty home in Lidcombe to a child in need. She also believed a foster child could provide the companionship she craved. The department assigned a young boy called Jimmie Boyd to her care.

The symbolic significance of Lidcombe to Jimmie's narrative is one that can't be overlooked. In Sydney, Lidcombe has long-held significance as a site for family reunions and healing. In a city where the geography almost incites parochialism because the harbour, rivers and mountains entrench the insularity and separateness of communities, Lidcombe is a little different. It is a meeting place. Train junctions from across the city converge there. And along with accommodating a good portion of the city's working class, Lidcombe houses the vast majority of Sydney's dead. Sooner or later, most Sydneysiders will make a trip to Lidcombe, and not just to switch train lines.

Rookwood necropolis takes up much of the landmass of Lidcombe between Auburn to the west and Strathfield to the east. Curtained by trees, and covering an expanse of over 700 acres (285 hectares), Rookwood was designed to provide a quiet place for family to congregate and commemorate, where a sense of reunion with lost loved ones can be felt. Though Jimmie did not know it, Lidcombe was a junction point for the Boyd family as well.

Just over the fence line of Rookwood was his sister's final resting place. After the post-mortem, her body had been transported there and laid to rest with other paupers, the homeless and those unclaimed by their families. Jimmie was now only walking distance away, just beyond the north side of the cemetery on Railway Street.

It is not known precisely when Jimmie went to live with Mrs McWilliam, though it is estimated he was moved from Scarba sometime in 1925. Whether he bounced through several foster-care placements – as many children did prior to being transferred to a long-term placement – cannot be confirmed. One newspaper suggests that he spent much of 1924 drifting through multiple placements and did not live consistently with one carer until 1925.

Trips to town were a regular outing for Mrs McWilliam and Jimmie. As he explored the city with his carer, those who passed them on the street would have seen them as the idealised image of a grandmother and grandson.

It is hard to visualise a more hopeful situation for Jimmie. His future certainly seemed more promising than it ever had. It is also hard not to sense the fragility of these optimistic imaginings for Jimmie's life.

The train trip into town would have offered a clear sight of the Rookwood grounds, and Jimmie would surely have been drawn to the immense green space and wild forest. It would have held the promise of discovery with sunshine, trees to climb and buried treasure to find. As he disembarked the train in the city, however, he would have undoubtedly faced complex emotional terrain as very early memories of life with his mother resurfaced.

But despite the traumas of his early life, Jimmie seemed to adjust remarkably well to a lot of change. He was enrolled in the local public school by Mrs McWilliam. Of the fragments of information available about his life at this time, what is most notable is how much time he spent on his own. He walked to and from school alone. He was permitted to walk to the local corner park and play, again alone. As a rare treat, he was permitted to attend the occasional movie at the local Arcadia cinema, which had only just opened. He was given sixpence in pocket money each week, double the amount that Sarah received from Long Bay prison management for a week's work.

It is not known how or why Mrs McWilliam gained access to information regarding Jimmie's family circumstances. What is most likely is that she wished to know more about a child to whom she was becoming increasingly attached and was considering to adopt. Child welfare conventions encouraged secrecy, and foster parents were rarely apprised of the family history of children in their care. Clearly, Mrs McWilliam showed a remarkably open view that was out of step with 1920s normative assumptions.

Mrs McWilliam took Jimmie to visit Sarah in prison. The act demonstrated an extraordinary level of acceptance and tolerance on the part of Mrs McWilliam, who had nothing to gain personally from this initiative. Though prison entry records pertaining to these visits have been lost, newspaper accounts are not saturated with emotion and sensationalism (like so many stories about Sarah were). If these reports can be taken as credible, Mrs McWilliam took Jimmie to the prison more than once.

Even more astounding, she also achieved what Sarah had been unable to. She reconnected with Sarah's family in Paisley, a process that started when she wrote them a very simple letter. William, Sarah's father, had passed away sometime after Sarah's imprisonment. Whether it was because the stern Irish patriarch was no longer leading the Boyd family, or because Mrs McWilliam had astonishing powers of persuasion, something had indeed shifted in the family's abject denial of Sarah. Mrs McWilliam shared details about Sarah's situation and talked very proudly of Jimmie. To everyone's surprise, most of all Sarah's, one of her sisters wrote back.

Around Christmas in 1926, a parcel arrived for Jimmie from overseas. There was no letter with long gushing sentiments enclosed. The contents of the parcel, however, conveyed much more than any letter could.

It was a hand-knitted jumper.

The gift highlighted the gulf between the Boyds in Scotland and those in Australia. A heavy ply had been used, and it was certainly a comforting and thoughtful gift in the context of a freezing Paisley winter. But as Jimmie opened the present on a sweltering Christmas Day, the poor choice of a thick jumper in an Australian summer could not have been more evident. By the following June, the earliest that Jimmie would be able to wear the item bearably in Sydney's climate, he would have outgrown it.

Sometime in February 1927, Mrs McWilliam took the jumper to the prison. For Sarah, it was a deeply meaningful keepsake made by her sister. It would have taken many hours to make, and smelled and felt like an artefact from a homeland that Sarah believed she would never see again.

•

By the time March rolled around, it became clear that the child welfare department was in a state of deep financial crisis and close to bankruptcy. Mismanagement claims were splashed across the newspapers. Whether these problems were a legacy of the previous conservative government or newly created by the reigning Labor government was unclear. Labor, however, would take the heat.

While many children had been leaving the care system, a great many more were still being absorbed into it. With the rising cost of living, the costs of state-supported child welfare had doubled in less than four years. Despite increasing attempts to make poor children a private charity problem by diverting them into the industrial school system and 'working farms' (something permitted from the age of fourteen), the system appeared to be at breaking point. For a newly formed child welfare portfolio very keen to prove its efficiency, the high rates of adoption were a good start, but clearly much more needed to be done to resolve a financial crisis of this scale.

In April, an official public inquiry was launched into the mismanagement of funds by child welfare. The opposition began to run a sustained campaign against Labor, and journalists were provided with endless material for dramatic headlines about government incompetence. By June, the Lang government was in economic freefall, in need of revenue and desperately in need of good press.

Meanwhile, over in Redfern, strange stirrings occurred in a home on Pitt Street. Since Sarah's imprisonment, Annie Lee had certainly been busy, but her efforts had focused on politicking and protesting at the local level and in the most polite way. Local meetings had been held to discuss the unfairness of Sarah's case, but they had not been particularly well attended. Attendees had shaken their heads and sadly reflected on the injustices for women in the state, but many believed that little could be done to help Sarah.

In 1926, Annie had baked a fruitcake, donned her gloves and hat, and called on Sarah at the prison. She had written courteous but firm letters to the government urging Sarah's release. While this had clearly helped by providing personal support to Sarah, it had yielded little in terms of forcing the executive's hand to use its discretionary power to release a prisoner.

Then, on a morning sometime in June 1927, Annie was reading the newspaper in the front room of her small terrace. Journalists were consumed with the crises facing the Labor government. Child welfare was in a shambles. The state lay on the brink of financial ruin.

Annie began reading the paper from its top left-hand corner, scanning the summary column featuring the head-line stories of the day. The date for the state general election had been tentatively set for 24 September. Bavin had just launched the Nationalist campaign with 'caustic criticism' of Lang: 'This state has been governed from the gutter' and 'all moral consideration had been eliminated from public affairs by Labor'. As the government's popularity slumped, support for the Nationalists appeared to be rising rapidly It was widely predicted that the conservatives would win the next election, and on their return they would dismantle the policies of Labor they perceived to be the most liberal and most immoral.

As Annie read further, the location of keywords across the page triggered a string of free associations within her mind. Steamship passengers were leaving for Scotland. The Supreme Court had a heavy schedule that week, with many probate matters under consideration; the firm 'Boyd' appeared on the page as the legal representative in one case, responsible for managing the affairs of a deceased estate sale. Boyd, death, sentence, Supreme Court, Scotland. Her thoughts kept aligning around how ominous the re-election of the conser-vatives would be for Sarah. If things did not change, Sarah was doomed. She would die in prison unless radical steps were taken.

Labor was in crisis, that was clear. But did this present an opportunity for leverage? Timing a campaign for Sarah's release suddenly became extremely important. Annie would have to move swiftly.

She reconsidered the slow and steady campaign she had been using to seek Sarah's release. A ladylike campaign involving cucumber sandwiches and raffles had got Annie near to nowhere. If a dignified protest had not worked, perhaps it was time for something undignified? She still held the newspaper in her hand, and this led to another idea. Sarah needed more public exposure, and she needed it quickly. Annie decided to approach an ideal conspirator and protesting partner, and the mogul of Sydney muckraking: the *Truth* newspaper. More than any other paper in Australia at the time, *Truth* was known for its sensationalist and outrageous stories. It was extremely popular with working-class readers, and its offices were nearby.

June was also an important turning point in the relationship between Mrs McWilliam and Jimmie. Without warning, he was struck down with a severe fever that left him weak, lethargic and unresponsive. Almost overnight he became gravely ill. Mrs McWilliam called a doctor who seemed baffled by the boy's symptoms.

In hospital, and fighting for his life, Jimmie was finally diagnosed with whooping cough. He had caught the infection from a child at school. By July, the NSW government declared an epidemic as whooping cough swept through the capital and most of the major regional towns. After his eventual discharge from hospital, Jimmie's recovery was long and difficult, with a body-racking cough persisting for ten weeks.

All visits to the prison stopped.

On a frugal budget, Mrs McWilliam prepared home remedies to ease the boy's wretched coughing fits. She mixed a solution of large quantities of garlic and rum (both expensive commodities), then rubbed it on the palms of his hands, the soles of his feet, his back and chest. When his cough became unbearable, in the early hours of the morning when the air was at its coldest, she dissolved the potent solution in a teaspoon of sugar and made him drink it.

Contracting whooping cough had cemented the bond between Mrs McWilliam and Jimmie. She had shown uncompromising commitment in her care for the boy, and he had bonded to her like a son to a mother. Frontline practitioners began to advocate strongly for Jimmie to be placed with his carer permanently. It would mean another child off the books. Mrs McWilliam, now completely smitten with the boy, could imagine herself being a mother again. She began to agree with the child welfare view that adoption would be the best option.

Annie visited the *Truth* newspaper offices sometime in July 1927, with the intention of carrying out her plan to remind the general public of Sarah's imprisonment. The election was looming. Just over three years before, the state had gaoled a woman who many believed had not received a fair trial.

The next time Annie organised a public meeting to agitate for Sarah's release, a journalist would be there.

Annie had been at the courthouse on the day of Sarah's trial. She had seen the hundreds of women who had turned up to watch the proceedings. Annie knew support existed for Sarah in Sydney, it was just dormant – and she hoped this was where the *Truth* newspaper would step in to wake up the sleeping masses.

In Annie's local member for Redfern, William McKell, she found a strong ally. McKell understood Sarah's story both politically and personally, in a way that many politicians did not. He had been Minister for Justice, and he understood the broad details of Sarah's case and knew the machinations of the prison system in New South Wales.

In a deeply personal way, Sarah's case also resonated with McKell. At nine years old, his father had deserted the family, leaving his mother and siblings with no means of support. McKell knew firsthand what financial vulnerability could do to a family when a father failed to meet his obligations. His mother had struggled to survive, earning money as a seamstress and laundering clothes, just as Sarah had done. McKell's older sister had died of tuberculous meningitis, a fact that he attributed to the cramped conditions of inner-city Sydney. He had always been particularly close to his mother, so Sarah's story immediately spoke to him. It was a tragic tale of a desperate mother trying, against all odds, to protect her son. He also knew what shame could do to someone. For his entire life, McKell had claimed his father had died, denying all suggestions that his father had started an affair and left one family to begin another.

Annie began organising a local army to 'Save Sarah'. The key figures in the campaign were all women, all living within walking distance of one another in Redfern and Surry Hills. Annie Lee was still living in Pitt Street and her close friend, Mary Trewhella, lived nearby in Centre Street. The campaign snowballed. They spoke to neighbours, who spoke to their neighbours.

The date for a local meeting – an open forum about Sarah's case and her subsequent imprisonment – was set. At the old Redfern coffee palace, a daytime meeting was organised. The timing was carefully planned to garner grassroots support from local women: a midday meeting would permit large numbers to attend because it was after husbands left for work and before children returned home from school.

Women in the Redfern area sympathised with Sarah in ways that not even Annie had expected. Spontaneously, and somewhat to Annie's surprise, women volunteered to get up and speak about the sadness of Sarah's situation and about the tragedy of separating a mother from a son.

'We as mothers understand better than men could. How this poor girl, a stranger in a strange land, came to commit this terrible act. And we say emphatically that Sarah Boyd has suffered enough – more than enough,' said one woman.

'We believe that when the facts of this case are brought by the women of Sydney before a humane minister like Mr Lysaght he will declare that the gaol gates should be opened to this woman,' declared another woman with great confidence.

Migrant women spoke of their own hardships of living in Sydney while trying to raise a family. One woman, at work while the meeting was held, submitted a letter of personal support.

I write to you to say that I admire you for the defence you are putting up on behalf of Sarah Boyd. I only read the case for the first time in Sunday's *Truth*. I am a Scotch girl myself and know what I suffered when I first came out here. I was in a similar position to Miss Boyd only I wasn't so unfortunate. Anyhow my case was bad enough. And I can sympathise with the poor woman. There are a good many women wronged in this world and no woman should be gaoled over men such as the one mentioned. I wish I could help to fight for Sarah Boyd but I am as poor as she. I have often like Sarah thought of murder or suicide. Oh if these judges knew half what women put up with they would not be so harsh in their sentences.

Another Scotch girl, who had lived in Wellington just as Sarah had a few years before, also expressed her support for Sarah's situation. 'With a feeling of great pity I read the case of Sarah Boyd in *Truth*. I think it is splendid of Mrs Annie Lee to take up the cause of this unfortunate girl whom she does not even know. I do hope with all my heart that she will be successful. Being Scotch myself and a deserted wife with a little girl of about three years my heart goes out in sympathy to Sarah.'

McKell agreed to enter into direct negotiations with Andrew Lysaght, Minister for Justice, and advocate for Sarah's release.

A further meeting on Sunday, 7 August was organised – an outdoor rally for Sarah. A staggering four hundred women, all from the local Redfern, Surry Hills and Darlinghurst area, turned up to sign the petition. The event was again covered by the *Truth* newspaper.

Sarah's public image was undergoing a careful reinvention, all of it beyond her control. In November 1923, she was a calculating murderer. In December 1923 and January 1924, she was a vulnerable woman at the mercy of powerful men. By July 1927, she was transformed into something else entirely. The *Truth* had successfully manipulated her image, portraying her as a simpleton and someone utterly incapable of solving her own problems. In other words, the *Truth* was selling her as a complete idiot. She had seen a black cat in her prison cell that very week and this made her believe that her luck was about to change, the paper reported. The paper implied that she had little to no awareness of the relentless campaign to secure her release.

The following Sunday, the *Truth* again set the tone for the coming campaign week. This time, the character of the Minister for Justice was in the firing line of journalists: 'Ironbark not Ironheart: Minister Andy Lysaght Knows What to Do' was the headline. The title of one article was overshadowed by an enormous pen sketch. Beautiful crosshatching and shading produced a very dignified representation of the man. His eyes were fixed with a determined stare towards the reader. It was a far cry from the crude sketches used to illustrate the suitcase baby story four years before, in which Sarah was depicted as a Scottish hag with heavy mandible and deep-set eyes.

On Monday, McKell arranged another meeting with Lysaght. McKell took the petition of four hundred signatures collected at the rally.

Less than a week later an envelope arrived at Annie Lee's home, printed with 'OHMS' and having the distinct oblong shape associated with government correspondence. She held it nervously and felt the absolute weight of it in her hands. She believed its contents would mean either triumph or tragedy for Sarah.

Strangely, the letter was both good and bad. The government was prepared to give Sarah a reprieve, but some strict conditions were associated with her release. Sarah had to leave the country immediately and return to her homeland. The letter further noted that the state was not in a position to and under no circumstances would meet the costs of deporting Sarah.

The Save Sarah campaign had reached an impasse.

Annie was shocked. Could this mean that all of her work had come to nothing? She sat down and collected her thoughts. The *Sydney Morning Herald* was spread out before her at the table. A pot of warm tea sat beside her.

Annie was not a wealthy woman. She could not pay for Sarah's ticket out of her own pocket. She was also not aligned to any upper-crust women's organisations with access to substantial funds.

Right before her in the open broadsheet was a lengthy story about the Women's Reform League, which had only that week held a lavish fundraiser. A long summary of the event was printed on page twelve. Prominent ladies had decorated the Town Hall with pot plants and garlands of red berries. Music was played and framed needlework was raffled. The event was attended by brigadier generals and mayors, alongside many women with double surnames such as Stanhope-Swift and Crouch-Waugh.

Annie's Save Sarah campaign held rallies in the hot midday sun in public parks in Redfern and passed around a collection plate. Annie did not network with the wives of parliamentary members on a regular basis, and she knew no wealthy benefactors that she could approach. The Women's Reform League even had access to a donated war plane. Annie's campaign had been run with women foot soldiers and use of the tram system alone.

Annie read the letter again more closely. This time she noticed a line that she had missed: 'If funds could be raised for her passage home to Scotland the state of NSW would release her forthwith.'

The letter from Lysaght conveyed a sense of urgency. An offer was being made, but by the incumbent government, and this meant the clock was ticking. If the Nationalists won the election it was unlikely they would honour any agreement of this kind.

If anything could be done to save Sarah, and Annie still believed it could, it needed to be done now. Letter in hand, she rushed out of the house.

She went first to the prison to share the news with Sarah, and immediately after went to the offices of *Truth*. She would again ask for their help. The Save Sarah campaign was about to become the Save Sarah Fund. If there was to be a fight, Annie still had plenty of fight in her.

While Annie launched the fundraising campaign, Sarah busied herself in prison with a renewed enthusiasm. She now had real hope. She had read the letter with her own eyes. Matron Grace, an advocate for Sarah of long standing, permitted her to sew three dresses in anticipation of her release. She was provided a pattern book for a fashionable straight-line dress, which she commented to the matron looked vastly different from the fuller style she had worn into prison. Annie had also promised her a new pair of shoes, a hat and three pairs of stockings. With the three pounds that Sarah had earned in prison, Grace permitted her to buy any additional luxuries she felt she might need for her voyage home. Sarah declined to buy anything but she did make a request – the first personal request she had made of the Long Bay administration since her arrival. She asked Grace for a mirror. The matron obliged. It was the first time Sarah had seen her own reflection in nearly four years.

Annie's front sitting room in her narrow broken-down terrace became a war room. General Annie and her 2IC Mary Trewhella developed their strategy. The campaign would need to extend far beyond sandwiches and tea urns and church hall–style fundraising.

Annie and Mary worked closely with *Truth*. A collection plate would be taken around to workplaces filled with working men who carried cash in their pockets. The women would fan out from the Redfern rail yards towards other industrial sites across the city. They marked out the map on a grid. Local agents would take responsibility for hitting the streets and collecting from housewife sponsors within their suburbs. *Truth* would print lists of contributors to ensure the entire city was reminded that supporting Sarah was now something to be proud of.

It had all the elements of a modern-day tabloid campaign, including photographs worthy of what now might be described, using internet slang, as a 'photoshop fail'. Large emotive images accompanied lengthy articles. Photos of a tiny Jimmie had clearly been cut from others. It was also clear that the original images had been taken surreptitiously, without anyone's permission, while he was walking home from school. His body, head to toe, was glued in front of the terrifying gothic archway at Long Bay. He was dwarfed by the menacing black gates, his back turned to the camera as if he was desperately banging on the doors for his poor mother's release. There were also pictures of Sarah, her feet eerily hovering just above the ground because her mug shot had been inexpertly pasted to an external shot of the prison.

Truth was holding nothing back and made it clear where the city of Sydney must stand with regard to Sarah Boyd:

'mother love was threatened', it proclaimed in boldly printed letters across the front page.

The campaign gathered significant momentum. A Mrs Fulmer collected from the residents of Botany, an eclectic area comprising tightly knit pockets of working-class villages. Mary Trewhella collected from Redfern. A Mrs Macpherson covered the affluent area of Haberfield, known for its grand gardens and large homes, hoping this might yield larger donations. A Mr Sidebottom collected from returned soldiers in Mortdale.

Small businesses took the opportunity to promote themselves in the newspaper by making generous donations. Others took the opportunity to show union solidarity and pride. The Caterers and Waiters Union, the Waterboard Pipe Head Workers of Guildford, and the New World Café Owners and Employees were all listed as contributors. Both employers and unions seemed keen to help and were happy to be listed alongside each other.

The list of individual sponsors was long. Each made a donation of around ten shillings. Some preferred to remain anonymous. Their aliases reveal a good deal about the diverse base of the Save Sarah movement: 'Three Miranda Well Wishers', 'Digger and a Digger's Friend', 'Fitters Wife', 'Scottish Social Club Committee of Lakemba', 'Butcher Boy', 'Country Mother', 'Gardener', 'Teacher', 'Little Jack', 'Mother of Three', 'Caledonian Lass and Lad', 'Scots Sympathiser'. All contributions were listed down to the pounds, shillings and pence. This was a clever strategy: it implied that the

Save Sarah Fund was truly a people's campaign and was of such great importance that no amount of money would be considered too small.

The Labor Party, still trying to improve their public image in the wake of more in-fighting between Lang and his ministers, and the ongoing financial scandals of the year, used the Save Sarah Fund very effectively too. Local branches were listed over and over again as key contributors. Their donations were generous and outweighed those made by others tenfold.

Annie's plan was detailed. Large-scale worksites were targeted, particularly in industries known for employing a large number of Scots. She would speak to the shop steward on arrival, typically arriving on or just after payday when the men were more likely to be feeling generous. As soon as the lunch whistle blew, the shop steward called the men over to listen to Annie speak.

Annie also connected the Save Sarah Fund directly to issues that were important to all Sydneysiders. The Harbour Bridge construction had begun, and newspapers closely followed its development. It was the most important piece of infrastructure ever built in Sydney because it finally connected the north and south of the city. It was also a source of intense pride for Sydney Scots: Scottish architects, stonemasons and engineers were involved in every aspect of the project. A key contractor, Dorman Long & Company, was an engineering company with a high proportion of Scottish workers that had large-scale sites at Milsons Point and Alexandria to fabricate the steel girders. The visits to Dorman's worksites across Sydney would prove to be the most successful of the funding drive.

From her speeches in Redfern, Annie now knew how to deliver a message powerfully and had become an accomplished and charismatic public speaker. The expression 'stranger in a strange land' had become a regular catchphrase, used in every speech. Sarah was a poor Scottish girl. She was a victim of circumstance and of men who had been unwilling to honour their responsibilities of fatherhood. The messaging was consistent and strong, and had always struck a chord with the poor women of Sydney. Now it struck a chord with the hundreds of men on industrial sites, working hard to support their families.

In the last week of August, everyone involved in the campaign assembled at the offices of *Truth*. An announcement was made. The fundraising goal had been more than reached. Annie immediately made arrangements to book a berth for Sarah and Jimmie to travel within the week, on Friday, 2 September, before even contacting Lysaght's office. She felt no need, as she had the proof of their guarantee to release Sarah.

Annie had no inkling that while she had been campaigning for Sarah's release, other decision-makers in other parts of the government had been solidifying arrangements regarding the care of Sarah's son.

A total of fifty-five pounds and ten shillings had been raised for Sarah's and Jimmie's passage to Scotland. A further five pounds was provided for clothing. The government deemed fifty pounds to be sufficient for Sarah to start a new life, far away from Sydney – this too was provided by the Save Sarah Fund. The final pound gathered by the campaign drive was spent on a cablegram to Scotland in order to notify Sarah's sister of her release.

Annie rushed to Long Bay to deliver the news to Sarah. She gloried in her personal triumph. In less than a week, Sarah and Jimmie would be on board a steamship, the *Barrabool*, travelling home via Liverpool.

But when Annie arrived at the prison, she immediately knew something was wrong. As she was a frequent visitor, prison staff had become accustomed to her presence, and over time protocol had become almost relaxed about her visits. On this day, however, there was a delay: Annie was asked to wait. Prison staff offered no explanation and seemed to be avoiding her questions. An exacting and impatient woman, Annie Lee did not like it.

When she was finally permitted to meet with Sarah in the garden, closely observed by a warder, Sarah struggled even more than normal to talk to her. The women sat together on a narrow garden seat. Annie's signature floral hat, which had always looked jarringly out of place against the grey stone prison walls, was completely in keeping with the low-lying gardens.

A man from justice and a man from the prisons had visited her, Sarah said. They had presented her with legal papers. Jimmie would be formally adopted by Mrs McWilliam, and the state had made a commitment to apprentice him to a good trade if Sarah would give her consent and relinquish all parental rights.

Annie was already aghast, and yet Sarah had even more to tell her. The state had also offered to pay for her passage to Melbourne so she might depart to Scotland from there, if she would agree to the adoption.

Sarah had read the documents and signed the papers.

Annie rose slowly from the garden seat. Her eyes, peering with fury from beneath the brim of flowers, stared Sarah down. She spoke carefully; a simmering rage could be heard within her voice. 'If you do this, you can stop in gaol so far as I am concerned because you will not be worthy to leave it.'

It was not the reaction that Sarah had expected.

Annie stormed back into the main building and promptly left the grounds. She did not wait to hear if it was something that Sarah had wanted or if she believed this all might be in Jimmie's best interests. The state was interfering in the sanctity of motherhood again, and Annie would not have it.

From the prison, Annie caught the tram to the *Truth* offices. If good press would not work to force the hand of the government, then perhaps bad press would. She pleaded with the *Truth* to write a scathing article about the actions of the child welfare department and the comptroller of prisons.

Annie then went directly to the office of Mr Bethel, the head administrator of child welfare. She refused to leave until he agreed to meet with her.

As Sarah had already signed the papers, there was little that could be done, Bethel argued. But Annie was determined. She argued that Sarah, in prison and vulnerable to intimidation and pressure, had signed the papers not fully realising their implications. Sarah had been distressed and confused, said Annie. Sarah had believed that conceding to this arrangement was the only way she would be freed, Annie added.

Bethel, believing himself to be a man of great rectitude, and not one easily swayed by emotion, stated that he would see the mother and the son for himself. If he could make a personal assessment of them when they were together, this would be resolved once and for all, he said.

For three days, nothing happened. Then Bethel sent word to the prison and Annie Lee. He asked Sarah and Annie to attend a meeting in his office.

Sarah was released at six-thirty in the morning, on the very same day she was scheduled to leave Australia. As she left, Matron Grace took the very unusual step of hugging a prisoner farewell.

Annie and Mary took Sarah back to the Pitt Street terrace. Annie sat Sarah down at the kitchen table. She cooked her a large plate of bacon and eggs. Though there is no way of knowing what passed between the women in those waiting hours, and whether warmth or intimidation ultimately defined their relationship, Sarah's thoughts would have been elsewhere. After nearly four years in prison, she must have been consumed with the anticipation of finally leaving a city that had come to represent tragedy and loss for her. She would leave Australia that very afternoon. Whether Jimmie would leave with her would come down to a senior public servant's 'on the spot assessment' of a woman's innate capacity for motherhood, as he sat behind his desk in a city office.

At Bethel's office, Sarah, Annie and Mary waited patiently outside. In an adjoining room, out of sight, Jimmie waited in the company of a child welfare officer.

After the women were led into the room and the door was closed, it can't be known what transpired. *Truth* claimed that Bethel commenced with something along the lines of, 'This is all very hard to believe. I will let the mother tell me herself that she does not want her child.' Despite *Truth*'s tendency for bluster and bullshit, Bethel's comments seem plausible. As head of child welfare, he was keen to ensure that Sarah's words – not a journalist's commentary nor the rally cry of a forceful female advocate in a flowery hat – were the last ones he heard on the subject. Bethel's comments also reflect the prevailing and unshakeable belief that governed social mores of motherhood: that it is natural instinct for mothers to always want a first-born son, and if Sarah did not agree, it would be her responsibility to explain why.

To the very end, however, Sarah remained an elusive character. No newspaper report, no transcript nor office minute is available to shed light on exactly how she responded to Bethel's questioning.

Whatever was said, Bethel came to a decision quickly and apparently very easily. He ordered that Jimmie be released into Sarah's care once again. The adoption would not proceed.

Jimmie was led into the room by a child welfare officer. 'Jimmie, aren't you glad to have your mummy again?' is the only thing that Sarah said.

On 4 September the story of Sarah Boyd and her son, Jimmie, filled the front page of a Sydney newspaper for the very last time. It was the 'first step into the paradise of liberty', said *Truth*.

Annie would no doubt have been satisfied with the article. The official part of the Boyd family reunion was chronicled using photographs. One is of an office, the walls lined with bound books, and a desk front and centre. Around the desk are Annie Lee, Mr Bethel and Mr Davies (the Minister for Public Instruction). Sarah is towards the back, standing behind Davies. Mary Trewhella is not pictured.

The photograph was intended to capture Annie in her most triumphant moment. Yet she looks far from happy. No sense of joy is present in the image. Annie stares past Sarah, her expression bearing a strong resemblance to hatred. Her large decorative hat is pulled low but her steely gaze can still be seen clearly. Her eyes are fixed on the head of child welfare.

Sarah is grasping Jimmie firmly by the shoulders in front of her as if using him to steady herself. Mrs McWilliam is nowhere in sight.

The *Truth* newspaper celebrated the victory of Annie Lee and shared in the spoils. Shamelessly, in the centre of an array of photographs, articles and quotes about the Save Sarah Fund, *Truth* boasts of the sales it has achieved. 'The Pinnacle Achieved by "Truth"' is the gloating headline above this text:

The latest net sales certificate deals with Truth's position in NSW for July. The figure reached is a satisfactory one – 191 020 per issue. This represents practically a constant cumulative gain of almost one thousand new readers on every issue during the past twelve months . . . That is a most satisfactory position but Truth is not content to let it stay at that.

For *Truth*, the campaign had been a resounding financial success.

Annie's planning and execution of the campaign had been immaculately timed. A month later, on 8 October 1927, Jack Lang and the Labor government lost the election. Had Annie delayed and not fought such a hard battle, Sarah would have remained in gaol indefinitely.

The boat was shot with streamers. Tears were shed. Annie handed Sarah a heavy coat, suitable for the fast-approaching Paisley winter. Annie and Mary watched the steamship as it passed through the Heads and out of sight.

It is hard to imagine what it must have been like for the two on board. At 5 p.m. on 2 September 1927, they sat in a cabin sailing towards a homeland that Jimmie had never seen. He was seated beside a woman he hardly knew. Though they were mother and son, they remained little more than strangers.

20

BAGGAGE

They had with them a trunk or suitcase full of clothing provided by the sending organisations. Most never returned to their place of birth.

Curator, Australian National Maritime Museum Exhibition:
On Their Own: Britain's child migrants

ON 24 NOVEMBER 1928, 438 SOULS BOARDED THE *EURIPIDES* AT Liverpool, en route to Sydney. One of these souls, a young boy who had just turned eight, would disembark there about five weeks later. He had two travelling companions. One was a complete stranger to him: a social worker, whom he had only just met, would accompany him to Sydney. His other companion, a trusty and reliable suitcase, he carried in his hand. A large oblong object that opened like a book with two large clasps, it was inscribed inside with his name.

There were other boys on board, also surrendered by their British parents to travel to Australia with the hope they could achieve a better life there than their biological families felt they could provide. One boy, George Griffiths, fourteen years old, was listed as a 'farm pupil'; another was listed simply as a 'scholar'. A few rows down, the name James Orvieto Boyd is listed in neat cursive script.

What led Sarah to transport her son back to Sydney, only a year after their return to Scotland, is one of the least cryptic elements of her life. Although there is little verifiable documentation available regarding Sarah's life after she returned to Scotland, nor indeed Jean's life in New Zealand post-release, some conclusions can still be drawn about what might have occurred for Sarah.

In the context of broader social welfare policy of the time, Sarah was both a social and economic problem. Though she would have experienced the exhilaration of prison release and held the very highest hopes for a triumphant return home, she would have very quickly realised that single parenthood and unemployment were no more surmountable in Scotland than Sydney.

In the late 1920s, welfare was simultaneously experiencing great shifts in thinking on the care philosophies surrounding children. Child welfare was being redefined as a collective international problem, one best solved using international means and interventions. In 1927, overseas migration settlement programs that targeted the relocation of British children to Canada and Australia were in full swing. In 1928 throughout Scotland and England, the advertising campaign for this program was ramped up significantly. The newspapers that Sarah read were saturated with them. The town centre of Paisley was covered in posters promoting the value of the scheme to families who were struggling.

In policy terms, Jimmie conformed to the criteria considered ideal for a child worker migrant. He was white. He was healthy. He had an unwed mother and absent father: this was a particularly important factor for administrators of work programs for children. His mother faced little opportunity of achieving economic independence without marriage, and the boy would inevitably grow up to be another jobless and delinquent socioeconomic problem. Removing him from this unsuitable situation was seen as the optimal outcome for both the family and the economy.

At eight years old, James was younger than many of his travelling companions, but extensive reviews of the records available on British child migrants, fragmented as they are, show the youngest documented child surrendered to these schemes was aged four. Jimmie, a self-reliant, quiet and compliant child for his age, would have been seen as an ideal candidate. Sarah would have felt lucky to have secured him a place in the scheme.

Jimmie's solo migration also shows where Sarah stood within her family. The disconnected dynamic that had prompted her departure from Scotland in the first place had clearly not healed in the way she had hoped. Perhaps she believed that by sending Jimmie away for good, she would break the cycle of poverty and shame that had overshadowed her life.

What is less understandable is Sarah's persisting enchantment with the dream of migration. The idealised notion that travel could heal their family was a fantasy that post-murder, trial and imprisonment should have been more than a little worse for wear in her eyes. Yet it was clearly still a dream onto which she held tight. Jimmie was very young, completely on his own, but somehow Sarah remained enraptured with the delusion that her son would be able to achieve what she herself had been unable to.

21

SUNKEN GARDEN

WHEN JIMMIE RETURNED TO AUSTRALIA IN 1928, THE TRAIL OF investigation into his life briefly runs cold. His story bears remarkable similarity to the experiences of thousands of child migrants separated from their parents and sent away to Australia to work their way to a better life through organised and indentured labour schemes. Records from this time, including documents on Jimmie's life as a young man, have been destroyed.

Retrospectively, historians identify some particularly shameful and misguided elements of social welfare practice to be associated with the provision of services and supports to children like Jimmie. Some of the worst include: time in residential care (which in some cases reassigned children with numbers instead of names); the act of unaccompanied child migration; the absolute severance of ties to birth family; and concerted and deliberate attempts to hide children from their biological history. Jimmie lived not one but all of these things. He experienced a statutory care system known for its brutality and widespread failure to acknowledge that all children, no matter their circumstances, need care, love and acceptance. The narrative trajectory of his life would be intimately familiar to many a Forgotten Australian.

Though no specific records regarding Jimmie's time in institutional care now exist, the stories of ex-Scarba kids are well known in Sydney. The custom and practice of social welfare institutions at the time dictated that the vast majority of records regarding children be destroyed, thereby ensuring any shameful history could not be accessed at a later time. To understand Jimmie's life, however, there is now an accumulated body of evidence on the collective trauma of children just like him. This ever-growing database continues to be assembled as more and more adults come forward to share stories about the effect that social welfare has had on their lives. Evidence given to several inquiries by ex-Scarba children demonstrates that even well into old age these people experienced 'continuing adverse consequences'. It is a most polite and euphemistic way to describe indescribable pain and loss.

Outwardly Jimmie's life followed the desirable economic trajectory of a working man in Sydney in the post World War II period. To society he would have been perceived as a man who had achieved a stable, certain and secure life, if not an abundantly prosperous one. As a young man he started in a brickworking trade in which he would spend the rest of his working life.

Like many industries during the Depression, brickworking faced decline. However, by the time Jimmie reached the apprentice age of fourteen, the industry was beginning to rebuild. Brickmaking then became uniquely important to New South Wales in the postwar years. Sydney has one of the most brick-dense cityscapes in the world, and the demand for product experienced long periods of boom. Those in the industry could be assured of a steady income. Jimmie was never out of work.

The security of employment afforded him the opportunity to make the kind of property purchase envied by working-class families – a corner block with a large yard.

Jimmie made his home in the south-west of the city, in Punchbowl, an area that more-affluent Sydneysiders dismissed as 'rough'. The private homes in the area were owned by men just like Jimmie, working class and hardworking. In between, urban expansion was peppered with the building of large-scale public-housing projects. He worked hard enough in a low-paying job to take out a mortgage on a home.

A local artist, Reg Mombassa, has sought to convey the aspirational significance of home ownership and suburbia to Australia and the complexity these desires present to the psyche. For Mombassa, the suburbs represent both landscape and portrait. Telephone poles laced together by wires dot his paintings in measured ways. A solitary mailbox or a water tank might be painted as a stand-alone object to the very side of the image. The houses, however, are bold character portraits. Each is a lonely figure set back beyond the reach of the viewer, its darkened windows making it inscrutable. The vibrancy of the coloured house paint both calls to and unsettles the viewer as it is cut through with solid washes of tan and brown that signify a precise and ordered section of lawn. Housing in Australia, argues Mombassa, provides an ancestral shrine and paints a metaphysical portrait of those who dwell within it.

Jimmie's house could have been any one of the brick veneers featured in Mombassa's artworks of postwar Australian homes. It was single storey, had a featureless facade, a man's shed out the back and a lawn to mow. The small alcove verandah provided a place to park workboots. Mombassa once said the suburban home 'can serve as a substitute for a tribal homeland for people who no longer have access to such things'. It is comforting to imagine that Jimmie's brick veneer might have offered him this kind of stability, after the tragedy and sense of displacement that must have defined his early years.

The interior trajectory of Jimmie's life, his emotional and psychological landscape, was much darker and sadder than appearances suggested. Jimmie's life was completely absent of those emotional milestones typically used to define a fulfilling life for a working man in Sydney in the postwar period. Jimmie never married and never had children.

Jimmie struggled with depression and battled severe alcoholism throughout his adult life. Based on current theoretical understandings of psychosocial development, he would have been an emotionally troubled man who had difficulty forming trusting relationships. For long periods of time he lived alone. He would have spent a lifetime trying to come to terms with the effects of an abrupt, traumatic severance from a primary attachment figure at an early age.

Nearer to his death, a friend moved into his house with him. Jimmie was experiencing the painful effects of chronic ill health and the comorbidities of liver disease, diabetes and heart disease. Still, he continued to smoke and drink heavily. His liver had lost the ability to heal itself. His gut often bloated with fluid. He suffered massive gastrointestinal bleeding on a regular basis and required frequent emergency trips to the local hospital. These are all conditions consistent with someone having experienced a lifetime of struggle with post-traumatic stress disorder.

During the 1970s, the sixtieth birthday was considered an important turning point for men in Australia because it signalled the transition towards retirement after a lifetime of work.

James never reached this milestone. He died at fifty-nine.

In the final twenty-four hours of his life, Jimmie was rushed to the hospital after violently vomiting blood. The relationship with his housemate was sufficiently close for this person to make the arrangements for Jimmie's funeral and prepare and submit the documentation required to process his death. An optimistic interpretation pictures a stoic and caring friend, or perhaps lover, looking after Jimmie in his final months. A more depressing and perhaps more realistic interpretation suggests that the companion was little more than a housemate who helped meet the costs of a mortgage that Jimmie could no longer afford thanks to increasingly poor health and an inability to maintain work. The bond between the two was not sufficiently close for the friend to claim Jimmie's ashes after his death.

It is clear that the shame and stigma of illegitimacy that Jimmie felt as a young man overshadowed him for his entire life. His father's name was reported as John – a fact that could never be confirmed by anyone, including the police who investigated Sarah's life in Scotland after her arrest in Sydney. John's death, as described by Sarah, was most likely a convenient explanation, a fable offered to provide legitimacy for Jimmie and thereby protect her son from shame.

The way in which Jimmie wrote the narrative of his own life and imparted family history to others is also poignant. Throughout his life, he carefully and subtly rearranged facts to create a more acceptable and respectable life than the one he had lived. Jimmie swapped the surnames of his mother and father. On official documentation, Sarah's married surname is recorded as Boyd, her maiden name as Aitken, all to create an impression that she had been married and given birth after wedlock. It was a lie that she may have vehemently maintained in all her conversations with her son about his father. Or it may have been a lie that Jimmie crafted for himself. It is perhaps most likely that the lie was both of these things: a description of a fantasy narrative in which Jimmie and

Sarah actively participated in order to hide the shame of illegitimacy that shaped Sarah's life and the murderous act that would ultimately flow from it.

Jimmie and Josephine were close in age, and there is every chance they would have been close throughout life had she lived. As many migrant families in Sydney will attest, the bonds of family cement in particularly strong ways when life is built far from the shores of ancestral homelands.

On his death, Jimmie returned to a place not far from where he had lived with Mrs McWilliam in Lidcombe. His remains were scattered at Rookwood necropolis. No doubt they were handled respectfully, and scattered with compassion and care, but the hands that cradled his ashes were unknown to him. As required by the crematorium protocols, day-shift staff scattered Jimmie in an unmarked area devoted to those who have no family and no loved ones.

The synchronicity of the two sibling deaths, separated by more than fifty years, is breathtaking. While they could not share mortal life, they were reunited in a mass grave for the unclaimed.

Their home together now is in part of the cemetery that looks forgotten compared to some of the other meticulously tended plots at Rookwood. The plants look less well tended by cemetery staff. Though the heirloom roses for which Rookwood is famous do still bloom prolifically, the dry Australian dirt is deeply cracked and furrowed in many places. It is curious indeed that the area is called the sunken garden. The terrain is largely flat and the only water feature is a small, dark and stagnant pond. Occasionally a large bright orange koi, seemingly unconcerned by the filth of the bricked pool in which it lives, bobs up between the water weeds to catch a glimpse of light.

Rookwood necropolis is a perfect and eternal echo of the Sydney metropolis in which it is located. Those who lived with a sense of celebration and joy rest shoulder to shoulder with those who carried burdens unseen and untold. Here though, in this meeting place, all is finally laid to rest.

Jimmie and Josephine now lie together in soil consecrated as a special place, reserved exclusively for the city's lost and unwanted. But unlike the watery grave that Sarah had intended for each of her babies when they were newly born, the soil is always warm and dry here, even in winter.

ACKNOWLEDGEMENTS

I WOULD LIKE TO THANK THE FOLLOWING FOR THEIR ASSISTANCE in the writing and production of *The Suitcase Baby*:

The National Library of Australia's 'Trove' online portal and repository of digital resources. This search engine is vital because it encourages everyone to explore history and offers them the hands-on opportunity to do so.

The hardworking, committed and patient archivists and staff of State Archives NSW, Kingswood, Sydney.

Nerida Campbell, Sydney Living Museums.

Thank you sincerely to my publisher, Sophie Hamley, and the team at Hachette Australia: Fiona Hazard, Anne Macpherson, Isabel Staas, Karen Ward, Daniel Pilkington, Tom Saras, Kate Goldsworthy and Christa Moffitt. There are no words for how grateful I am.

ENDNOTES

1. HARBOURING SECRETS

p.4, 'In contrast to Eunice's clinical notes': Statements by Eunice Clare and
William Lodder, and biographical details about the children, drawn from
archived materials: City Coroner's Court, Sydney, 6 December 1923.
Documents held by Kingswood Archives, NSW.

2. CORNERING A SUSPECT

p. 13, 'Police force operations in New South Wales': D. Dixon, *A Culture of
Corruption: Changing an Australian Police Service*, Hawkins Press, Leichhardt, 1999, p. 10.

p. 14, 'Alchin was from Young': NSW Heritage Office, *Thematic History of
Young Shire Council*, Young Shire Council, 2008. http://www.young.nsw.
gov.au/Building-and-Planning/heritage

p. 14, 'Alchin led a high-profile investigation': 'Donnybrook tragedy', *Western
Mail*, 12 July 1923, p. 16; 'The Donnybrook tragedy: A lad arrested',
Sunday Times, 8 July 1923, p. 1.

p. 15, 'Brookes was found guilty of manslaughter': 'Donnybrook tragedy',
Western Mail, 12 July 1923, p. 16. 'Thomas Brooks [sic] Sentenced', *The
West Australian*, 2 August 1923, p. 8.

p. 16, 'pickpockets': 'Works of "art"', *Truth*, 12 November 1911, p. 9.

p. 16, 'find bank robbers': '"A perfect day": And its abrupt finish', *Sunday Times*, 29 October 1922, p. 1.

p. 16, 'mould pennies into florins': 'Spurious coins', *The Richmond River Herald and Northern Districts Advertiser*, 31 December 1926.

p. 16, 'stolen watches from George Street': 'Man arrested in city', *Sydney Morning Herald*, 30 September 1922, p. 14.

p. 16, 'a primitive version of a Ponzi scheme': 'Get rich quick scheme', *Richmond River Express and Casino Kyogle Advertiser*, 21 March 1923.

p. 16, 'well before the intended marriage had occurred': 'Married man's deceit', *Geelong Advertiser*, 22 January 1923, p. 5. 'Sergeant D Alchin', *Sydney Morning Herald*, 1 June 1931, p. 10. 'Engaged to married man girl's escape', *Newcastle Sun*, 20 January 1923, p. 5.

p. 17, 'Alchin had led an unusual': 'My oath!', *The Richmond River Express and Casino Kyogle Advertiser*, 5 May 1922, p. 6.

p. 18, 'aspirational pastoralists': Croydon Pioneer Association, *A Register of Pioneer Families, Volume 1*, The 1788–1820 Pioneer Association, Croydon, 1989.

p. 19, 'imprinted on the minds of the public': 'Mosman Baby Case', *Evening News*, 6 December 1923, p. 7.

p. 22, 'The laundry code system': P. Malcolmson, *English Laundresses: A Social History, 1850–1930*, University of Illinois Press, Urbana and Chicago, 1986.

4. GONE TO GROUND

p. 37, 'By 1923, the inner-city streets': City of Sydney 1912 City Engineers Department Plans S4-175/9.

5. ABLACH

p. 45, 'the NSW police force had an image problem': D. Dixon, op. cit., p. 8.

p. 45, 'A historian at Deakin University': R. Evans 2015, '"The police are rottenly corrupt"': Policing, scandal, and the regulation of illegal betting in Depression-era Sydney', *Australian and New Zealand Journal of Criminology*, 48, 4: 572–587.

p. 46, 'the now overstaffed Irish police force': 'Imported police men from Ireland: Question for NSW', *Newcastle Sun*, 19 April 1922.

6. PLOTTING A BOYD CURVE

p. 55, 'While this was not Ireland's only potato famine': D. Harkness, 'Irish Immigration', in W. F. Willcox (ed.), *International Migrations, Volume II: Interpretations*, National Bureau of Economic Research, Belfast, 1931, p. 264.

p. 55, 'mass migration from Ireland': S. C. Johnson, *A History of Emigration from the United Kingdom*, Routledge, London, 1913, p. 276.

p. 55, 'Historian Dr Frank Costello': 'Famine misery "targeted Ulster's Catholic and Protestant poor"', BBC News Northern Ireland, 20 January 2015. Available at: http://www.bbc.com/news/uk-northern-ireland-30898074

p. 56, 'vulnerable families had to develop astute coping': R. Dodgshon, 'Coping with risk: subsistence crises in the Scottish Highlands and Islands, 1600–1800', *Rural History*, vol. 15, no. 1, 2004, pp. 1–25.

p. 58, 'Steven King, Professor of Economic and Social History': S. King & J. Stewart (eds), *Welfare Peripheries: The development of welfare states in nineteenth and twentieth century Europe*, Verlag Peter Lang, New York, 2007, p. 76.

p. 59, 'they accessed the only institutional provision': R. Houston, *Bride Ales and Penny Weddings: Recreations, reciprocity, and regions in Britain from the sixteenth to the nineteenth centuries*, Oxford University Press, Oxford, 2014.

p. 60, 'W.R. Curtler continued to describe': W. H. R. Curtler, *A Short History of English Agriculture*, Clarendon Press, Oxford, 1909.

p. 61, 'Prior to the 1880s': J. Rosenbloom, *The Challenges of Economic Maturity: New England, 1880–1940*, Federal Reserve Bank of Boston Conference on the Economic History of New England, Boston, Massachusetts, 1998.

p. 61, 'New England's early industrialisation': ibid.

p. 62, 'only small-framed workers could move': J. Humphries, *Childhood and Child Labour in the British Industrial Revolution*, Cambridge University Press, Cambridge, 2010.

p. 62, 'to ensure production was not halted': A. Cooke, *The Rise and Fall of the Scottish Cotton Industry 1778–1914: 'The Secret Spring'*, Manchester University Press, Manchester, 2010.

p. 65, 'comparable to the higher incomes in England': W. Knox, *A History of the Scottish people: Poverty, income and wealth in Scotland, 1840–1940*, SCRAN [www.scran.ac.uk].

p. 67, 'Drylie was captured': 'Leaving his family to the parish', *Edinburgh Evening News*, 30 September 1896.

p. 68, 'A sixty-year-old local labourer': *Edinburgh Evening News*, 16 July 1894.

p. 69, 'But the bullet had lodged': 'The tragic shooting affair at Paisley', *Edinburgh Evening News*, 2 November 1899, p. 5.

p. 69, 'Paisley gained a reputation': 'Paisley crime increasing', *Edinburgh Evening News*, 13 January 1897.

p. 70, 'the market for Paisley-made goods': 'The Scottish textile trade', *Edinburgh Evening News*, 27 March 1897.

p. 70, 'more efficient production in Lancashire': W. Knox, op. cit.

p. 70, 'Renfrewshire had long maintained': F. Mort, *Renfrewshire*, Cambridge County Geographies, Cambridge University Press, 1912.

p. 71, 'They were also more likely to experience': R. Botsch, *Organizing the Breathless: Cotton dust, Southern politics and the brown lung association*, University Press of Kentucky, Lexington, 1993.

p. 71, ' "influenza-like symptoms" ': *Sickness in Scotland*, Department of Health report 1932, *Falkirk Herald*, 3 September 1932, p. 2.

p. 73, 'Glasgow Sarah was found guilty': 'Glasgow woman suffocates child', *Aberdeen Journal*, 1 July 1920.

p. 74, 'According to Professor Andrew Blaikie': A. Blaikie, 'Infant survival chances, unmarried motherhood and domestic arrangements in rural Scotland 1845–1945', *Local Population Studies*, University of Aberdeen, no. 60, Spring 1998, p. 8.

7. SUITOR

p. 78, 'While Iris Wilkinson's first column': A. Fensome, 'Literary giant: MPs "are the most awful liars"', *The Dominion Post*, 16 December 2014.

p. 80, 'an early incarnation of modern institutional child care': 'Residential Nursery: How women's national reserve cares for children. Problem solved for parents', *NZ Truth*, Issue 1285, 17 July 1930, p. 22.

p. 83, 'Sarah later described her occupation': J. Malthus, 'Worse Than Picking Up Pins? The search for dressmakers in nineteenth-century New Zealand',

Stout Centre Review Paper, *The Journal of New Zealand Studies*, vol. 1, no. 2, 1991.

8. IN SIGHT OF THE SEA

p. 102, 'Joseph talked with great pride about the area': *Evening News*, 21 April 1924.

p. 104, 'For the important matter of settling returned soldiers': *Wyong Correspondent Gosford Times and Wyong District Advocate*, 28 June 1917, p. 14.

p. 106, 'A Wyong news correspondent': *Wyong Correspondent Gosford Times and Wyong District Advocate*, 28 June 1917, p. 14.

p. 106, 'one local claimed': 'Sunrise oats at Wyong', *Sydney Morning Herald*, 6 October 1923.

p. 108, 'Colonial botanist Joseph Maiden': J. H. Maiden, *The Forest Flora of New South Wales: 4 volumes*, held at the University of Sydney Library, 1908.

10. FLAPPERS AND FLOPPERS

p. 128, 'Many a young life is battered': B. Ehrenreich & D. English, *For Her Own Good: 150 years of the experts' advice to women*, Pluto Press, London, 1979, p. 99.

p. 128, 'In 1931, William Boyd': 'Insanities Associated With Child-Bearing', *British Medical Journal*, vol. 2, no. 3701, 1931, pp. 1087–1088.

p. 131, 'Hunter claimed that most mothers': W. Hunter, 'On the uncertainty of the signs of murder in the case of bastard children', *Medical Observations and Enquiries*, vol. 6, 1784, 266–290.

p. 131, 'There is a widespread belief': R. Halliday 'The roadside burial of suicides: an east Anglian study', *Folklore*, vol. 121, no. 1, 2010, pp. 81–93.

p. 132, 'William Acton, surgeon to the Islington': W. Acton, 'Child-murder and wet-nursing', *British Medical Journal*, vol. 1, no. 7, 1861, pp. 183–184.

p. 133, 'In a post-mortem process': J. Braxton Hicks, 'The effects of artificial respiration on the stillborn', *British Medical Journal*, vol. 2, no. 2601, 1910, pp. 1416–1418.

p. 133, 'The widow received a custodial sentence': (author unknown), 'Infanticide and concealed birth source', *British Medical Journal*, vol. 1, no. 846, 1877, p. 329.

p. 133, 'wrapped in an old skirt': 'Medical Evidence in Cases of Child-Murder: The New Criminal Code', *British Medical Journal*, vol. 2, no. 915, 13 July 1878, pp. 63–64.

p. 134, 'A year before Sarah's trial': Hansard Second reading speech Infanticide bill, 22 March 1938, vol. 108, 292–310.

pp. 135–7, 'George King, a gynaecologist in Bath': G. King, 'On the comparative size of the hand of the accoucheur and of the female pelvis', *Provincial Medical & Surgical Journal*, vol. 15, no. 1, 1851, pp. 7–12.

p. 138, 'As late as 1940': *British Medical Journal,* vol. 2, no. 4166, 1940, pp. 652–653.

p. 138, 'To this day, an ongoing debate': P. Bahadoran, H.R. Oreizi & S. Safari, 'Meta-analysis of the role of delivery mode in postpartum depression (Iran 1997–2011)', *Journal of Education and Health Promotion*, 2014, 3: 118.

p. 138, 'One British infanticide case': *British Medical Journal*, vol. 2, no. 2273, 23 July 1904, pp. 214–215.

p. 141, 'the *Mudgee Guardian*': *Mudgee Guardian*, 31 October 1932, p. 6.

p. 142, 'Down the street trips the winsome': *Truth*, 19 April 1924, p. 1.

p. 142, 'My flapper': Anonymous poem, *West Gippsland Gazette*, 4 July 1916, p. 3.

p. 143, '*Daughters of Today* and *The Romantic Age*': 'Union Theatres', *Sydney Morning Herald*, 18 October 1924, p. 14. 'Theatre attractions for the day', *Sydney Morning Herald*, 14 February 1928, p. 12.

p. 143, 'In *Daughters of Today*': *Truth*, 25 March 1928, p. 10.

p. 143, 'An alphabet of the flapper': *The Wyalong Advocate and Mining, Agricultural and Pastoral Gazette,* 3 July 1925, p. 2.

p. 145, 'the Perth *Sunday Times*': Perth *Sunday Times*, 22 August 1920, p. 1.

p. 145, 'Evidence from British legal cases': 'Poor fool: Jealous of flapper', *Uralla Times*, 16 April 1925, p. 2.

p. 146, 'In 1889, Jane Culpitt': The analysis of these cases is based on information provided by the Capital Convictions Database, managed by Francis Forbes Society for Australian Legal History. The primary source used to populate this database is: 'N. S. W. Death Sentence Register, Nov. 1839 – Nov. 1968', Department of Corrective Services Archive, Long Bay.

11. HARD AND FAST

p. 149, 'From the establishment of the first colony': Statistical analysis conducted from data drawn from the NSW Capital Convictions database maintained by Francis Forbes Society for Australian Legal History 2013.

p. 153, 'Over the next twenty-five years': ibid.

p. 155, 'As one newspaper noted': 'Reported executions', *The Australian*, 18 July 1826.

p. 156, 'The formal statement made': Goulburn Circuit Court, 26 March 1860.

p. 156, 'The sentence of death': 'Goulburn Circuit Court. Monday, March 26. (Before his Honour Mr Justice Wise.) Sentence of death upon Ellen Monks for the murder of her husband,' *Bell's Life in Sydney and Sporting Reviewer*, 31 March 1860: 3.

p. 158, 'For those women who were forced': 'A woman sentenced to death for child murder', *Empire*, 6 April 1872, p. 3.

p. 159, 'In 1892, when the extent of their enterprise': A. Cossins, *The Baby Farmers*, Allen & Unwin, Sydney, 2013.

12. INQUEST NO. 482

p. 168, 'In 1887, the office had spearheaded': Sydney, Coroner's Office, 1887.

p. 169, 'Coroner James Murphy': 'Infanticide: Sydney Coroner's report 1909', *The Mercury*, 20 August 1909: 5.

13. BOUNCING BABY

p. 181, 'Historians have described Fuller': D. Clune, 'Sir George Warburton Fuller', in D. Clune & K. Turner (eds), *The Premiers of New South Wales 1856–2005*, Federation Press, Sydney, 2006, p. 167.

p. 181, 'in the words of political historian David Clune': ibid., p. 168.

p. 181, 'Jack Lang was everything that Fuller was not': B. Nairn, *The 'Big Fella': Jack Lang and the Australian Labor Party 1891–1949*, Bede Nairn, Carlton, 1986.

p. 181, 'Lang's Labor government could offer': R. Dixon, *The Story of J T Lang*, Mastercraft Publishing, 1943.

p. 182, 'The *Evening News* dispensed with referring to Puddifoot': 'Arncliffe murder', *Evening News*, 29 May 1923.

p. 183, 'Bavin was cornered in parliament': 'Arncliffe murder, sentence upon Puddifoot discussed in Assembly', *Barrier Miner*, 21 September 1923, p. 1.

p. 185, 'Historical research on media hyperbole': P. King, 'Making crime news: Newspapers, violent crime and the selective reporting of Old Bailey trials in the late eighteenth century', *Crime, History and Societies*, vol. 13, no. 1, 2009, pp. 91–116. C. Casey, 'Common misperceptions: the press and Victorian views of crime', *Journal of Interdisciplinary History*, XLI, 3, 2011, pp. 367–391.

p. 186, 'Grace brought a personal libel suit': 'Writ against newspaper', *Singleton Argus*, 6 March 1923.

14. IN DECEMBER 1923

p. 194, 'One newspaper headline': 'Bush fire peril', *Cootamundra Herald*, 12 December 1923, p. 4.

p. 199, 'social historian Shurlee Swain': S. Swain, *History of Child Protection Legislation*, Australian Catholic University, Canberra, 2014, p. 13.

p. 202, 'Local regions paid an annual stipend': 'Saving the babies', *Singleton Argus*, 4 December 1920, p. 1.

p. 204, 'Two weeks before Sarah and Jean's trial': 'Women jurors', *Don Dorrigo Gazette and Guy Fawkes Advocate*, 5 December 1923, p. 2.

p. 205, 'Women, they argued, had the intellectual': 'Women's right to jury service', *Sydney Morning Herald*, 20 December 1923, p. 9.

p. 205, 'They identified two key problems': 'Women jurors? Representations to the Minister of Justice', *Daily Advertiser,* 20 December 1923, p. 2.

p. 205, 'As one campaigner argued': ibid.

p. 207, 'Journalists were equally dispassionate': *Tweed Daily*, 18 December 1923, p. 3.

p. 208, 'In the second week of December': 'Equal pay for women', *Northern Star*, 10 December 1923, p. 5.

p. 208, 'The women employed by the force would have to go': 'Women police equal status with men: Dismissal threatened', *Sydney Morning Herald*, 13 December 1923, p. 9.

p. 208, 'Colloquially called "social workers in uniform"': L. Straw, *Kate Leigh: The Worst Woman in Sydney*, UNSW Press, Sydney, 2016, p. 120.

p. 209, 'Justice Curlewis, in particular': 'Women's dresses', *Northern Star*, 19 December 1923, p. 4.

p. 210, 'Another Infant Assaulted': *The Advocate*, 20 December 1923, p. 2.

p. 210, 'Sexual offences butcher remanded': *The Age*, 20 December 1923, p. 11.

p. 211, '"Sticky beaks," he called them': 'Sticky beaks – women in court – judge's rub', *Evening News*, 19 December 1923, p. 10.

15. THE TRIAL

p. 223, 'Jean's bold red lipstick': Information drawn from transcription of court proceedings 20 December 1923 and other archived documentation (subpoenas, witness statements) Supreme Court Rex V. Boyd and Olliver, Sydney, 20 December 1923. Documents held by Kingswood Archives, NSW.

p. 223, 'each standing at a little over 5 feet': H. King, 'Lillian May Armfield', *Australian Dictionary of Biography: Volume 7*, MUP, Melbourne, 1979.

p. 228, 'A key focus of Catholic welfare': Sr Kath Burford, 1989, R.S.J. St Anthony Family Care.

p. 229, 'St Margaret's Home for Unwed Mothers': G. Abbott, *Australian Dictionary of Biography*.

p. 235, 'Although legal historians have noted': Robyn Lansdowne, Child killing and the offence of infanticide: The development of the offence and its operation in New South Wales 1976–1980, thesis submitted for the degree of Master of Laws, University of New South Wales, 1987.

p. 235, 'Mark Tedeschi QC has written extensively': M. Tedeschi, *Eugenia: A true story of adversity, tragedy, crime and courage,* Simon & Schuster, Cammeray, 2012.

p. 238, 'When the two women had huddled together': 'Cruelly strangled', *NZ Truth*, Issue 944, 29 December 1923, p. 6.

17. SUITCASE

p. 251, 'At the Court of Criminal Appeal they would seek': 'Murdered her baby', *Chronicle*, 19 January 1924, p. 50.

p. 252, 'By 1928, more than 260 doctors': Parliamentary Archives and Parliamentary Education NSW 2011, *History Bulletin 8*, Parliament of NSW, Sydney.

p. 253, 'Another Macquarie Street doctor, Terrence Green': 'Tragic end of girl who loved too well and not too wisely', *Truth*, 13 April 1923, p. 9.

p. 254, 'They also claimed that all of the doctors': 'Condemned woman: Medical men's views', *Daily Examiner*, 25 December 1923, p. 3.

p. 254, 'These assessments would need to occur': 'Impulse impropriety', *Truth*, 10 December 1922, p. 14.

p. 258, 'Researchers have identified the 1920s': H. Hendrick, *Children, Childhood and English Society 1880–1990*, Cambridge University Press, Cambridge, 1997.

p. 258, 'Nell Musgrove wrote of Australian institutional': N. Musgrove, *The Scars Remain: A long history of forgotten Australians and children's institutions*, Australian Scholarly Publishing, Melbourne, 2013.

p. 259, 'Authorities were weighing options regarding Jimmie's': 'Child welfare: A special study', *Evening News*, 11 March 1925, p. 8.

p. 260, 'Foster-care benefits provided an additional': 'Child welfare and Catholic orphanages', *Freemans Journal*, 11 November 1926, p. 24.

p. 260, 'work was often a requirement': M. Murray, *Working Boarders: The boarding out scheme in New South Wales, 1820–1920*, Faculty of Economics Working Papers, Faculty of Business, University of Wollongong, 1999.

p. 262, 'With a view to fairness, Scarba arbitrarily': 'Child welfare adoption system', *Sydney Morning Herald*, 8 November 1926, p. 10.

18. DOING TIME

p. 265, 'Eugenia Falleni was impoverished': Tedeschi, *Eugenia*.

p. 266, 'And there was a library': 'Modern ideas succeed virtues of clemency', *The Sunday Times*, 11 June 1916.

p. 267, 'many women criminals were victims': 'Class conscious prisoners out at the bay', *Truth*, 10 August 1930, p. 11.

p. 267, 'Sydney Hospital was reputed to be dirtier': 'At Long Bay', *Sunday Times*, 11 June 1916, p. 6.

p. 270, 'New South Wales records still retain the letter': Cossins, *The Baby Farmers*, p. 135.

19. STRANGERS IN A STRANGE LAND

p. 275, 'In the 1920s, a popular syndicated children's': 'Poppy Penmore Children's Column', *Tumut Advocate and Farmers and Settlers Advisor*, 6 January 1925, p. 1.

p. 281, 'With the rising cost of living': 'Child welfare: Relieving the destitute: Increasing cost', *The Farmer and Settler*, 27 March 1925, p. 15.

p. 281, 'Despite increasing attempts to make poor children': 'Child welfare: Parramatta industrial school: Minister's statement', *Maitland Weekly*, 2 July 1927, p. 9.

p. 282, 'In April, an official public inquiry was launched': 'Child welfare: Mr Lang's comments', *Maitland Daily Mercury*, 15 June 1927, p. 6.

p. 283, 'Bavin had just launched the Nationalist campaign': 'NSW government governed from the gutter', *The Sun*, 11 June 1927, p. 3.

p. 288, 'Migrant women spoke of their own hardships': 'Sarah Boyd', *Truth*, 7 August 1927, p. 1.

p. 134, '"Being Scotch myself and a deserted wife"': 'For her ain countee', *Truth*, 14 August 1927, p. 24.

p. 301, 'On 4 September the story of Sarah Boyd': 'Suffer little children come unto me', *Truth*, 4 September 1927, p. 1.

20. BAGGAGE

p. 303, 'They had with them a trunk or suitcase': *On Their Own: Britain's child migrants*. A collaboration between the Australian National Maritime Museum and National Museums Liverpool, UK. Opened in Sydney, November 2010.

21. SUNKEN GARDEN

p. 308, 'Evidence given to several inquiries': K. Squires & L. Slater, *Living at Scarba Home for Children*, Benevolent Society, Sydney, 2006, p. 9.

p. 308, 'Those in the industry could be assured': R. E. Ringer, *The Brickmasters: 1788–2008*, Dry Press Publishing, Wetherill Park, 2008.

p. 310, 'Mombassa once said the suburban home': Reg Mombassa, aka Chris O'Doherty, verbatim quotes on Suburban Housing. regmombassa.com/post/5347203405/suburbanhouses